I0815981

AC/DC

SONG BY SONG

BILL VOCCIA

FONTHILL

First published in Great Britain and the United States of America 2025 by
Fonthill
An imprint of
Pen & Sword Books Ltd
Yorkshire – Philadelphia
www.fonthill.media

ISBN 978-1-78155-949-9

A CIP catalogue record for this book is available from the British Library.

Typeset in Sabon LT 10/13
Typeset by Fonthill
Printed and bound in the UK by CPI Group (UK) Ltd, Croydon, CR0 4YY

The Publisher's authorised representative in the EU for product safety is Authorised Rep Compliance Ltd., Ground Floor, 71 Lower Baggot Street, Dublin D02 P593, Ireland.
www.arccompliance.com

For a complete list of Pen & Sword titles please contact
PEN & SWORD BOOKS LIMITED
47 Church Street, Barnsley, South Yorkshire, S70 2AS, England
E-mail: enquiries@pen-and-sword.co.uk
Website: www.pen-and-sword.co.uk

Or
PEN AND SWORD BOOKS
1950 Lawrence Rd, Havertown, PA 19083, USA
E-mail: Uspen-and-sword@casematepublishers.com
Website: www.penandswordbooks.com

A very special thanks to my wife, Cynthia,
for your love and support and for your awesome photos.

Very special thanks to my mom and dad for your encouragement and support.

This book is also dedicated to the memories of
Bon Scott and Malcolm Young of AC/DC.

All photographs were taken by Cynthia Voccia.

Preface

"In the beginning, back in 1955, rock and roll was born." The infamous quote from AC/DC's 1977 title track "Let There Be Rock" takes you on a journey through time, starting with how rock 'n' roll music began.

AC/DC are a band that emerged from Australia and defied all odds. They did not have the support, encouragement, or praise from most critics in their early days. The band were deemed as "Punk rock from Australia," vulgar, sexist, and outright dirty by media, yet despite this, they were successful every step of the way. Though it may have taken quite a long time before the band reached worldwide acclaim, they did it without much support from critics or the charts. Bon Scott joined the band in 1974 soon after their first single, and he brought experience and confidence to the then-new band called AC/DC. Angus and Malcolm's elder brother, George, was already a famous musician, songwriter, and producer in Australia, having been in the Easybeats. With his counterpart Harry Vanda, Young would take AC/DC under wing during the inception of the band and help graduate them toward success. Angus and Malcolm strived very hard to work and succeed, probably more so trying to gain acceptance from their older brother. *Highway to Hell* in 1979 was the ice breaker for AC/DC to finally achieve the next level of success, finally breaking into the *Billboard* Top 100 charts in the USA, reaching #17 as the band continued to tour extensively. An untimely tragedy struck in 1980 with the loss of singer Bon Scott, but AC/DC decided to carry on and released their definitive album *Back in Black*, featuring singer Brian Johnson. *Back in Black* has since become the world's second biggest-selling album of all time—and that's not just rock albums, that's albums of any genre of all time. Now fifty years since their inception, AC/DC have survived some of the most difficult tragedies during their career. Despite these challenges, they have become one of the world's most successful rock bands and the most successful Australian band of all time.

AC/DC (Acca Dacca to their fans down under) are an Australian band, Australia's most successful and influential band in history. AC/DC define rock music, from every song since their early beginnings in Australia's pubs to the platinum-selling albums and stadium tours of today, they have never strayed from their own consistent, recognizable formula. What is so special about AC/DC one might ask? They are a band that have always remained true to their roots. They stuck to their own proven formula and never veered away from playing rock music. Guitars, drums, bass, and raspy, powerful vocals, never any gimmicks, keyboards, or ballads. The ingredients that make up any typical AC/DC song are just that: guitar, more guitar, powerful vocals with big choruses, and that unmistakable AC/DC groove. Over the years, many critics have underestimated their ability as musicians and songwriters, when it is otherwise almost blatantly obvious that this band has the ultimate recipe for rock music. AC/DC were often labeled as a 'three-chord' band, but that is certainly not the case once one actually listens to their music or tries to emulate it on a guitar. Their guitar tones are unmistakable, as are their vocals, whether it is the late Bon Scott or if it is Brian Johnson belting out the verses, many can recognize an AC/DC track after the first few seconds, and then there is that solid, driving groove. Producer Rick Rubin (*Ballbreaker*, 1995) notes: "I'll go on record as saying they're the greatest rock n roll band of all time. They didn't write emotional lyrics. They didn't play emotional songs. The emotion is all in that groove. And the groove is timeless." I concur with Rick Rubin's statement and could not have said it better myself.

AC/DC songs are predominantly about the same topics: sex, booze, and rock 'n' roll, with the heavy use of metaphors. Some of the other topics interweaved with the main subjects are tales of life on the road, hardships and problematic relationships, defiance of authority and societal norms, and living life by one's own terms. The remaining percentage goes off the beaten path of exploring different topics such as historical events, war, and few other areas of interest, likely because of Angus Young' interest in history. I will dive deeper into the inner meanings of these songs, their history, and their longevity to describe to you what I hope to be a meaningful transcription of what makes AC/DC tick. The masterful songwriting team of Angus Young and Malcolm Young when accompanied by the genius songwriting abilities of Bon Scott would be a huge part of what made AC/DC special and very successful. I refer to Bon as a genius songwriter, because quite frankly, that best describes who he was and his unique ability to twist words throughout AC/DC's songs to create poetic, yet clever verses that often had hidden or subtle meanings. Although the band struggled financially when trying to gain that big-time success and stardom that they always yearned for, the band made vast impressions among every audience they performed for. As they continued to play, their fanbase grew, as did their paychecks, eventually. Despite having practically no support from critics, some who referred to them as a "punk" band in the early days and others who did not take them seriously enough, AC/DC never got the radio airplay or critic-friendly help to elevate their reputation. Instead, the band relied on relentless live performances, touring almost non-stop in between writing and releasing the next album. The untimely death of Bon in 1980 led the band to an unfortunate crossroads, but they defied all odds and found Brian Johnson, formerly of the band Geordie, interestingly as a recommendation from Bon himself who had toured with Geordie in the early 1970s with his previous band Fraternity. The addition of Brian prevailed for AC/DC, his unique stage presence and vocal style complimented AC/DC's music while at the same time welcomed him as not a replacement for Bon, but as a new addition to the family. A new AC/DC was born in 1980, and now, some forty-four years later, they have cemented their legacy as the all-time greatest rock band in history. AC/DC survived the domination of disco and punk in the '70s, glam and "hair metal" trends in the '80s, and grunge, alternative, rap, hip hop, and pop in the '90s, and to this day, they have stayed true to their own form: straightforward, hard, rock 'n' roll music without compromising their sound or style to accommodate any trends, and they have remained one of the most successful music acts in history.

I have been an AC/DC fan since I first heard them on the radio, sometime in the early summer of 1980, and I was instantly hooked and a fan ever since. Although I am a huge fan of music in general, particularly many hard rock and heavy metal bands for the past four decades, AC/DC have never strayed from being my all-time favorite. The initial songs I heard were with Bon Scott, and between Bon's unique and distinctive voice coupled with the aggressive-sounding crunchy guitar tones and electrifying lead guitar solos, I was an instant fan and never looked back. Ever since, I have been immersed in AC/DC's music and I have become an avid collector of the band's music, collectibles, and memorabilia (amassing one of the world's largest AC/DC collections), as well as having the opportunity to manage content for their official website acdc.com (Sony Music/Columbia Records) for about three years (shortly after the Black Ice Tour). I was also fortunate enough to meet the members of AC/DC on a few occasions, and every one of them were the nicest, most down to earth, genuine, and humble "rock stars" one could ever imagine. I still hope to one day be able to sit down and have a beer with Brian and the boys—maybe one day. AC/DC's music is timeless and the epitome of rock 'n' roll music. There never was, nor will there ever be, a band as significant, dedicated, and relevant to the longevity of rock music as AC/DC. Thank you for your music. As we fans say, AC/DC isn't just a love for their music, but a way of life. For those about to rock ...

Malcolm Young
Angus Young
Bon Scott
Phil Rudd
Cliff Williams
Brian Johnson
Mark Evans
Simon Wright
Chris Slade
Stevie Young

... we salute you!

Contents

Preface 5

1 *High Voltage* 11
2 *T.N.T.* 21
3 *Dirty Deeds Done Dirt Cheap* 31
4 *Let There Be Rock* 41
5 *Powerage* 49
6 *Highway to Hell* 58
7 *Back in Black* 68
8 *For Those About to Rock (We Salute You)* 77
9 *Flick of the Switch* 86
10 *Fly on the Wall* 96
11 *Who Made Who* 104
12 *Blow Up Your Video* 108
13 *The Razors Edge* 117
14 *Ballbreaker* 128
15 *Stiff Upper Lip* 139
16 *Black Ice* 149
17 *Rock or Bust* 160
18 *Power Up* 168
19 Non-Album Tracks (*Bonfire*, *Backtracks*, & B-Sides) 179

Bibliography 189

1

High Voltage

Release date:	February 17, 1975 (Australia)
Current edition:	Albert Productions/EMI, CD
Personnel:	Bon Scott, lead vocals
	Angus Young, guitar
	Malcolm Young, guitar
Contributions:	George Young (bass guitar), Tony Currenti (drums), Peter Clack (select drum portions)
Duration:	39:51
Recorded at:	Albert Studios, Sydney, Australia, November 1974
Produced by:	Harry Vanda & George Young
Chart position:	#14 Australian Albums

Notable info: AC/DC's first album recorded in late 1974 at Albert Studios in Sydney, Australia, with the mentoring and guidance from George Young and Harry Vanda, Australia's iconic rock stars, producers, and songwriting team. It was released in Australia and New Zealand only. Two tracks from this album were combined with the majority of the songs from the *T.N.T.* album for AC/DC's internationally released album, also titled *High Voltage*. Some of the remaining unreleased Australian-only tracks from this album were released internationally in 1984 on the *'74 Jailbreak* EP and ultimately the remaining tracks became available on the *Backtracks* release in 2009. *High Voltage* received certifications of 5x platinum in Australia.

AC/DC's debut album, appropriately titled *High Voltage*, was released in Australia and New Zealand only on February 17, 1974 through Albert Productions. Distinct from the international release, this album consists of a total of eight tracks, six of which are unique to this version. The album was recorded in late 1974 at Albert Studios in Sydney, Australia, with the mentoring and guidance from George Young and Harry Vanda,

Australia's iconic rock stars, producers, and songwriting team. The band was on a rigorous schedule of performing the Australian club circuit and had recently fared through a few lineup changes with bass players and drummers. Ultimately, they decided to record their debut album without a dedicated bassist or drummer and recruited session drummer Tony Currenti for the studio sessions along with elder brother, George Young, to handle most of the bass, who was also handling production duties along with Harry Vanda. The Vanda and Young team were already a well-known and established songwriting team, producers, and rock stars themselves, having been in The Easybeats, one of Australia's most well-known acts of the '60s. The album cover depicts a large electrical box inscribed with "AC/DC, High Voltage" as a dog is seen at the bottom left corner relieving himself on it, which gives the impression of the sarcastic and cheeky lyrics the listener would be about to experience. *High Voltage* is not to be confused with the more well-known album also titled *High Voltage*, which was released worldwide a year later with different tracks. Many of the tracks from the original *High Voltage* were held back and not available outside of Australia (and New Zealand) until the 1984 EP release *'74 Jailbreak*, which contained four of the eight songs. Two of the others were released on the worldwide version of *High Voltage*, while the remaining two ("Love Song" and "Stick Around") were held back for decades until they became available as part of the 2009 *Backtracks* box set release. The album showcases the band's journey in finding their unique sound and style.

AC/DC were around the Australian club circuits by this time and had previously released a single titled "Can I Sit Next to You Girl" in mid-1974 with an early, pre-Bon Scott lineup including lead singer Dave Evans. The B-side of the single was "Rockin' in the Parlour." By September 1974, Bon Scott had joined the band as they continued to make an impressible impact upon the Aussie pub circuit. Entering the studio in November that year, AC/DC's lineup was in flux with the current rhythm section, so the band commissioned session drummer Tony Currenti to record with them along with elder brother and producer George Young taking on a majority of the bass guitar. AC/DC at this stage were still finding their own sound, which was immensely influenced by the input of the Harry Vanda and George Young production team, which was quite evident in the final recordings. It was certainly an advantage to have the direct influence and advice of Australia's greatest songwriting team at your fingertips, but at the same time it was not an easy road. Malcolm and Angus worked very, very hard for their success, and achieving that level of success may have even proved to be more difficult trying to live up to the standards and expectations of what they felt their elder peers were anticipating.

High Voltage would be released in Australia and New Zealand just three months later, hitting shelves on February 17, 1975. As of January, Phil Rudd had already joined AC/DC as their permanent drummer, and they were ready to take on Australia by storm.

The international version of *High Voltage* released in 1976 is a compilation album that combines selected tracks from the band's first two Australian-only albums, *High Voltage* (1975) and *T.N.T.* (1975). Only two tracks ("She's Got Balls" and "Little Lover") were selected from the original Australian *High Voltage* album for the compilation. The remaining tracks were taken from *T.N.T.* Five of the songs from the original Australian *High Voltage* were held back for nearly ten years until their international release as part of the *'74 Jailbreak* EP released in 1984. "Love Song (Oh Jean)" and "Stick Around" were held back and did not receive international release until they became available as part of the 2009 *Backtracks* box set. As Angus Young stated in an interview:

> High Voltage ... I think that sums up, pretty much, the band, in general ... the title. Yea ... and the title itself, you know, in the beginning it was our way of saying, you know, what was AC/DC? You know, a high voltage band, full of energy, and lighting, and power, and that's what always sticks in my head. It was a way of describing your sound, wasn't it? High Voltage Rock n Roll.

"Baby Please Don't Go"

The intro track to AC/DC's debut album makes its instant impact with the raw, blues-driven guitar sound that would later become the band's forte. As the opening track on the album, the fast-paced boogie-style version of Joe Williams' classic blues track "Baby Please Don't Go" kicks off the album with a bang. There have been many renditions of this song performed and recorded by numerous artists over the years, and with bias aside, I truly feel that AC/DC's version is the icing on the cake. The version on the record is arguably the best and most powerful-sounding rendition of this early blues classic, complimented by Bon Scott's raspy howl and Angus Young's interplaying lead guitar. The energy captured in the studio recording brings the song to life in with a rock 'n' roll vibe that sets the stage for the rest of the album. Certainly, at this phase, AC/DC were still finding themselves and their sound; a cover song as the opening track on their debut album was what was decided for the release. The song was released as the B-side on AC/DC's first single from the album; "Love Song (Oh Jene)" was intended as the single, however, radio stations picked up on the harder rocking "Baby Please Don't Go," which received all of the airplay instead. The track became a staple in AC/DC's early Australian shows and would typically be extended as Angus stripped his school uniform down to his knickers and hopped around the crowd improvising guitar solos. AC/DC also made impact across Australia with their performance on *Countdown* TV in April 1975, where Bon surprised the rest of the band and came out on stage dressed in drag as a schoolgirl. While the rest of the band continued to perform while visibly cracking up laughing, Bon lit up a cigarette and continued to play the role with Angus.

"She's Got Balls"

"She's Got Balls" is a song that combines raw energy with a playful, somewhat sarcastic attitude. The song kicks off with the guitar riff of overdriven amplifiers and the combination of a Gibson SG and Gretsch, oozing with an almost bluesey yet sinister feel. Bon once told the tale of how his wife was complaining that he never wrote any songs about her, so he wrote "She's Got Balls" and "then she left me," Bon would reminisce with a grin. The second track on the album is a raunchy hard rock number that has one of those signature AC/DC riffs. "No one has to tell her what a feller is for" sneers Bon during the pre-chorus, showcasing his witty lyrical writing style. Bon's cheeky wordplay adds an extra layer of charm and wit to the song, painting a vivid picture of a woman who exudes confidence and sexual allure. The lyrics describe a woman with a strong, assertive personality, using the phrase "she's got balls" as a metaphor for her boldness and resilience. This is a common theme in AC/DC's music, where women are often portrayed as powerful, confident, and in control. The song opens with lines that highlight her various attributes: "She's got style, that woman, makes me smile, that woman, she's got spunk, that woman, funk that woman." Throughout the song, the woman's characteristics are celebrated in a manner that combines admiration with a touch of humorous irreverence. The chorus emphasizes this with the repeated line, "But most important of all, let me tell you, the lady's got balls." It's a playful, yet direct way of acknowledging her strength and independence. Additionally, the song touches on themes of sexual attraction and desire, which are common in AC/DC's repertoire. The lines "She's got soul, likes to crawl, my baby, all around the floor on her hands and knees, Ooh, because she likes to please me" portray a more direct and unapologetic sexual scene. The song could also perhaps be somewhat of a spin-off tribute to AC/DC's early club days, when they would often get bookings to perform at drag bars due to the band name, which by no means had been the intention of the Young's when they selected it. A tongue-in-cheek track, "She's Got Balls" is one of the finest earlier examples of Bon Scott's masterful lyrical style, where he leaves the listener wondering how to interpret the words, whether figuratively or literally.

"Little Lover"

"Little Lover" is a song that delves into themes of infatuation and desire, focusing on a young woman that Bon observes at a concert. This encounter leads to a thrilling motorcycle ride, which is depicted with sensual and vivid imagery. The chorus, "Little lover, I can't get you off my mind," repeated throughout the song, emphasizes a deep infatuation or obsession with the woman described in the song. This repeated sentiment emphasizes the depth of his fascination and desire. This is complemented by the line, "I tried so hard to find someone like you," which suggests a longing for a specific kind of connection or relationship that the singer has been unable to find elsewhere. The verse "You had my picture on your bedroom wall, next to Gary Glitter" paints a picture of a fan's admiration, possibly hinting at a younger, perhaps more innocent attraction or the idolization of rock stars. This line also places the song within the context of rock 'n' roll culture, where musicians are often idolized by their fans. The focus on personal relationships, sexual desire, and the rock 'n' roll lifestyle is a recurring theme in their music, often delivered with a direct and unapologetic approach. The mention of a "wet patch on your seat" is provocative and suggestive, adding a risqué element to the song, typical of AC/DC's songs throughout their discography. Although the exact inspiration behind the song is not clearly known, it is believed to be influenced by real-life experiences, a common theme in many of AC/DC's songs.

"Stick Around"

The track "Stick Around" was a hidden gem that would not see a worldwide release until much later than the majority of the songs from this album which were released on the 1984 *'74 Jailbreak* EP. "Stick Around" finally made it to international release as part of the 2009 *Backtracks* box set. The opening riff packs a rock 'n' roll punch, and Bon weaves a tale through the verses of this track, which paints the story of a love relationship gone bad and him wondering why things have gone the way they have. "Stick Around" is essentially about a rocky relationship, where Bon is experiencing uncertainty and anxiety over his partner's potential departure. The song begins with the lines, "Well you came on like a hurricane, about a month ago, Blowing like a stiff breeze, always on the go." This introduction sets a tone of intensity and dynamism, possibly referring to a tumultuous relationship or a passionate encounter. The hurricane metaphor suggests something overwhelming and powerful, indicative of the impact the subject has had on Bon's life. The chorus, "Stick around yeah stick around, stick around babe stick around," is a straightforward plea or request for someone to stay. This simplicity is characteristic of AC/DC's lyrical style, where directness often takes precedence over complexity. The lyrics express a mix of confusion, plea, and nostalgia for better times in the relationship. Towards the end, the lines, "I take you out dancing, Honey we can go out to a show, spend a night romancing, Nights out on the town," suggest an attempt to rekindle a relationship or keep the excitement alive. This again ties into the theme of trying to hold onto something or someone enjoyable yet ephemeral. There is a sense of regret and a quest for understanding in lines like, "What have I been doing lately, to make you wanna go." Bon now questioning his actions and considering how they might have contributed to the current situation. The latter part of the song portrays Bon's attempts to rekindle their romance, suggesting going out dancing or spending a night on the town. This shows his willingness to make efforts to salvage the relationship and bring back the joy they once shared. Overall, the song captures the emotional turmoil of a relationship on the brink of ending. The lyrics convey confusion, longing for the past, and a desperate desire to keep his partner from leaving.

"Soul Stripper"

"Soul Stripper," my favorite track from this album, is a song that delves into themes of seduction, lust, manipulation, and emotional upheaval, common motifs in many rock songs, particularly those by AC/DC. The atmospheric intro sets a mysterious and alluring tone, creating a dark and enigmatic scene. As the song progresses, the rhythm section establishes a steady and pulsating groove that creates the foundation for the track. A really cool and unique aspect to this track is that it features a trade-off of guitar leads between brothers Angus and Malcolm Young. The opening lines, "Well I met her in the garden, underneath that old apple tree, sitting with a handful of flowers, looking as cool as can be," set a scene of idyllic innocence that might subtly nod to the biblical story of Adam and Eve and the theme of temptation. This imagery is quickly subverted as the song progresses, revealing a more manipulative and seductive scenario: "Then she laid her hand on my lap, Oh I thought I got to be dreaming, I didn't know I fell in her trap." The guitar work in "Soul Stripper" is exceptional and highlights the virtuosity of Angus Young. His ability to weave intricate and emotive melodies is on full display, as he effortlessly showcases his soulful, blues-inspired licks. Bon Scott's voice intertwines with the music, creating an atmosphere of sensuality and intrigue. The song creates a seductive and captivating theme of temptation, lust, and the power of the music itself. The chorus, "She was a soul stripper, yeah, she took my heart, she was a soul stripper, ooh, and tore me apart," uses the metaphor of a "soul stripper" to describe a woman who is captivating yet ultimately destructive. This figure metaphorically "strips" the narrator of his defenses, leaving him emotionally exposed and vulnerable. The lines, "Then she made me say things I didn't want to say, then she made me play games I didn't want to play," further emphasize the idea of being controlled or manipulated, a theme that is often explored in rock music, particularly in the context of romantic relationships. The imagery of the woman "moving nice and easy," getting "near to my spine," and leaving him "hollow and naked" intensifies the sense of vulnerability and exploitation. The dramatic turn of the knife scene could be interpreted as a metaphor for betrayal and the deep, lasting impact of such a relationship, where the protagonist is left emotionally wounded and scarred. AC/DC would perform "Soul Stripper" live during their early days performing in Australia.

"You Ain't Got a Hold on Me"

"You Ain't Got a Hold on Me" is a song that speaks to themes of independence and defiance, a recurring thread in many of AC/DC's works. The lyrics convey a strong sense of self-assurance and the refusal to be dominated or possessed by another person. The opening lines, "You can roll me round your finger, you can roll me if I'm blind, you can roll me tally ho ho, I'm the easy rollin' kind," initially suggest a willingness to go along with what the other person wants. However, this apparent compliance is quickly countered by the assertion in the following part of the verse: "but don't think I'm facin' downhill, 'cause soon you'll see, you'll lose your grip and slip, 'cause you ain't got a hold on me." The repeated lines, "You ain't got a hold on me," serve as a bold declaration of freedom, emphasizing the unwillingness to be dominated in any relational context. The song navigates through various scenarios, from intimate moments to general interactions, yet consistently returns to the central theme of maintaining self-control and not yielding to external influences. The song's structure is straightforward, with the chorus being the central element, driving home its message repeatedly. This theme is further reinforced in the lines "You can take me to your bedroom, you can take me to your heart, you can take me to a climax, I won't fall apart." Here, Bon recognizes the allure and potential influence of romantic or sexual encounters but asserts a strong sense of self, unaffected by these experiences. This is a classic example of hard rock music, where themes of resilience, self-sufficiency, and a certain nonchalance towards convention and expectation are predominant. Overall, the track reflects the principles of AC/DC's music: freedom, individuality, and a rebellious spirit against any form of control.

"Love Song (Oh Jene)"

Perhaps AC/DC's only "ballad" if you were to dare call it that, "Love Song (Oh Jene)" was set to be the very first single release from their debut album *High Voltage* in Australia. The intended B-side "Baby Please Don't Go" overshadowed it and received more airplay, effectively becoming the hit. "Love Song" tells likely a true story of a former lover whose name was Jene; the song was originally known as "Fell in Love" in AC/DC's earlier days with the first lineup. Bon Scott, who joined AC/DC in 1974, altered the lyrics during the recording process. Angus Young later expressed regret over this song, considering it the band's most regrettable one. He was not sure if they were trying to parody love songs of the time, and he mentioned that the song did not represent their sound, leading radio stations to flip the record over and play "Baby, Please Don't Go" instead. "Love Song" diverges from the band's typical hard rock style, expressing the singer's love and devotion to someone named Jean and delving into themes of love, longing, and vulnerability. The lyrics convey deep emotional connection and fear of loss, with the chorus repeating the name "Jean" to emphasize her significance in the singer's life. Bon Scott's vocals on "Love Song" are filled with sincerity and a touch of longing. His voice resonates with emotion, capturing the nuances of the lyrics and delivering them with heartfelt conviction. Bon's performance adds a layer of vulnerability to the song, showcasing his versatility as a vocalist. The imagery in the lyrics, such as "When you smile, I see stars in the sky, when you smile, I see sunrise," is poetic and romantic, a departure from AC/DC's usual straightforward and aggressive style. These lines evoke a sense of awe and admiration for the person being sung about. Towards the end, the lyrics, "If you leave me, you'll make me cry, When I think of you saying goodbye, Oh the sky turns to a deeper blue, that's how I'd feel if I lost you," express vulnerability and fear of loss, which is not commonly found in AC/DC's more upbeat and rebellious songs. Overall, "Love Song (Oh Jene)" is a unique piece and deviates from AC/DC's repertoire, a more subdued and heartfelt approach which offers a contrast to their usual high-energy rock style. The song would also be held back from the '74 *Jailbreak* EP released in 1984 (along with "Stick Around") and would not receive international release until its inclusion as part of the 2009 *Backtracks* box set.

"Show Business"

"Show Business" offers a candid and somewhat cynical look at the music industry, reflecting on the challenges and realities faced by musicians. Exactly as the title says, this song is about show business and the reality of the hardships of the business, the struggle of making it as a band, and the fact that the record companies and managers get rich and the musicians are stuck with the debt and the challenges while doing all of the hard work. The recurring phrase "That's show business" serves as a sardonic chorus, underscoring the various challenges and paradoxes faced by musicians—a tale of life as a band, performing the pubs and bars of the early Australian circuit, tiring, draining, and working hard, sometimes multiple shows in a day without much pay. A real boogie-blues, rock 'n' roll-style riff, "Show Business" finishes the album with introspective lyrics that shed light on the hardships of the music industry, providing a perspective to the listener of the world of show business. The opening lines, "You learn to sing, you learn to play, why don't the businessmen, ever learn to pay," immediately set a tone of frustration and irony. It highlights the contrast between the artist's passion and dedication to their craft and the business side of the music industry, which is often seen as exploitative or unfair. The chorus, "That's show business, show business, show business, That's the way it goes," is repeated multiple times, underlining a sense of resignation to the realities of the music industry. It suggests that the hardships and injustices faced by musicians are just a part of the business. Musically, "Show Business" showcases the band's versatility with a more restrained and atmospheric approach. The Young brothers demonstrate their skillful guitar work by crafting melodic lines that complement the introspective nature of the song, which also features trade-off guitar solos between them, something that had tapered off by the following year when Angus took over the lead guitar role. The guitars weave together intricately, creating a tapestry of sound that adds depth and richness to the overall composition. Bon Scott's vocal performance adds an additional layer of depth and authenticity to the already captivating track. The verse, "You play in halls, play in bars, you're climbin' walls, chasing' stars," speaks to the grind and struggle of trying to make it in the music world. Playing in small venues, constantly striving for success, and metaphorically "climbing walls" paints a picture of the constant uphill battle artists face. Towards the end, the lyrics "You pay the man, you pay your dues, when it's all gone, ooh, you sing the blues" reflects the financial challenges and the emotional toll of pursuing a career in music. The idea of paying dues and eventually being left with nothing but the blues encapsulates the often-harsh reality of the industry. The final verses delve into the physical and emotional exhaustion faced by musicians, where even personal relationships and pleasures become taxing and unrewarding. This represents the often-overlooked aspect of the musician's lifestyle—the weariness and personal sacrifices made behind the scenes. "Show Business" is a great rock track that captures the essence of AC/DC's early struggles as a band and delivers a message that remains relevant in the music industry today.

Interesting Facts

AC/DC endured several lineup changes in their early days, having gone through several bassists and drummers after the original lineup that had included singer Dave Evans. At the time of recording the *High Voltage* album, they did not have a full-time bassist or drummer, so George Young stepped in to record the bass parts and they hired session drummer Tony Currenti to handle the drum parts. Peter Clack had also contributed to drum portions of the recording. The album was likely left intentionally vague due to this fact, with no mention of band members or a lineup and a slightly blurred photo collage on the reverse cover of the sleeve. The track Baby Please Don't Go was originally credited to Broonzy (Big Bill Broonzy); however, later pressings of the album were updated to reflect the correct song writing credit to Joe Williams.

2

T.N.T.

Release date:	December 1, 1975 (Australia)
Current edition:	Albert Productions/EMI, CD
Personnel:	Bon Scott, lead vocals
	Angus Young, lead guitar
	Malcolm Young, rhythm guitar
	Mark Evans, bass guitar
	Phil Rudd, drums
	George Young, bass guitar on "High Voltage" and "School Days"
Duration:	41:55
Recorded at:	Albert Studios, Sydney, Australia, March–July 1975
Produced by:	Harry Vanda & George Young
Chart position:	#2 Australian Albums

Notable info: Released in Australia and New Zealand only. The first album with the classic AC/DC lineup. A combination of tracks from the majority of the *T.N.T.* album and two tracks from the previous *High Voltage* album were released as the international album titled *High Voltage* in 1976. *High Voltage* is certified 9x platinum in Australia.

AC/DC's follow-up and second studio album, *T.N.T.*, was released exclusively in Australia and New Zealand in 1975; it showcases the foundation of what AC/DC as a band, both lyrically and musically, were to become. The raunchy, rock 'n' roll pub sounds are captured on this recording and begin to reveal the genius songwriting talents of Bon Scott. This album captures the band's raw energy and sound at its formative stage. Produced by Harry Vanda and George Young, *T.N.T.* is characterized by its straightforward hard rock and blues-rock influences. Bon was truly a genius with his double-entendre, tongue-in-cheek lyrics telling tales of sex, booze, and life on the road. The lyrics are filled with a sense of rebellion, humor, and a celebration of the rock 'n' roll lifestyle. *T.N.T.* played a significant role in establishing AC/DC's popularity in Australia and laid the foundation for their international success. If *T.N.T.* had been AC/DC's debut, it would very well be the finest debut album ever released by a rock band. Everything that AC/DC embodies, in both name and live performance, is summed up on this record, which delivers the power and rock guitar assault one could only expect from an album called *T.N.T.* The album cover is no exception; the gatefold sleeve depicts several broken boards spraypainted in red with "AC / DC T. N. T." laid across a background of broken rocks and debris. The inner sleeve was typewritten and included the lyrics to the songs as well as mock police files of each of the band members. The packaging reinforced AC/DC's high-voltage rock 'n' roll sound and attitude to fans and critics alike. The majority of the tracks from the nine-track album would make up most of AC/DC's first internationally released album, titled *High Voltage*. Along with the seven tracks taken from *T.N.T.*, the international version of the *High Voltage* album also included two tracks from the original Australian *High Voltage* album, "She's Got Balls" and "Little Lover." The two tracks held back from *T.N.T.* were "Rocker" and "School Days." "Rocker" would later find its way on the international version of *Dirty Deeds Done Dirt Cheap*, while "School Days" would remain a rarity until its international release as part of the 2009 *Backtracks* box set.

The international version of the *High Voltage* album featured mock letters written to each of the band members on the reverse side of the album cover, illustrating their trouble-making reputations. The letter addressed to Angus and Malcolm's mother was from their school, complaining about the brothers' illicit behavior. The letter to Phil was from a father threatening to press charges for an incident the night before where Phil allegedly cracked a drumstick over his daughter's head; the broken drumstick is laid across the image of the letter. Mark's letter is from the Shakedown Club, banning him from the establishment based on his previous antics, which are now deemed worse having joined AC/DC. Lastly, Bon's letter is from a smitten girl who claims that her father, the mayor of her town, would pull Bon's arms off if he ever saw him in person. Quite candid and similar to the police files depicted on the inner fold out of the *T.N.T.* album cover.

"It's a Long Way to the Top (If You Wanna Rock 'n' Roll)"

Probably one of the most recognized and epic rock 'n' roll anthems of all time, "It's a Long Way to the Top (If You Wanna Rock 'n' Roll)" is one of the most significant AC/DC songs ever released. Not only does Bon Scott's poetic verses in this song describe the long and challenging feat it would be to make it in the music business, but as a tribute to his Scottish heritage, Bon plays bagpipes in the song, which he had to learn to play during the recording sessions. From the opening riff, which is later accompanied by the wailing bagpipe notes, a sense of grandeur and uniqueness immediately grabs the listener's attention. It was true that Bon played in a pipe band when he was a youth, but he was the drummer—something the band found out last minute with the expectation that he already knew how to play the pipes. Although Bon did play the recorder during his days with Fraternity, the bagpipes proved to be more challenging. The unconventional use of bagpipes in a rock song sets "It's a Long Way to the Top" apart from the rest, giving it a distinct flavor and an unmistakable identity. The bagpipes provide a powerful and soaring introduction that ignites the track with an irresistible allure. Bon's vocals are charismatic and filled with a rebellious rock 'n' roll spirit. His powerful and soulful delivery captures the essence of the lyrics, which depict the hardships and sacrifices of a life dedicated to rock 'n' roll. "Gettin' had, gettin' took, I tell you folks, it's harder than it looks" tells the tale of the struggles of life on the road and making it in the music business. Bon's voice exudes authenticity and determination; this song would ultimately become one of the world's most iconic rock music anthems after Bon's tragic death in 1980. The chorus is undeniably anthemic, with its sing-along quality and memorable lyrics. "It's a Long Way to the Top" is a timeless classic that continues to inspire generations of rock 'n' roll enthusiasts, reminding us that the road to success may be arduous, but the journey is what defines us. On February 23, 1976, the band recorded an iconic promotional video for the song on the back of a flatbed truck as it drove down Swanston Street in Melbourne, Australia. The video was aired on the Australian TV program *Countdown* and was made commercially available on the AC/DC *Family Jewels* DVD. AC/DC would perform this track live on many occasions in their earlier days in Australia and in the UK, with Bon handling the bagpipe duties live on stage. The song was eventually retired from the live set list; however, it made a surprise return to the set during the band's performance at the Hammersmith Odeon in London on December 17, 1979 with the bagpipe portion being played on a synthesizer from behind the stage.

"The Rock 'n' Roll Singer"

"The Rock 'n' Roll Singer" is a gritty and electrifying rocker that embodies the essence of the rock 'n' roll lifestyle and serves as a tribute to those who live and breathe the music. Likely drawing inspiration from Stevie Wright's "Guitar Band," Bon Scott's vocals are the centerpiece of "The

Rock 'n' Roll Singer." His gravelly voice exudes charisma and attitude, capturing the essence of a true rock 'n' roll frontman. Bon's powerful delivery and emotive storytelling transport the listener into the world of a struggling musician, grappling with the challenges and sacrifices of chasing their rock 'n' roll dreams. The lyrics are a powerful expression of the rebellious and nonconformist ethos that defines rock and roll. The song begins with a bold rejection of conventional societal expectations, as evidenced by the lines, "You can stick your moral standards 'cause it's all a dirty lie" and "You can stick your golden handshake and you can stick your silly rules and all the other shit that they teach to kids in school." This sets the tone for a narrative of defiance and self-determination. "They wanted me to be respected as a doctor or a lawyer man," Bon sings, as he wittingly responds "but I had other plans..." Bon chooses a different path, symbolized by the act of leaving school, growing his hair, and embracing the identity of a rock 'n' roll singer. The chorus, "Gonna be a rock 'n' roll singer ... Gonna be a rock 'n' roll star," repeated throughout the song, serves as a mantra of aspiration and determination. It is a declaration of an unwavering commitment to their dream, despite societal disapproval and the challenges inherent in such a lifestyle. Moreover, the song also touches upon the allure of fame and the desire to see one's name in lights, as highlighted by the lines, "I can see my name in lights, And I can see the queue." This reflects the ambitious side of the band's dream, driven by a desire for recognition and success in the rock 'n' roll world. Overall, "The Rock 'n' Roll Singer" encapsulates the spirit of rock 'n' roll, characterized by a rejection of societal norms, a pursuit of personal dreams against all odds, and an unyielding passion for rock music. The song is a vivid portrayal of the rock 'n' roll lifestyle, emphasizing individualism, rebellion, and the pursuit of one's true calling.

"The Jack"

"The Jack" by AC/DC is a cleverly veiled narrative set within the context of a poker game, using card game metaphors to depict a sexual encounter. "She's Got the Jack" as it is otherwise known is a classic AC/DC track that showcases the brilliance of Bon Scott's lyrical genius and play on words. To the unsuspecting listener, the song is about a game of poker, with the usual sexual overtones interweaved through each word. The wittiness of the lyrics makes it a stand-out AC/DC track from their repertoire. This is reinforced by the line, "But how was I to know that she'd been dealt with before?" suggesting the woman's past sexual experiences. In poker, a "jack" is a middle-ranked card, but here, it is a play on words, referring to a sexually transmitted disease. The live version, however, gets more to the point with completely different verses than what is heard on the studio track, essentially removing the metaphors and getting straight to the point of "She's got the clap." A standard blues-rock riff, "The Jack" chugs along as Bon tells his story, and the listener can almost see Bon smirking as he sings the words. Angus delivers a blistering guitar solo, which compliments the track's sexuality. The song opens with Bon being enticed by a woman, represented through the metaphor of her giving him the "queen" and the "king," suggesting a seemingly favorable situation in a card game. However, the lyrics soon reveal that the situation is more complex and riskier, as indicated by references to her "deuce" and his "ace." Lyrically, "The Jack" tells a tale of love, lust, and the consequences that can come with it. Bon's witty lyrics create a playful and provocative narrative, making the song both intriguing and memorable. Throughout the song, the woman is described as skilled in deception, much like a poker player. Her expertise in the game symbolizes her prowess and control in her interactions. The protagonist's realization of being outplayed comes too late, as he acknowledges that he should have seen the signs of her "dealing" from the "bottom of the pack." Essentially, the song is about the misfortune of getting venereal disease, likely based on real-life experiences of the band's early Australian pub days. Bon Scott's vocals on "The Jack" are gritty and filled with attitude, perfectly embodying the spirit of the song. Bon Scott's charismatic performance adds an extra layer of authenticity, making the track feel like a live performance in a smoky, dimly lit venue. The clever wordplay and double meanings in the lyrics showcase AC/DC's ability to embed deeper stories within seemingly straightforward rock songs, making it a classic example of their lyrical ingenuity.

"Live Wire"

One of my personal all-time favorite AC/DC tracks, "Live Wire" is a high-energy song that epitomizes the band's raw and powerful approach to rock music. AC/DC have always been an "electric" band, hence the band name and titles like *High Voltage*, and "Live Wire" fits this theme. After its release in 1975, it became a staple in the band's setlist, as the opening live track for most of their concerts through 1979. The song would also be the B-side on the "High Voltage" single released in the UK in 1976. "Live Wire" is a high-octane rock masterpiece that unleashes a relentless assault on the senses, from the moment the song kicks off with its explosive guitar riff along with its driving rhythm section; the song is a memorable AC/DC classic. Bon Scott's vocals are a standout feature of "Live Wire." His gritty and charismatic voice oozes with attitude and intensity as he delivers the lyrics with a captivating blend of power and swagger. The opening lines set the tone, with Bon positioning himself as the go-to person for trouble and satisfaction, implying a rebellious and adventurous spirit. The imagery used, such as being "cool as a body on ice" and "hotter than the rolling dice," further emphasizes the duality of his character—both calm and collected, yet capable of explosive energy. The rhythmic interplay between Angus and Malcolm Young is the backbone of the song, creating a pulsating energy and an irresistible groove that drives the track to its explosive climax. The song itself is electrifying, and Bon's delivery is masterful: "Oh come on honey, you've got nothin' to lose, you've got the thirst, and I've got the booze." Mötley Crüe would also borrow the title for one of their own songs, along with much of their early album lyrics, which were heavily influenced by AC/DC and Bon Scott ("Public Enemy Number 1" is another example, among several others). The chorus, "I'm a live wire, gonna set this town on fire," encapsulates the song's essence—a declaration of Bon's intent to bring dynamic excitement wherever he goes. Moreover, the song exudes a sense of spontaneity, as seen in lines like "You've got the phone and the number, and I got no future plans." This reflects a live-for-the-moment attitude, where plans are irrelevant, and the focus is on immediate gratification, an attitude which will be found throughout AC/DC's fifty-year discography. This track is a bold assertion of energy, sexuality, and fearlessness, delivered with AC/DC's characteristic hard rock flair.

"T.N.T."

The title track of their second Australian album, "T.N.T." is a high-voltage rock anthem that has become synonymous with the band's iconic sound and electrifying performances. It exudes a raw energy and rock 'n' roll power that has solidified its status as one of AC/DC's most beloved songs. The song is a brash proclamation of Bon Scott's unapologetic and explosive rock 'n' roll personality, akin to the volatile nature of the explosive T.N.T. itself. The introduction to the song following the E power chord is at first a gravelly throated chant of "Oi, oi, oi, oi/Oi, oi, oi, oi, oi, oi, oi," which emerges into a loud unifying chant. It is reminiscent of the Marcus Hook Roll Band recording of "Ape Man" with the ongoing grunts in the background, likely a testament to the original concept, where traces of this sort of approach can also be heard on the title track to the following studio album *Dirty Deeds Done Dirt Cheap*. The track exemplifies what AC/DC is all about—power, energy, and a tough rock 'n' roll street attitude. Bon Scott's lyrics, filled with playful wordplay and clever innuendos, tell a tale of explosive power and the irresistible allure of the band's music. The opening lines, "See me ride out of the sunset on your color TV screen," immediately establish Bon as a larger-than-life figure, akin to a modern, rebellious outlaw. The imagery of riding out of the sunset, traditionally associated with Western heroes, is subverted here to introduce a character who is out for personal gain and indulgence ("Out for all that I can get"). Lines like "Lock up your daughter, lock up your wife, lock up your back door and run for your life" have become a rallying cry for fans, inviting them to embrace the rebellious, high-voltage spirit of rock 'n' roll. The song's anthemic quality is further enhanced by the powerful backing vocals, adding a layer of depth and intensity to the already explosive sound. The song captures the essence of rock 'n' roll with its rebellious attitude and unadulterated power, making it an enduring classic whose popularity is a testament to its ability to resonate with fans indefinitely.

"Rocker"

"Rocker" is a high-octane rock 'n' roll song. The track would later appear on the non-Australian versions of *Dirty Deeds Done Dirt Cheap*, but with a fade out rather than the sudden and abrupt cut heard here on *T.N.T.* The song exudes a sense of liberation and the wild abandon of rock 'n' roll music. Bon describes himself using a series of bold, assertive statements: "I'm a rocker, I'm a roller, I'm a right out of controller." These lines immediately establish his identity as someone who lives on the edge, embodying the spirit of rock 'n' roll. The repetition of "I'm a rocker, I'm a roller" throughout the song acts as a chant, reinforcing this identity. The track would become a staple in AC/DC's live repertoire during the mid-'70s through the early '80s. The song's lyrics are a straightforward and unabashed celebration of the rock 'n' roll identity, characterized by a sense of freedom, rebellion, and a carefree attitude. The track also delves into the aesthetics and symbols associated with the classic rock culture, taking much inspiration from AC/DC's own early influences from the 1950s rock era. References to "slicked black hair, skin-tight jeans, Cadillac car, and a teenage dream" paint a vivid picture of the classic rock 'n' roll look and lifestyle. This is further emphasized with mentions of "lurex socks, blue suede shoes, V8 car, and tattoos," all of which are iconic elements of the rock 'n' roll image. The lyrics convey a sense of invincibility and confidence, attributes often idolized in rock culture. Phrases like "I'm a wicked woman stealer," "I'm a bruiser," and "I'm a cruiser" depict the narrator as someone who is tough, irresistible, and constantly on the move. "Rocker" is an ode to the rock 'n' roll lifestyle, celebrating the freedom, rebellion, and the persona of being a "rock 'n' roll man." The song's energy and straightforward lyrics make it an enduring anthem, embodying the spirit of rock music as envisioned by AC/DC. An extended version of the song would also serve as Angus Young's guitar solo track for some of AC/DC's early live performances.

"Can I Sit Next to You Girl"

AC/DC's original single released in 1974, "Can I Sit Next to You Girl" was rearranged and recorded for *T.N.T.*, now with the band's first solidified studio and touring lineup. The song captures the essence of AC/DC's early sound with a very noticeable The Easybeats influence, likely a derivative of working directly with producers George Young and Harry Vanda, which can be heard heavily throughout this track. The Young brothers deliver a very catchy, foot-stomping groove that is characteristic of AC/DC's early sound accompanied by the driving groove of the rhythm section duo Phil Rudd and Mark Evans. Their contribution forms the backbone of the track, creating a solid platform for the guitars and vocals to shine. Bon's voice brings the track to life with charisma and confidence, singing about his cheeky pursuit of a girl. Scott's dynamic performance adds an extra layer of personality, making the song feel alive and vibrant. Bon adds his own twists to the song in comparison to the original version of the track, which was sung by AC/DC's first singer Dave Evans. "Oh, I took him by surprise, when I gave him one of my lines, she started smiling at me real fine, and that's when I said ... Can I sit next to you girl?" sings Bon with the upmost confidence that he would win this girl over from the guy she was with. AC/DC would perform this song during their live sets in the early days, but it would later be replaced with higher-energy rock tracks.

"High Voltage"

"High Voltage" is a spirited homage to the electrifying essence of rock 'n' roll, both as a genre and a lifestyle. The repeated chorus, "High voltage rock 'n' roll," serves as the heart of the song, symbolizing the intense energy and power of rock music, specifically done the AC/DC way. The term "high voltage," typically associated with electric power, is the perfect metaphor that summarizes not only AC/DC's high-energy rock style, but

AC/DC as a band. This metaphor extends to the description of the band's performance as needing to be "plugged in" to unleash their full potential, much like an electric device. The lyrics also touch upon themes of freedom and self-expression. Questions like "Why do I grow my hair?" or "Why am I in a band?" are answered in a way that emphasizes the commitment to personal freedom and non-conformity in the rock 'n' roll lifestyle. Phrases like "I dig doin' one-night stands" and "I got to get my kicks some way" reflect a desire for spontaneity and living in the moment, key elements of the rock 'n' roll spirit. Furthermore, the song invites the audience to participate in this high-energy experience, the track would be a live staple during many of AC/DC's early shows with audience participation as Bon demanded the crowd to loudly shout "High" at his command. The song is an anthem celebrating the power, energy, and rebellious spirit of rock 'n' roll. Through its straightforward lyrics and driving rhythm, AC/DC captures the essence of what makes rock music captivating and enduring and essentially defines AC/DC's overall music style. Although AC/DC's first album was titled *High Voltage*, the album did not have a title track, at least not at the time. "High Voltage" would eventually become a title track once it became part of the international version of the *High Voltage* album released in 1976; however, the first album appearance of this song was a year earlier as part of *T.N.T.* The version of "High Voltage" on this album is a longer version than the fade-out version included on the international version of the album where it is the title track. On *T.N.T.*, the song and guitar solo continues until the ending lead guitar note, which fades into the very beginning of "School Days." "High Voltage" summarizes essentially what AC/DC is all about, much like some of their other tracks on this album ("Live Wire" and "T.N.T." respectively)—high-voltage rock 'n' roll, power, energy, electricity. Angus even came up with the guitar riff, trying to come up with an A, C, D, C chord progression for the song. The song is a salute to what AC/DC stands for and was the band's way of saying this is who we are, and we are here to conquer the world.

"School Days"

The final track on *T.N.T.* is a cover song of Chuck Berry's "School Days." *T.N.T.* was the second and final AC/DC album to feature a cover song. Chuck Berry was a huge influence on the band, especially in the early days when they would often perform cover songs of '50s rock hits by Chuck Berry in addition to songs by Little Richard, Elvis Presley, and others. It was rare for the band to include cover songs on their albums, but on the first two records ("Baby Please Don't Go" on the original

High Voltage album), they decided to include a cover song. The AC/DC rendition of "School Days" is a great rocker and presents itself just as that, a straightforward rock 'n' roll, guitar-driven song that you can stomp your foot to. I think that Chuck would have been proud.

Interesting Facts

"The Rock 'n' Roll Singer" is titled as "Rock 'n' Roll Singer" (dropping "The") on the international release of *High Voltage*. The remake of the song "Can I Sit Next to You, Girl" from the prior year with the original AC/DC lineup featured on *T.N.T.* drops the comma in the title. "Rocker" is shorter than the fade-out version included on the international version of *Dirty Deeds Done Dirt Cheap*. On *T.N.T.*, "High Voltage" is a longer version than that issued on the international *High Voltage* album. On the tracks "High Voltage" and "School Days," George Young played bass guitar.

3

Dirty Deeds Done Dirt Cheap

Release date:	September 20, 1976 (Australia) December 17, 1976 (U.K.) March 23, 1981 (U.S.)
Current edition:	Albert/EMI, CD, Sony/Columbia CD, LP
Personnel:	Bon Scott, lead vocals Angus Young, lead guitar Malcolm Young, rhythm guitar Mark Evans, bass guitar Phil Rudd, drums
Duration:	42:24 (Australia), 39:59 (international)
Recorded at:	Albert Studios, Sydney, Australia, December–March 1976 & Vineyard Studios, London, England, September 1976 ("Love at First Feel")
Produced by:	Harry Vanda & George Young
Chart position:	#5 Australian Albums #3 U.S. *Billboard* 200

Notable info: This album was not released in North America until 1981. The Australian and New Zealand version of the album had a different picture sleeve and track listing than the rest of the world. *Dirty Deeds Done Dirt Cheap* is certified 6x platinum in the USA, 6x platinum in Australia with additional platinum and gold certifications in other countries.

AC/DC's third studio album, *Dirty Deeds Done Dirt Cheap*, was recorded at Albert Studios in Sydney, Australia, once again and produced by the mastermind team Vanda and Young. It is another album originally only released in Australia, but it would later follow with a UK and European release later the same year. The album was held back for release in North America, finally releasing shortly after AC/DC struck an international record deal with Atlantic Records (Atco); the record company decided to restrict the album's release and focus on the band's next album to make a bigger impact, especially for the United States. Produced by Harry Vanda and George Young, the album exhibits a more unrefined and gritty sound compared to the band's later, more polished works. The album is notable for its straightforward, no-nonsense, blues-infused rock 'n' roll, driven by powerful guitar riffs, steady rhythms, and Bon Scott's distinctive, raspy vocals. The lyrics are characterized by humor, rebelliousness, and a touch of menace, reflecting the band's usual themes. According to Angus Young:

> When I was younger, there was this cartoon, with a sea serpent and some guy called Beanie. But the bad guy in it was this guy called Dishonest John and he used to pop out every now and again, he'd pop up with this card and it went "Dirty Deeds Done Dirt Cheap" and you know, special rates, holidays, you know, and Sunday's. So, as a kid I always saw that, it always stuck in my head, so it seemed a good idea, you know to come up with a title like that. Especially from this band.

The original Australian version of the album features completely different album cover artwork depicting cartoon-like caricatures of the band members romping around in a billiard hall as well as a different track listing than any of the other international versions of the record. The international album featured a different album cover design as well as a different track listing. Songs such as "Jailbreak" and "R.I.P. (Rock in Peace)" were completely omitted and were replaced with "Love at First Feel," a track recorded later during a recording session that took place in the UK, and "Rocker," taken from the Australian-only *T.N.T.*, but with a fade out of the song. The track order of the Australian and New Zealand release is also different than the other releases, and there are additional subtle differences in some songs; "Ain't No Fun Waiting Around to Be a Millionaire" goes on for a bit longer before the fade out on the Australian version. The title track on the Australian version also features a longer version of the song with a different mix. The album release in 1981 to North American markets was a poorly timed decision by Atlantic Records at the time. AC/DC were just about to release their second studio album with then-new singer Brian Johnson as the follow up to their extremely successful *Back in Black* album, and although *For Those About to Rock (We Salute You)* catapulted up the U.S. *Billboard* charts to #1 and quickly went platinum, the release of *Dirty Deeds Done Dirt Cheap* at the time impacted what could have otherwise been additional success of *For Those About to Rock* and also led to confusion among many newer fans who AC/DC's singer was.

"Dirty Deeds Done Dirt Cheap"

The title track and opening song on the album *Dirty Deeds Done Dirt Cheap* is a tongue-in-cheek exploration of organized crime, revenge, and clandestine activities. In the song, Bon presents himself as a mercenary of sorts, offering illicit services to those seeking retribution or solutions to their problems. The guitar riff and AC/DC's distinctive and unmistakable guitar tone opens the album, accompanied by a rhythmic groove. The opening verse sets the tone, addressing a student having trouble with a high school authority figure. Bon offers a solution, a criminal approach to resolving this issue. "Pick up the phone, I'm always home, call me anytime, just ring 36-24-36 hey, I lead a life of crime." This establishes the song's central theme: offering "dirty deeds" as a means to deal with life's problems, albeit in a morally questionable way. This line resulted in a fair bit of unwanted, although slightly humorous publicity, where people started calling this "telephone number" in different parts of Australia at late night and early morning hours asking about getting their dirty deeds done dirt cheap. The gravely throated, repeated chorus, "Dirty deeds, done dirt cheap," is catchy and emphasizes the underhanded nature of the services offered, reminiscent of the chorus in "T.N.T." The backing vocals are purposefully gritty to give the track an overall sinister feel. The lyrics are filled with references to various forms of underhanded tactics, like "concrete shoes, cyanide, TNT," "neckties, contracts, high voltage," all which serve to exaggerate the extent of the Bon's willingness to engage in illicit activities. Moreover, the song touches on themes of infidelity and relationship issues, which Bon quickly offers his services to eliminate the source of her troubles. "Come right in, forget about him, we'll have ourselves a ball." The song's blend of dark humor, catchy chorus, and rock rhythm makes it a unique and memorable track in AC/DC's discography, capturing the band's ability to combine edgy themes with an energetic rock sound. "Dirty Deeds Done Dirt Cheap" has since become a fan favorite over the years, ever since its North American release, and has remained a staple in AC/DC's live set.

"Ain't No Fun (Waiting Around to Be a Millionaire)"

"Ain't No Fun (Waiting Around to Be a Millionaire)" offers a satirical and somewhat cynical take on the pursuit of fame and fortune, particularly in the music industry. A testament to AC/DC's early struggles for stardom, much like "Rock 'n' Roll Singer" and "It's a Long Way to the Top (If You Wanna Rock 'n' Roll)" from the year before, the song is a celebration of rock 'n' roll and the band's vision for superstardom. The song narrates the story of leaving a mundane life behind with dreams of becoming a rock star, only to face the harsh realities of this pursuit. The song chugs along with a slow rock 'n' roll groove and raw guitar with the opening lines, "Well, I left my job in my hometown, and I headed for the smoke," setting the stage for a classic tale of chasing dreams. The line, "I got holes in my shoes, I got holes in my teeth, I got holes in my socks, I can't get no sleep," highlights the financial and personal hardships faced while on the road, all of which were likely truthful testaments to AC/DC's own hardships. "One of these days see me driving around town in my rockin' rolls Royce with the sun roof down..." Bon's vision for stardom was definite and his determination shines throughout the song. The lyrics paint a gleeful tale of the struggle and commitment to finally achieving success and stardom in rock 'n' roll music, something that the band would later achieve, likely to a magnitude that they never even dreamt of. "Hey Howard, how are you doing, friend? Oh yea, get your fuckin' jumbo jet outta my airport" sneers Bon with a cheeky tone toward the end of the track, a testament that he finally made it big. The song is a long one, compared to most AC/DC tracks, at 7:31 in length. Midway through the song, the riff picks up pace and becomes a faster rocker with the repeated chorus "Ain't No Fun" and Bon ad-libbing through the fade out.

"There's Gonna Be Some Rockin'"

An old school rock 'n' roll groover, "There's Gonna Be Some Rockin'" is one of those laid-back AC/DC tracks that tells the tales of playing in a rock 'n' roll band on stage. A classic '50s-rock-inspired riff opens the song, and Bon begins to tell the story, focusing on the promise of a lively and memorable night: "Well, me and the boys are out to have some fun, gonna put on a show, come on, let's go... There's gonna be some rockin'.... Every night there's a rock n roll queen, gonna quiver and quake, gonna shake her thing." The guitar riff is similar to some of the other AC/DC songs on the album—namely "Rocker" and "Ain't No Fun (Waiting Around to be a Millionaire)"—and features a classic rock 'n' roll blues chord progression. Malcolm once stated in an interview that it was not one of his favorite AC/DC tracks, likely a reason why it was never part of AC/DC's live set. "Theres Gonne Be Some Rockin'" is essentially a straightforward celebration of live rock music. The song encapsulates the essence of live rock performances, emphasizing the anticipation, excitement, and the shared experience between the band and the audience.

"Problem Child"

"Problem Child" is a powerful AC/DC track that is a tribute to the band's rebellious spirit and high-voltage, rock 'n' roll sound. The lyrics present Bon as an archetype of a rebellious youth, embodying traits of defiance, danger, and nonconformity. The song interplays the problematic snotnosed schoolboy attitude of Angus and the street-tough brawler attitude of Bon, perfectly illustrating the onstage banter that would take place as the two would feed off of each other's energy during live performances. The opening lines, "I'm hot, and when I'm not, I'm cold as ice," immediately establish Bon's unpredictable and extreme nature. This is further emphasized by the lines "Get out my way, just step aside, or pay the price," which convey a no-nonsense attitude and a readiness to confront anyone who stands in his way. The chorus, "I'm a problem child, and I'm wild," serves as a bold declaration and perhaps even the self-acceptance and pride in being a troublemaker and someone who lives by their own rules. Lines like "Make my stand, no man's land, on my own" and "Man in blue, it's up to you, the seed is sown" suggest a sense of solitary defiance against authority figures, further cementing the central theme of one's rebellious nature. Bon's delivery is filled with charisma and a devil-may-care attitude, capturing the essence of being a "problem child" and embracing it without reservation. Through its lyrics, AC/DC captures the essence of the rebellious spirit that often characterizes youth, particularly within the context of rock music. The song's raw energy and straightforward lyrics resonate as a powerful expression of teenage rebellion and nonconformity, a popular theme that will be found in many AC/DC songs. "Problem Child" would later find itself as part of the international release (most versions) of *Let There Be Rock* the following year, as it was decided that *Dirty Deeds Done Dirt Cheap* would be held back for release in America at the time. "Problem Child" would again later be reissued on the North American version of *Dirty Deeds Done Dirt Cheap*, despite the track already being available on *Let There Be Rock*.

"Squealer"

"Squealer" gets right to the point as a song with sexually explicit lyrics that describe a sexual encounter with a woman. The rhythm section, consisting of bassist Mark Evans and drummer Phil Rudd, provides a solid groove and pulsating bass line. The song's content reflects themes of seduction, sexual foreplay, and dominance, charismatically illustrated by Bon. The opening lines, "She said she'd never been, never been touched before, she said she'd never been, this far before," introduce a scenario where the woman is portrayed as inexperienced or naive in sexual matters. The gradual foreplay described in the song later becomes more intense as the track continues on "When I held her hand, I made her understand" and "When I kissed her lips, sucked her finger tips." The chorus, consisting of the repeated word "Squealer!" suggests a response or reaction from the woman during the sexual encounter as Bon delightfully sings "She was a squealer." The song also contains a boastful tone with the lines "Fixed her good" and "I think I've got the magic touch!" which sets off an intense guitar solo by Angus Young that lasts for the remainder of the song. Angus really goes all out during this track, laying down a very memorable blazing and lengthy lead guitar solo through the fade out. The song's straightforward and unapologetic approach is typical of many AC/DC songs found throughout their discography.

"Big Balls"

AC/DC's "Big Balls" is a sarcastic and playful rock track that showcases Bon Scott's wit and his unique ability to craft dual-meaning lyrics, a trademark of his. "Big Balls" is a testament to Bon Scott's lyrical genius and AC/DC's ability to deliver rock tracks that combine catchy melodies with clever wordplay. The song cleverly plays on the dual meaning of the term "balls," referring both to elegant social gatherings (ballroom events) and to a more vulgar reference to male genitalia. This play on words creates a comedic and cheeky tone throughout the song. Bon positions himself as a prominent figure within this social setting, boasting about his status and the grandeur of his events, metaphorically described as "balls." The chorus, "I've got big balls, and they're such big balls, dirty big balls," is where the double entendre is most evident. The song continues to play with this double meaning in lines like, "And my balls are always bouncing, my ballroom always full." Here, the imagery of a crowded ballroom event doubles as a humorous reference to male genitalia. Bon's vocal delivery is laced with a mischievous charm that adds an extra layer of enjoyment to the song. The backup vocals at the end in a chant-like chorus of "bollocks, knackers" adds an additional layer of humor to the track as it fades out. It was never really a live song, although there is one time in the early days after the release of the *Dirty Deeds* album in Australia that the band performed it; however, it was never performed live again after that. "Big Balls" is a comical and satirical take on high society, using wordplay and double meanings to create humor, resulting in a witty and memorable song.

"R.I.P. (Rock in Peace)"

"R.I.P. (Rock in Peace)" is a boogie-blues, rock 'n' roll standard track that pays tribute to the pure joy and freedom found in rock 'n' roll. The lyrics are a straightforward celebration of the rock lifestyle, emphasizing a desire for unbridled musical expression and independence. The song pays homage to the power of rock music and the thrill of living life on the edge playing in a rock band. The opening lines, "Leave me alone, like a dog with a bone, like a stone that's been thrown, let me be on my own," set the tone for the entire song, expressing a yearning to be free from restrictions and to live in the moment. The chorus, "Let me rock, let me roll, let me rock, let me rock in peace," is a simple but powerful request to enjoy the act of rocking out without interference. This refrain is the heart of the song, encapsulating the essence of what it means to be absorbed in the energy and spirit of rock music. The lines "Outta my way, got a boogie to play, every dog has his day, rock 'n' roll's here to stay" further emphasize the enduring and unapologetic nature of rock 'n' roll. The lyrics also mention rock legends "Little Richard, Oh Jerry Lee, Chuck baby," which pay homage to the roots of rock 'n' roll and AC/DC's primary influences as a band. The song was kept back from the international version of *Dirty Deeds Done Dirt Cheap* and was also not included on the 1984 *'74 Jailbreak* EP release, so it remained an obscurity to mainstream fans until it was finally released internationally as part of the 2009 *Backtracks* box set release.

"Ride On"

"Ride On" is a standout track in AC/DC's extensive discography, showcasing the band's versatility and their ability to delve into emotional depths beyond their usual in-your-face rock tracks. The song encapsulates the pain of heartbreak and the longing for redemption. The lyrics paint a vivid picture of being at the crossroads of life, seeking solace and redemption after a tumultuous relationship. The song reflects on loneliness, regret, and the continuous search for redemption and change. The opening lines, "It's another lonely evening, in another lonely town," set a tone of isolation and wandering. This mood is carried throughout the song, as Bon speaks of his experiences with failed relationships and the consequent emptiness that follows, as depicted in "Got another empty bottle, mmh and another empty bed." With lines like "Broke another promise, and I broke another heart, But I ain't too young to realize, that I ain't too old to try, try to get back to the start," the song conveys a raw vulnerability rarely seen in AC/DC's early catalog. There is a recurring theme of confronting one's own flaws and the struggle to change. Lines like "one of these days I'm gonna change my evil ways" indicate a recognition of personal shortcomings and an aspiration to improve, although the journey towards change is ongoing, "for now I'll just keep 'em." "Ride On" features a fantastic and intense, blues-inspired guitar solo by Angus Young, which further elevates the emotions of the song. "Ride On" would eventually become "Bon's" song after his death in 1980, often cited as a tribute by fans around the world. "Ride On" takes listeners on an introspective journey of heartbreak, resilience, and redemption. It stands as a testament to the band's artistic range and their ability to craft deeply moving and timeless music. AC/DC have only performed this song live once, in Paris, France, in 2001.

"Jailbreak"

The song's foundation is built on the driving force of Malcolm Young's rhythm guitar, laying the groundwork to start the track. "Jailbreak" tells a dramatic and gritty story of a fugitive on the run and the prisoner's desperate attempt to regain his freedom and defying authority. Bon came up with the idea for the song after being arrested in Perth about a year prior to joining AC/DC. The song narrates a tale of incarceration, rebellion, and the ultimate cost of seeking liberty under extreme circumstances. The opening lines set the scene of a man sentenced to a long prison term: "There was a friend of mine on murder, and the judge's gavel fell, jury found him guilty, gave him 16 years in Hell." This introduction immediately establishes the song's dark and somber tone, highlighting the severity of the situation. The chorus, "Gonna make a (jailbreak) and I'm lookin' towards the sky, I'm gonna make a (jailbreak), Oh, how I wish that I could fly," captures the prisoner's longing for freedom and his determination to escape. The repeated use of the word "jailbreak" emphasizes the central theme of the song, and the line "Oh, how I wish that I could fly" metaphorically expresses the inmate's desire for liberation. "All in the name of liberty, all in the name of liberty, got to be free!" is declared before the chorus, conveying the pursuit of liberty and freedom no matter the cost. "He said he'd seen his lady being fooled with, by another man," describes a violent encounter when another man is found with his woman. "She was down and he was up" sneers Bon "he had a gun in his hand," a cheeky double-entendre. The song concludes with a dramatic escape, marked by "Heartbeats they were racin', freedom, he was chasin' ... but he made it out ... with a bullet in his back!" describing the ultimate fate of the prisoner. This line was recorded several times as drunken Bon made his way through the recording session to get that very perfect take you hear on the final recording. The song, for some reason, was held back from the international release of *Dirty Deeds Done Dirt Cheap* and would not see a worldwide release until 1984 as the title track of the *'74 Jailbreak* EP. The song's energy and narrative drive make it a standout track in the band's catalog. AC/DC would then incorporate it in their live set later, replacing "Bad Boy Boogie" as Angus' "striptease" song after many years.

"Love at First Feel"

"Love at First Feel" was not part of the original *Dirty Deeds Done Dirt* Cheap album released in Australia; however, it would be part of the international version of the album. The track would be released in Australia as the B-side of "Problem Child" in 1977. "Love at First Feel" was recorded at Vineyard studios in London in September 1976. The song was recorded during the same time the band recorded "Carry Me Home" and "Dirty Eyes" (and early version of "Whole Lotta Rosie"), possibly intended for an EP at the time. "Love at First Feel" explores the provocative theme of instant attraction and physical desire. The lyrics paint a vivid picture of a risqué, captivating encounter with an alluring, younger partner. The opening lines, "You never told me where you came from, you never told me your name," suggest a spontaneous and mysterious connection between Bon and the girl in the song. The phrase "Love at first feel" is a play on the more commonly heard "love at first sight," indicating that the connection is based more on physical sensation and immediate attraction rather than a visual or romantic ideal. This theme is further reinforced by the line "First touch was too much," suggesting an overwhelming and instant physical connection. Bon's playful and suggestive delivery adds an extra layer of charisma to the words, amplifying the song's sensual nature. The lines "They told me it was disgusting, they told me it was a sin" reflect the external criticism and moral judgment faced by Bon. This disapproval, however, seems to only intensify the allure and excitement of the relationship, as seen in "Saw me smile when you let me in," mischievously sang by Bon. Additionally, the setting of the song, implied in "Let's get something going, while your mum and dad ain't home," underscores the youthful and somewhat secretive nature of this affair. The reference to the absence of parents suggests a sneaking around and a sense of forbidden love, a common tale in young romance. The song captures the rebellious spirit of youth, challenging societal norms and embracing the impulsive and passionate nature of relationships, a theme common in many AC/DC tracks.

Interesting Facts

The title track "Dirty Deeds Done Dirt Cheap" from the Australian version of the album is longer, with an extended chorus portion towards the end of the song. When the album was reissued internationally in 1981, it featured a shortened version of the title track. The original version was subsequently released on certain international reissues of the album later. The Australian version of the album also features a slightly longer version of "Ain't No Fun (Waiting Around to Be a Millionaire)" which extends a bit more during the fade out than the version found on the international release.

"Jailbreak" and "R.I.P. (Rock in Peace)" were both held back from the Australian version for the international release. The international release had "Rocker" and "Love at First Feel" in their place. The version of "Rocker" is longer than the version found on *T.N.T.*, as it fades out at the end of the track.

4

Let There Be Rock

Release date:	March 21, 1977 (Australia) July 25, 1977 (U.K.) July 25, 1977 (U.S.)
Current edition:	Albert/EMI, CD, Sony/Columbia CD, LP
Personnel:	Bon Scott, lead vocals Angus Young, lead guitar Malcolm Young, rhythm guitar Mark Evans, bass guitar Phil Rudd, drums
Duration:	40:19 (Australia), 41:01 (International)
Recorded at:	Albert Studios, Sydney, Australia
Produced by:	Harry Vanda & George Young
Chart position:	#19 Australian Albums #17 U.K. Albums #154 U.S. *Billboard* 200

Notable info: The Australian version has a different picture sleeve and track listing. This was the last AC/DC album with Mark Evans on bass. *Let There Be Rock* is certified 2x platinum in the USA, 5x platinum in Australia, with additional platinum and gold certifications in other countries. "Problem Child," previously available on *Dirty Deeds Done Dirt Cheap*, was added in place of "Crabsody in Blue" for versions in North America and Japan.

Let There Be Rock is, to me, one of the definitive and defining moments of AC/DC's career as a band, and as a guitar player myself, this album is one of the greatest and quintessential rock albums ever written and recorded in music history. The album is raw, to the point, and what every rock 'n' roll enthusiast craves. Malcolm Young stated in an interview: "We thought, just from touring, especially in the states, you know, we need a bit more hard-edge rock here. So, me an Angus said we want more louder guitars, we want bigger solos, you know and let's take it to the max, you know and it came off." *Let There Be Rock*—recorded and produced at Albert Studios in Sydney, Australia, once again by the infamous Vanda and Young production team—sets AC/DC up for their trek to worldwide stardom. The album would be the first to get the much-needed attention from Atlantic Records (Atco) from a promotional perspective in North America but would also be the first AC/DC album to launch the band's first live appearances in the states. As Angus Young reminisced:

> We wanted a good guitar album and because you know, you had the different trends at the time. You had punk music coming out in Europe, you had America, was into the disco thing, so ... and we thought it would be totally different, hey you know, we'll go out and make a good hard rock album. You know, with plenty of guitars up front. And we thought that was our calling card. So, if you were going to go see AC/DC, you know you were going to get these big loud brash guitars in your face. You know, there would be no room for the timid.

Once again, the Australian version features a completely different album cover, as well as a different track listing. The European version had the same track listing; however, the album artwork would match the rest of the world's international release. The international album cover is a photo of the band performing on stage taken on March 19, 1977 at the Kursaal Ballroom in Southend, England. The image was overlayed with paint and illustrates an almost majestic, Godlike sky above and also featured the first rendition of the now classic AC/DC logo. The Australian album cover depicts a set of fingers in motion on a guitar neck set on black background and opens as a gatefold with several black and white live photos of the band on the inner sleeve. The fingers shown on the Australian cover are actually not Angus or Malcolm's but that of Chris Turner (Buffalo, Rose Tattoo). *Let There Be Rock* features only eight tracks, each epitomizing AC/DC's straightforward and powerful approach to music. The title track, "Let There Be Rock," is an anthemic song with a memorable riff, setting a hard-hitting tone for the album. "Bad Boy Boogie" and "Problem Child" offer a rhythmic drive and lyrical playfulness, typical of AC/DC's style. "Overdose" showcases a heavier, more intense aspect of the band's music. "Hell Ain't a Bad Place to Be" stands out for its raw energy and engaging rhythm. The album concludes with "Whole Lotta Rosie," a high-powered track that has become one of the band's most iconic songs. The track "Crabsody in Blue" was deemed too much of a risk, particularly for American markets at the time, so it was decided to include "Problem

Child" (taken from the previous year's *Dirty Deeds Done Dirt Cheap* album, released only in Australia) in its place. The record company also wanted more radio-friendly tracks and ultimately decided that "Crabsody in Blue" would be too risqué for North American markets. *Let There Be Rock* would solidify AC/DC's place in the rock genre and is revered for its influence on hard rock and heavy metal music.

"Go Down"

Speaking of risqué, "Go Down" kicks off *Let There Be Rock* and is essentially a song about fellatio, which couldn't be more direct in its lyrics. The song is a celebration of sexual encounters and pleasure, using vivid imagery and euphemisms to convey experiences and desire. It could not be more obvious to see what the song is about, likely an intentional effort by the band to show the record company who was really in charge of things. The song begins with references to two women, Ruby and Mary, each described in terms that highlight their sexual prowess and appeal. Ruby's skills with the "lickin' stick" and her ability to "make a strong man weak and a heathen pray" imply a powerful sexual allure and capability. Similarly, Mary is likened to a sting from a bumblebee, adding a sense of intensity and excitement to the sexual imagery. "Mary, Mary, you're the one for me, and the way you hum, stings me like a bumble bee," sings Bon gleefully as the tells the tales of his sexual encounters with various women throughout the song. Following the guitar solo, Bon essentially voices a climax, likely to the disapproval of the record company at the time. Overall, the song is straightforward, hard-rocking track, with in-your-face guitars and a driving rhythm section that is coupled with unapologetic themes of desire and physical attraction, direct sexual themes, and living life your own way.

"Dog Eat Dog"

"Dog Eat Dog" is a hard-hitting track, which captures the dog-eat-dog nature of the world, creating a sense of urgency and defiance. The song's title and chorus, "It's a dog eat dog," is a well-known idiom that encapsulates the competitive and ruthless environment, where self-interest reigns supreme. Perhaps written even as a reflection of the woes faced by the corporate music industry or bad dealings with previous management, Bon injects some humor in the mix with lines like "Eat cat too, the French eat frog, And I eat you." The brilliance of the lyrics in this track shines throughout the song and the verses truly tell the tale of a dog-eat-dog, vicious world: "See a blind man on the street, looking for something free, Hear the kind man ask his friends, Hey, what's in it for me." The chorus is memorable, with the catchy phrase of "hey hey hey, every dog has his day, it's a dog eat dog." Concluding with the repetitive chant of "Dog eat dog," the song reinforces the relentless and unforgiving nature of this survivalist ethos. Perhaps a direct message regarding AC/DC's own ill experiences with management, the track could possibly be referring to the ruthlessness and unethical action often found in the music industry.

"Let There Be Rock"

AC/DC's "Let There Be Rock" is a high-energy and electrifying rock anthem that narrates the history and spirit of rock 'n' roll. To me, this song is essentially the defining and greatest rock anthem ever written. The song begins by setting a historical context, referencing 1955 as a pivotal year in the birth of rock 'n' roll. It highlights the cultural amalgamation of different musical styles: the "white man had the schmaltz" and the "black man had the blues," pointing to the fusion of various musical traditions that gave birth to rock music. The first line Bon sings, "In the beginning, back in 1955," is not only a tribute to the roots of rock music that heavily influenced the band's music but is also a nod to the year Angus Young was born. The song cleverly uses biblical-style language, with phrases like "Let there be sound," "Let there be light," and "Let there be rock," paralleling the Genesis creation story. This stylistic choice elevates the emergence of rock 'n' roll to a near-mythical status, implying it was a revolutionary and divine intervention in the music world. This is further demonstrated in AC/DC's promotional video for the song, which depicts Bon behind a church alter preaching the lyrics to the attendees, while surrounded by the band who are dressed as choir boys and with haloes on their heads while performing their instruments. As the song progresses, it describes the explosion of rock 'n' roll across the land, highlighting the fame and fortune it brought to musicians and businessmen alike. The reference to a "guitar man" getting famous and a "businessman" getting rich encapsulates the dual artistic and commercial nature of the rock industry. The song culminates in a vivid scene in a club, capturing the raw energy and communal experience of a rock concert with the epic final verse, "One night in a club called the shakin' hand, there was a forty-two (ninety-two) decibel rockin' band, and the music was good and the music was loud, and the singer turned and he said to the crowd ... Let there be rock!" sings Bon with all of the passion and glory ever witnessed in a rock 'n' roll singer. That verse is probably one of my all-time favorites from any AC/DC song and quite honestly any song at all. It would be the song where Angus would incorporate his infamous audience walk-about and extended guitar solos as he would be transported on the shoulders of Bon Scott while not missing a lick; in later years, it was on Brian Johnson's shoulders back to the stage for the conclusion of the song. "Let There Be Rock" is a celebratory anthem that not only recounts the origins of rock 'n' roll but also encapsulates its enduring spirit and impact and has become one of AC/DC's most timeless and iconic tracks.

"Bad Boy Boogie"

Another powerful guitar-infused track from *Let There Be Rock*, "Bad Boy Boogie" is another of my all-time favorite AC/DC songs. The song celebrates rebelliousness and nonconformity through the lens of rock 'n' roll with lyrics that craft the image of an individual who has been a societal outcast since birth. "On the day I was born, the rain fell down, there was trouble brewin' in my home town, it was the seventh day I was the seventh son, and it scared the hell out of everyone" sings Bon with an almost sinister tone. The song's narrative is built around the idea of defiance and going against the grain. Phrases like "They said stop, I said go," "They said yes, I said no," and "I said right and they said left" illustrate a constant state of opposition to societal norms. Moreover, the song delves into themes of sexual prowess and freedom, with lines like "Bein' a bad boy ain't that bad, I had me more dirty women than most men ever had." The song's structure, with its call-and-response style, reinforces this rebellious attitude, creating a dynamic and defiant anthem. "Bad Boy Boogie" would become a serious staple in AC/DC's live repertoire over the years, where Angus would perform extended guitar solos and do his infamous schoolboy "striptease" routine along with mooning the crowd during the live performances of the song. The song captures the spirit of AC/DC's music: loud, unapologetic, and defiantly joyous in its embrace of the "bad boy" persona.

"Overdose"

Another of my favorite AC/DC tracks, "Overdose" is otherwise considered a "deep cut," since it was never a song to see commercial airplay or even been performed live by the band. "Overdose" cleverly uses the metaphor of addiction to describe an intense and overpowering romantic relationship. The opening guitar riff creates a solid foundation for the song, where the distinctive guitar tones at the beginning of the track build up to create a solid wall of sound. You can hear each note as it is picked out, gradually increasing in volume with overdriven Marshall's to deliver a powerful guitar riff that drives the song forward. The song portrays love as a form of intoxication, likening the emotional high and dependency to the effects of substance abuse. The opening lines set the stage contrasting lack of involvement in the relationship with traditional vices such as cigarettes and alcohol: "I never smoked with no cigarettes, I never drank much booze, But I'm only a man, don't you understand, and a man can sometimes lose." The chorus, "I overdosed on you," powerfully conveys the theme of excess and uncontrollable desire, suggesting the feelings are so overwhelming they have surpassed a safe, manageable level. "Overdose" creatively uses the metaphor of addiction to explore themes of love, obsession, and the overpowering nature of emotions of a consuming relationship.

"Crabsody in Blue"

"Crabsody in Blue" remained a hidden gem only available on the Australian version of *Let There Be Rock* and select UK and European versions. The song was held back from release in North America, a decision by Atlantic Records at the time who felt it would be too risqué for American markets (yet, surprisingly allowed "Go Down" to remain). Atlantic decided to replace it with "Problem Child," taken from the previous year's *Dirty Deeds Done Dirt Cheap* album, which was not released in North America at the time. "Crabsody in Blue" embraces a bluesey atmosphere that sets itself apart from most of AC/DC's other harder rocking tracks. It is a humorous and somewhat unconventional song that uses the metaphor of crabs (likely referring to pubic lice) to create a blues-infused narrative about dealing with an irritating and uncomfortable situation. The song's title is a play on words, combining "crabs" with "rhapsody" and playing on the blues music genre, setting a playful and ironic tone for the lyrics. The song humorously addresses the process of dealing with the infestation, from the initial realization ("when they start to bite, then it's time you saw the light") to seeking a remedy ("for an appointment, I know"). The mention of "blues ointment" is a clever play on words, combining the solution to the problem with the musical theme of the blues. The repetitive nature of the lyrics and the focus on the treatment process ("well you rub it on, and you rub it in") add a comedic element to the song, as it deals with a subject that is typically considered taboo or embarrassing in a light-hearted and candid manner. The song would remain a "rarity" until finally making its way to international release as part of the 2009 *Backtracks* box set.

"Hell Ain't a Bad Place to Be"

"Hell Ain't a Bad Place to Be" is a standout track that showcases the witty and clever lyrical genius of Bon Scott. The song stands as a testament to Bon's ability to craft compelling narratives infused with his unique brand of humor and wordplay. The song explores the complexities of a tumultuous and passionate relationship through vivid and gritty rock 'n' roll imagery. The lyrics portray a relationship that oscillates between attraction and frustration, reflecting the unpredictable and sometimes volatile nature of the situation. "Sometimes I think this woman is kinda hot, Sometimes I think this woman is sometimes not" sets the stage for a relationship characterized by highs and lows, where pleasure and pain coexist. The woman's actions, such as putting him down and fooling around, contribute to his confusion and dissatisfaction, yet there is an underlying attraction that keeps him engaged. The chorus, "Hell ain't a bad place to be," serves as a metaphor for the relationship. It suggests that despite the challenges and negative aspect, that there is something compelling and even enjoyable in the chaotic dynamic. The phrase "brings out the devil in me" further implies that the relationship brings out a wilder, more uninhibited side of him. Bon's lyrical prowess is evident in lines such as "Spends my money, drinks my booze, stays out every night, and I got to thinking, hey, just a minute, something ain't right" not only showcase his sharp sense of humor but also his ability to craft the complexities and frustration of this relationship. Overall, "Hell Ain't a Bad Place to Be" presents a raw and unfiltered look at a relationship where the lines between love, lust, frustration, and pleasure are blurred and has often remained as part of AC/DC's live set for decades.

"Whole Lotta Rosie"

"Whole Lotta Rosie" is a high-energy, rock 'n' roll anthem that is inspired by a true story—a raucous tale of Bon Scott's encounter with an extra-large woman from Tasmania named Rosie. The lyrics vividly describe Rosie's physical attributes in a manner that defies traditional perceptions of attractiveness: "She ain't exactly pretty, Ain't exactly small, Forty-two, thirty-nine, fifty-six, you could say she's got it all." Bon expresses admiration and awe for Rosie's capacity for love and her enduring stamina ("Honey, you can do it, do it to me all night long"). Angus' guitar amp literally blew up and caught on fire during the recording of the song, with his elder brother and producer George motioning from behind the glass of the recording studio's control room for Angus to keep playing and not to stop! The result: one of rock music's most blazing, blistering, and electric guitar solos on record. The song's energy builds throughout the entire track, fueled by Angus' climatic guitar solo. Throughout the years, AC/DC fans have culminated an "Angus" chant during the introduction of the song. This is another AC/DC song that has grown into one of their most influential and legendary tracks. It has remained a staple in AC/DC's live set ever since its release in 1977 and remains as one of AC/DC's most revered songs.

Interesting Facts

The song "Go Down" was always a fade-out at the end of the track. Later remastered versions of the album included a full version of the song with a complete ending.

5

Powerage

Release date:	May 5, 1978 (U.K.)
	May 25, 1975 (U.S.)
Current edition:	Sony/Columbia CD, LP
Personnel:	Bon Scott, lead vocals
	Angus Young, lead guitar
	Malcolm Young, rhythm guitar
	Cliff Williams, bass guitar
	Phil Rudd, drums
Duration:	39:47
Recorded at:	Albert Studios, Sydney, Australia, February–March 1978; Vineyard Studios, London, England, September 1976 ("Cold Hearted Man")
Produced by:	Harry Vanda & George Young
Chart position:	#22 Australian Albums
	#26 U.K. Albums
	#133 U.S. *Billboard* 200

Notable info: There are different track lists/mix variations between some European versions. "Cold Hearted Man" was only available on the European version of the vinyl LP release and some versions of the album also omitted "Rock 'n' Roll Damnation." It is the first AC/DC album to feature Cliff Williams on bass. *Powerage* is certified platinum in the USA, 3x platinum in Australia, and gold in multiple countries.

Powerage, AC/DC's fifth studio album, is an often-cited favorite among die-hard AC/DC fans, as well as celebrity musicians like Keith Richards of the Rolling Stones. The album, released on May 25, 1978 in the United States, has a more down-to-earth, bluesey feel than the previous year's *Let There Be Rock*, which was more of an outright, straightforward guitar-rock album. As stated by Angus: "We had that association with the lightning and the you know, the power and the High voltage thing. We just thought it be a good way to describe a newcoming, a coming of age." *Powerage* also reveals some of Bon Scott's most introspective lyrics, many of which contain subtle messages of sadness, loneliness, and perhaps even a hint of despair, much of which was heavily influenced by personal relationship issues at the time. *Powerage* is often praised for its raw energy and is considered by many fans and critics as one of the band's most underrated albums. Malcolm Young stated in an interview about the album: "We like to Rock n roll there, we just decided at the time we would lay down a good rock n roll album. Try and get to our influences when we first got together with Bon which was like Little Richard, Chuck Berry, and really sort of putting a rock edge to it." The album opens with "Rock 'n' Roll Damnation," a catchy, high-energy track that sets the tone. "Down Payment Blues" and "Gimme a Bullet" showcase the band's ability to blend strong riffs with memorable melodies. "Riff Raff," one of the album's standout tracks, is notable for its driving rhythm and guitar work. "Sin City" offers a darker, more rhythmic sound, while "What's Next to the Moon" continues the album's theme of energetic rock. "Gone Shootin'" stands out for its bluesy undertones. The album also includes "Up to My Neck in You" and "Kicked in the Teeth," which maintain the high-octane, guitar-driven sound characteristic of AC/DC. The album is another example of different track listings and even different song mixes this time, depending on the country of release. The track "Cold Hearted Man" was never released in North America until it appeared on the 2009 *Backtracks* box set release, like many of AC/DC's other more obscure B-side tracks. "Rock 'n' Roll Damnation" was also omitted from certain European releases, while there are others that contain all ten tracks. One European version also contains a completely different song mix with some differences and variations in the actual songs, in particular "What's Next to the Moon" and "Gone Shootin'," as well as a power chord that kicks off "Kicked in the Teeth" that is not heard on any of the other versions of the record. *Powerage* is a bridge between the raw energy of their early works and the polished brilliance of their later masterpieces. The album's commercial underperformance, often attributed to a lack of promotional support from the record label, did not deter the band. Instead, *Powerage* solidified the band's reputation as purveyors of authentic, no-nonsense rock 'n' roll and remains a fan favorite album to date.

"Rock 'n' Roll Damnation"

What the album was lacking, at least according to Atlantic Records at the time, was a radio-friendly single, so AC/DC wrote the song "Rock 'n'

Roll Damnation" to fill that gap. The opening track on the album was actually the last song to be recorded, which required the band to reenter the recording studio to complete. "Rock 'n' Roll Damnation" delves into themes of defiance, rebellion, and the struggles of living a rock 'n' roll lifestyle. The lyrics portray a narrative of someone criticized for their loud, unapologetic way of life, particularly in the realm of rock music. Phrases like "they say you play too loud" and being called "Ma's own whippin' boy" suggest a struggle against societal norms. The chorus, "rock 'n' roll damnation, take a chance while you still got the choice," reflects the spirit of seizing life despite the risks and judgments, embodying the rebellious essence of rock music. The song also touches on the challenges of this lifestyle, such as alienation ("left a happy home") and the pursuit of material gain ("dollars in your eye"), alluding to the potential moral and personal costs of fame and success in the rock 'n' roll industry. The song was released as the first single from *Powerage* in May 1978. The track is a strong song, and the recording resulted in a strong opener for the album, despite the rationale behind it being about writing a radio-friendly single. The song was also performed live on the 1978 Powerage Tour.

"Down Payment Blues"

The track "Down Payment Blues" delves deep into the realities of life's struggles and the pursuit of dreams, likely inspired much by challenges of the music industry faced by AC/DC since they started as a band. The song kicks off with a powerful guitar riff that instantly sets the stage and then picks up pace as the song begins. Another of Bon Scott's brilliant lyrical moments can be found within this song, which presents a brutally honest exploration of life's hardships and the unfulfilled dreams, perhaps the difficulties of making a living but at the same time borrowing money and ending up in debt to live like a king. The song, with its vivid imagery and straightforward language, tells the story of struggling financially, yet dreaming of a more lavish lifestyle. Phrases like "living on a shoestring" and "fifty cent millionaire" paint a picture of being financially strapped but trying to maintain successful and wealthy appearances. Lyrically, the struggles and frustrations of working-class life is vividly captured, painting a picture of being trapped in the cycle of longing and unattainable aspirations. Such lines as "Get myself a steady job, some responsibility, can't even feed my cat, with social security" and then on the flipside Bon sings in a later verse "Sittin' on my sailin' boat, Sippin' on my champagne, Suzie, baby, all at sea, Say she want to come again." The phrase "down payment blues" aptly captures the frustration and helplessness of being caught in a cycle of poverty and unfulfilled dreams. This song, like many others by AC/DC, encapsulates the struggles and the gritty realism mixed with a sense of longing for a better life and the strive to become successful.

"Gimme a Bullet"

"Gimme a Bullet" is a song that conveys the pain and frustration of heartbreak through visceral and metaphorical lyrics. Bon sings about his partner decisively ended their relationship, leaving him feeling betrayed and hurt. The line "She had the word, had the way, the way of letting me know" suggests a certain coldness or calculation in the way the break-up was handled. The song kicks off with an instant groove with its foot-stomping rhythm and the signature gritty AC/DC guitar riff chugging along as Bon Scott seamlessly enters with the first verse. The chorus, "Gimme a bullet to bite on, something to chew, I'll make believe it's you," uses the metaphor of a bullet as a means of coping with emotional pain. Bon Scott's poetic lyrics serve as a powerful exploration of emotions, capturing the turmoil and pain of a love turned sour. In non-typical AC/DC fashion, the track does not feature a guitar solo but is rather a short and sweet grooving rocker that is both catchy and memorable. Bon's soulful vocal delivery contributes to the overall atmosphere of the song, with the use of the metaphorical "bullet" suggests a desire for a swift resolution, whether it be the end of the relationship or a resolution to the emotional conflict at hand. Essentially, "Gimme a Bullet" is a track about heartbreak and the desperate measure one might face as a means of dealing with such deep emotional hurt.

"Riff Raff"

The introduction to "Riff Raff" starts with Angus ripping a raw guitar riff on his Gibson SG, who is then joined with a rumbling buildup of guitar, bass, and drums before kicking you directly in the face with a hard-hitting, fast-paced, high-voltage rocker. The riff is one of AC/DC's finest and, in my opinion, the finest on the *Powerage* album. Angus and Malcolm unleash an electrifying boogie-infused rock riff that drives the song forward with intensity. The lyrics of "Riff Raff" present a commentary on the rebellious and carefree rock 'n' roll attitude and refusal to conform to societal norms. The term "riff raff" is typically used to describe people with a disreputable or undesirable status, and the song seems to embrace this label with a sense of pride and defiance. Bon sings with an attitude that is nonchalant about societal judgments ("I'm the kinda guy that keep his big mouth shut, it don't bother me"). Perhaps a tribute to the music itself, the title "Riff Raff" could also be a nod to the guitar riff mastery. The repetitive chorus, emphasizing laughter and fun, reinforces the idea that the song is about finding joy and amusement in defiance of societal expectations. The song has become a timeless AC/DC fan favorite, and a live version is also featured on *If You Want Blood (You've Got It),* AC/DC's first live album released the same year as *Powerage*. This version was performed as the opening song during the Glasgow Apollo concert (April 30, 1978).

"Sin City"

"Sin City" is likely inspired by the city of Las Vegas—we can assume that the band likely visited the city during some days off during the 1977 Let There Be Rock Tour. Bon and the boys pay tribute to the nightlife, the women, the booze, and the gambling, which is essentially what the song is all about. The lyrics of "Sin City" depict a vivid portrayal of the allure and dangers of a hedonistic lifestyle, symbolized by "Sin City." The track encapsulates the AC/DC signature sound and delivers clever wordplay with vivid imagery by Bon Scott telling a tale of temptation and indulgence. The lyrics "Diamonds and dust, poor man last, rich man first, Lamborghini, caviar, Dry martini, Shangri-La" capture the allure and excess of the city. During the breakdown, the bass takes precedence as Bon sings "ladders, and snakes, ladders give, snakes take, rich man poor man, beggar man thief…" Such a clever and perfect verse that succinctly sums up the gambling and nightlife scene of Las Vegas. The chorus, "I'm going in, to sin city, I'm gonna win, in sin city," embodies a sense of reckless ambition and confidence, suggesting a dive into the world of indulgence and vice with the intention to succeed. "Ain't got a hope in Hell, that's my belief" sings Bon, knowing that the odds are against him. This is further amplified by the line "So spin that wheel, cut that pack, and roll them loaded dice," which invokes gambling imagery the city is known for. The performance of the song on the ABC *Midnight Special* TV show in 1978 (which can be found on AC/DC's *Family Jewels* DVD) is certainly a treat as it captures the intensity of the track perfectly. The track succinctly conveys the world of extravagance and risk associated with the place "Sin City" where the pursuit of pleasure and wealth is met with danger and uncertainty but at the same time excitement and triumph.

"What's Next to the Moon"

Another song that is a brilliant play on words, even from the title itself, "What's Next to the Moon" has one immediately guessing what they can be talking about. It is a tale of mystery, murder, and a relationship gone bad, which captivates the imagination with its poetic and enigmatic lyrics. The lyrics are characterized by vivid and somewhat surreal imagery, blending elements of danger, desire, and fantasy. The song opens with a dramatic and troubling metaphor of tying a lover to a railroad track, suggesting a relationship marked by intense, possibly destructive passion. This imagery evokes classic melodramatic scenarios from early silent films, where such acts were symbolic of dire situations and high stakes. "Heavenly body flying across the sky, Superman was out of town, come on honey, gotta change your tune, 'cause it's a long way down" sings Bon with an almost sinister sneer. The references to iconic characters like Casey Jones, Superman, and Clark Kent introduce a sense of myth and heroism. The line "It's a bird, it's a plane, it's a suicide, and that'd be a shame" intriguingly mixes comic book heroism with darker themes, illustrating the scenario where the woman was thrown from the building and the suspect is blaming her death on an accident. The rhythm section is overlayed with a mesmerizing guitar riff that sets the overall tone of the song. Bon's overall vocal delivery is both ethereal and commanding, playing on the words as the pre-chorus builds up with "It's your love that I want, it's your love that I need, it's your love, got to have." The culprit in the song, now guilty of murdering the woman he wanted, is under investigation, blaming the death on a heart attack in a smug yet humorous craft of wordplay. The brilliance of Bon's poetic lyrical ability really shines in this track and is a testament to AC/DC as a band to create memorable songs with thought-provoking lyrics leaving a sense of wonder and introspection. AC/DC performed this song live with Brian Johnson in 2003 during a handful of intimate live shows, including the Roseland Ballroom in New York City, which I attended.

"Gone Shootin'"

"Gone Shootin'" opens with a haunting guitar riff that immediately sets a moody and atmospheric tone. The lyrics delve into themes of addiction, loss, and despair, a common theme found on *Powerage*. Some of the deeper meaning lyrics penned by Bon Scott, "Gone Shootin'" is tale of an estranged relationship with a woman who chose a different path and who was likely involved with drug habit. The song is likely heavily inspired by

Bon's own relationship difficulties with his girlfriend at the time, Silver Smith. The narrative perspective of the song is from someone witnessing a loved one's struggle with substance abuse, depicted metaphorically as "gone shootin'." The lyrics describe the gradual disappearance of the person they once knew, encapsulated in lines like "Packed your heart in a travelling bag" and "never said bye bye," suggesting a departure not just physically but emotionally and mentally as well. The play on words leaves the listener pondering different meanings of the word shootin'—a drug addict, a sex addict, or is Bon referring to a handgun? Perhaps all three in different context throughout the track, as Bon sings "She never made it past the bedroom door, what was she aiming for?" as one example. Helplessness and regret are also evident with the repeated line "My baby's gone shootin'," emphasizing the irrevocable change in their loved one. "Gone Shootin'" is infused with the signature blues-rock style of AC/DC, featuring gritty guitar riffs and powerful, dynamic vocals. The song captures the essence of a relationship altered by the pursuit of personal freedom and leaving an unfilled void, conveying a mix of emotions, including sadness, nostalgia, and even a tinge of resentment.

"Up to My Neck in You"

Like many other AC/DC tracks, "Up to My Neck in You" isn't much different in its subject matter, and it is full of double-entendre and Bon's witty, lyrical genius and play on words throughout. This is another rocking track from *Powerage* with a really great rock 'n' roll guitar riff and a nice pace to the overall feel of the song. "Up to My Neck in You" uses the metaphor of being submerged or overwhelmed to express the intensity of experiences and emotions. Deeper exploration of the lyrics shows that aside from the play on words of sexual themes, the lyrics paint a vivid picture of being caught in a web of complicated relationships, where passion and frustration intertwine. The phrase "up to my neck" suggests being almost completely overwhelmed, yet not entirely consumed, by these difficulties. However, the tone shifts when the Bon describes the transformative impact of someone entering his life: "You came along when I needed you, now I'm up, I'm up to my neck in you." This change implies that the overwhelming experiences have turned from negative to positive because of this woman's influence. "I've been up to my neck in whiskey, I've been up to my neck in wine, I've been up to my neck in wishing, that this neck wasn't mine" indicates the use of alcohol as a way to deal with these relationship challenges and that the resulting effects were often regretful.

"Kicked in the Teeth"

The final track on *Powerage* is a powerhouse song that barrels forward with a driving rhythm section. The song is yet another example on this album of relationship turmoil, this time a story of a girl that was unfaithful. The song expresses feelings of betrayal and disillusionment in a relationship, using the metaphor of being physically "kicked in the teeth" to convey the emotional pain and disappointment faced in the situation. The lyrics paint a picture of a duplicitous partner, described as a "Two faced woman with the two-faced lies," indicating deceit and unfaithfulness. This portrayal of betrayal is intensified by Bon's initial belief in her innocence and virtue, as mentioned in "I used to think that you were sugar and spice." The chorus, "Kicked in the teeth again, sometimes you lose, sometimes you win," reflects a resigned acknowledgment of the ups and downs of life and relationships. The repeated phrase "kicked in the teeth" suggests a series of disappointments, highlighting a pattern of being let down or betrayed. This repetition also conveys a sense of inevitability and the harsh realities of love and trust: "Two faced woman, such a cryin' shame, don't know nothing, you're all the same" Bon's ability to infuse his vocals with a mix of vulnerability and defiance gives the song an attitude that resonates with the listener. "You never know who's gonna win till the race been run" resonates as a theme of unpredictability in relationships in general. The song is certainly a hard rocker track on *Powerage* and a blistering conclusion to this fantastic release.

"Cold Hearted Man"

"Cold Hearted Man" was not available on the American version of *Powerage* and the song itself was not commercially available in North America until it was issued on the 2009 *Backtracks* box set. The song, however, was available elsewhere in different European versions of *Powerage* and was also available in Australia as a B-side to "Rock 'n' Roll Damnation." A special 12-inch maxi single with a unique picture sleeve (flaming AC/DC logo) was also included in an Australian-only 5LP box set. The song narrates the story of an enigmatic and isolated figure, Leroy Kincaid, whose life is shrouded in mystery and fear. The song begins by highlighting the unknown origins of this character ("No one knew, where he came from"), immediately setting a tone of mystery and intrigue. The lyrics paint Kincaid as a feared and respected figure, with phrases like "No one fooled, or messed him around" and "Ice in the eyes," suggesting a man who commands respect and perhaps fear, due to his intimidating demeanor. "One time lover with his heart in his hand, two-time loser, a broken man" sings Bon in the midst of the song. The words paint a vivid picture of Leeroy Kincaid, the black sheep of the family, a rebellious bad seed, a man with a bad reputation.

Interesting Facts

The vinyl release of a few versions of *Powerage* released in Europe contained completely different mixes of the tracks and different song sequencing (as well as the inclusion of "Cold Hearted Man"). The most noticeable different mixes include "Down Payment Blues," "Kicked in the Teeth," "What's Next to the Moon," "Gimme a Bullet," "Up to My Neck in You," "Riff Raff," and "Gone Shootin'." The original versions of the UK and European *Powerage* album also did not include "Rock 'n' Roll Damnation." Later, some versions of the album released in Europe included ten tracks with both "Cold Hearted Man" and "Rock 'n' Roll Damnation." There are also other various song sequencing differences on other releases/formats/reissues over the years. In New Zealand, a rare version of *Powerage* was issued featuring an album cover with a blue AC/DC logo and album title, now a highly sought-after collectible among fans.

6

Highway to Hell

Release date:	July 27, 1979 (U.K.)
	July 27, 1979 (U.S.)
Current edition:	Sony/Columbia, CD, LP, Albert/EMI CD
Personnel:	Bon Scott, lead vocals
	Angus Young, lead guitar
	Malcolm Young, rhythm guitar
	Cliff Williams, bass guitar
	Phil Rudd, drums
Duration:	41:38
Recorded at:	Roundhouse Studios, London, England, March 24, 1979–April 14, 1979
Produced by:	Robert John "Mutt" Lange
Chart position:	#13 Australian Albums
	#8 U.K. Albums
	#17 U.S. *Billboard* 200

Notable info: This is the final AC/DC album with Bon Scott and the first time AC/DC would work with a different producer than Vanda & Young. *Highway to Hell* is certified 7x platinum in the USA, 5x platinum in Australia, 2x platinum in Canada, with multiple platinum and gold certifications in other countries.

Highway to Hell was the very first record I ever purchased. It was the summer of 1980, and I had already heard a few AC/DC songs on the radio at the time and instantly became a fan. My first album was this one, and it remains my favorite AC/DC album to this day, and yes, I still own my original vinyl copy. This album marked a pivotal moment in the band's illustrious career. The band initially went into the recording studio with producer Eddie Kramer, at the suggestion and recommendation (if not declaration) of the record company to try a different producer than the tried-and-true Vanda & Young production team. By the first few days, the band was fed up and could no longer work with Kramer, who was fired, and the band found Robert John "Mutt" Lange to begin working with. Producer Mutt Lange's production on *Highway to Hell* contributed significantly to the evolution of AC/DC's sound. It was part of a pivotal album that saw the continued evolution of the band's distinctive double-guitar sound and improved backing vocals, featuring Malcolm Young and Cliff Williams. *Highway to Hell* would be the first album in AC/DC's catalog not to be produced by Vanda & Young, a difficult breakaway, but perhaps an attempt to try something new to crack the charts open, especially in America. The title itself, laden with rebellious connotations, set the stage for an album that would not only solidify the band's status as one of the greatest rock acts but also serve as a poignant milestone in their history. The album cover features the iconic AC/DC photo depicting all five of the band members, with Angus in schoolboy uniform, his hat topped with devil horns, and holding a devil's tail in his hand. The photo was taken during a photoshoot from December 1977, the same shoot that featured a photo of the band on the back of the *Powerage* cover from the year before. The unmistakable chemistry between the Young brothers, Angus and Malcolm, and the band's signature blend of thunderous riffs, Bon Scott's gravely, powerful vocals, and the hard rockin' groove of drummer Phil Rudd and bassist Cliff Williams catapulted AC/DC into the mainstream and the album remains a timeless classic to this day. The title track, "Highway to Hell," is renowned for its iconic riff and anthemic chorus, becoming one of the band's most famous songs. Tracks like "Girls Got Rhythm" and "Walk All Over You" feature the classic AC/DC combination of catchy hooks and powerful guitar work. "Touch Too Much" offers a slightly more polished sound, while "Beating Around the Bush" displays the band's raw, energetic style. "Shot Down in Flames" and "Get It Hot" are typical of the band's straightforward rock approach. "If You Want Blood (You've Got It)" and "Love Hungry Man" continue the high-energy, riff-driven style. The album concludes with "Night Prowler," a slower, bluesier track that showcases a different side of the band's musical range as well as Bon Scott's dynamics as a singer. *Highway to Hell* stands as a significant achievement in AC/DC's career and a lasting tribute to Bon Scott's legacy. In retrospect, *Highway to Hell* not only defined a genre but also served as a bittersweet farewell to the Bon Scott era. The album's success paved the way for AC/DC's continued dominance in the rock scene, with Brian Johnson stepping in as the new frontman for the subsequent masterpiece, *Back in Black*, the following year.

"Highway to Hell"

"Highway to Hell," the title track from this masterpiece album, is arguably one of the most significant and greatest rock 'n' roll anthems ever written; a timeless classic, the song is one of the most enduring and recognizable AC/DC tracks in their catalog. The song is an anthem celebrating freedom, rebellion, and the rock 'n' roll lifestyle. The Canning Highway in Australia, which connects the Perth Kwinana freeway to its port Fremantle and was home to many of Bon Scott's favorite pubs, including the Raffles Hotel, inspired the song's title. This highway, particularly known for its steep decline near the Raffles Hotel, was a significant part of Bon Scott's life. Angus Young in the opening riff is one of rock music's defining moments, the simple, but so memorable chord progression, which is then joined by Phil Rudd's solid drumbeat sets the stage for the verse. The song's title and lyrics are a metaphor for the grueling and demanding nature of touring, with the traditional wittiness and word play of being on a highway to Hell, the song is not really about the devil after all. Music critics and evangelists of the 1970s (and even to this day) argue otherwise, convinced by the menacing album cover, which featured the iconic image of Angus Young with devil's horns and pointed devil tail and reinforced the rebellious and devil-may-care attitude that permeated the music within. Angus Young described their exhaustive touring schedule as being "on a highway to hell," reflecting the challenges and sacrifices involved in achieving success in the rock music industry. The lyrics convey a sense of carefree abandon and defiance against conventional norms. The opening lines, "Livin' easy, lovin' free, season ticket on a one-way ride," set the tone for a journey without return, suggesting a commitment to a life of unrestrained freedom and pleasure. "Don't need reason, don't need rhyme, ain't nothin' that I'd rather do, goin' down, party time, my friends are gonna be there too..." Lyrically, the song is genius and one of the best penned by Bon Scott. The song doesn't present this "highway to hell" as a negative path; rather, it is portrayed as a celebration of liberty and living life on one's own terms. Mentions of Satan and playing in a rock band further amplify the song's association with the rebellious and sometimes transgressive nature of rock music. The reference to "Hey mamma, look at me, I'm on the way to the promised land" can be seen as a nod to achieving success and recognition in their own unconventional way. The track's impact transcends generations, serving as a testament to the enduring power of rock music. The song won the Most Played Australian Work Overseas at the 2009 APRA Awards and has been featured in various rankings, including being placed #7 on *The Guardian*'s list of the forty greatest AC/DC songs in 2020. It also ranks highly on *Rolling Stone*'s list of the 500 Greatest Songs of All Time and

The Rock and Roll Hall of Fame's 500 Songs that Shaped Rock and Roll list. It was also selected by fans as part of an online campaign in 2013 to push the song to #1 in the UK by Christmas, reaching #4 by December 22 that year.

"Girls Got Rhythm"

Plain and simple, "Girls Got Rhythm" is another track that essentially paints a picture of his Bon's admiration for a woman with an irresistible allure and a captivating presence. Bon holds no bars when it comes to writing songs about his passions: women, booze, and rock 'n' roll music. The song kicks off with a catchy riff and an instant and irresistible groove and pulsating, foot-stomping rhythm. The lyrics portray a sense of admiration and awe for a woman who stands out from all others as Bon sings "I've been around the world, I've seen a million girls, ain't one of them got, what my lady, she's got..." Perhaps even a tribute to Bon's girlfriend at the time, Ana Baba, the song is full of steamy wordplay with lines like "You know she moves like sin, and when she lets me in, It's like liquid love." The song goes on describing the physically attractive aspects of the woman, the way she moves, and her seductive qualities, all themes that resonate throughout AC/DC's catalog. "Girls Got Rhythm" is a tribute to a woman whose presence embodies the vitality and rebellious spirit of rock and roll and is a standout track from *Highway to Hell.*

"Walk All Over You"

"Walk All Over You" is introduced with a slower, musical buildup between the guitars and drums before it unleashes a sonic blast of energy. Another track about a night of love, sexual desire, and passion, "Walk All Over You" is characterized by strong themes of sexual context and assertive energy. The lyrics portray a dynamic of power and dominance in a sexual context, evident in the repeated chorus, "I'm gonna walk all over you." The lines "Outta my way I'm running high, take a chance with me and give it a try" convey a sense of urgency and confidence, inviting a woman into a passionate and potentially wild experience. The imagery used in the song, such as "Take off your high heels and let down your hair, paradise ain't far from there," further exemplifies the uninhibited pleasure and passionate scenario portrayed in the song. This is further emphasized by the sensual descriptions of the encounter, like "Reflections on the bedroom wall, I'm glad you got to see it all, we're rising, falling, like at sea, you're lookin' so good, under me." Although it was never stated by anyone in the band, I have always thought the title of the song could have been inspired by a verse in the Lynyrd Skynyrd track "Gimme Back My Bullets," the title track from Skynyrd's 1976 album. Bon was a big fan of Lynyrd Skynyrd and there was a comradery between the two bands in the '70s. Bon would even sport a Lynyrd Skynyrd confederate flag belt buckle during a significant portion of the Highway to Hell Tour. The lyrics of the song are quite straightforward in their exploration of the overall theme of sex and passion, much like most AC/DC tracks. Overall, the song encapsulates the essence of a passionate and intense relationship rooted by sexual desire between a man and woman.

"Touch Too Much"

Dare we say, yet another track with similar themes of sexual desire, love, and passion? "Touch Too Much" is a seductive track that revolves around a complex narrative woven with themes of desire, excess, and the impact of overwhelming emotions. The lyrics describe a powerful, almost consuming sexual encounter, marked by a strong sense of urgency and desire. The song opens with an evocative scene setting: "It was one of those nights, when you turned out the lights, and everything comes into view," suggesting a moment of intimacy and revelation. The chorus, "Seems like a touch, a touch too much," encapsulates the core sentiment of the song—an experience that is thrilling yet almost overpowering. The lines "Too much for my body, too much for my brain, this damn woman's gonna drive me insane" convey the sense of being overtaken by these emotions and physical sensations. The song explores the idea of mutual desire and the intensity of physical connection, as seen in "She wanted it hard, and wanted it fast, she liked it done medium rare." These lines suggest a raw, primal aspect to their interaction, marked by a strong mutual, sexual desire. "Touch Too Much" is a song that combines vivid imagery with a powerful rock rhythm to convey a story of desire, temptation, and the irresistible pull of physical attraction. The track was the final single from *Highway to Hell* in January 1980 and was starting to chart quite successfully; the band even discussed adding it to the live set, however, it never made it there as Bon tragically passed away less than one month later. It was performed on live TV, to the studio track on the *Top of the Pops* TV show in the UK on February 7, 1980, just twelve days prior to Bon's tragic death.

"Beating Around the Bush"

"Beating Around the Bush" particularly focuses on themes of deception, trust, and the challenges of a strained relationship that is filled with dishonesty and an unfaithful partner. The title itself, a common phrase for avoiding directness or honesty, sets the tone for the song's exploration of the relationship at hand, but not without the expected trademark sexual overtones of Bon Scott. The song begins with an intense boogie-inspired guitar riff, which is quickly joined by the driving rhythm section of Phil Rudd and Cliff Williams. The lyrics portray the situation of grappling with a partner's deceit and infidelity. The opening lines, "Smiling face and loving eyes, but you keep on telling me all those lies," immediately set a tone of distrust and disappointment. Despite the evident pain and suspicion, there is a sense of resilience and determination, as highlighted in the lines "You're the meanest woman I've ever known, sticks and stones won't break my bones." This suggests a refusal to be completely broken down by the situation. The subtle innuendos that allude to sexual connotations heard in the lyric "I was talking birds and you was talking bees, and was he down on his knees, beatin' 'round the bush," further illustrating the partner's infidelity. Although never part of the AC/DC live set to date, just ten days before Bon's death, the band did perform the song during a TV appearance in Spain (*Aplauso* TV show) on February 9, 1980, which was synced to the studio track from the album.

"Shot Down in Flames"

"Shot Down in Flames," a powerhouse track from the album, is a song that captures the theme of rejection in the context of pursuing romantic interests. The song is fueled by the pulsating bass lines of Cliff Williams and the hard-hitting groove of Phil Rudd. The lyrics follow Bon's experiences as he attempts to engage with women, only to be repeatedly rebuffed "She was standing alone, over by the jukebox, like she's something to sell, I said 'Baby what's the going price?', she told me to go to Hell." Each unsuccessful attempt at engagement with women is metaphorically depicted as being "shot down in flames," a powerful expression of the pain associated with rejection, through the song's chorus, "Shot down in flames, ain't it a shame, to be shot down in flames?" Despite this, the lyrics carry a tone of determination and an unyielding spirit, showcasing the resilience often found in AC/DC songs. This song aligns well with the overarching themes of *Highway to Hell*, which delves into topics like rebellion, desire, and the trials of life on the road. The track was performed live on the

Highway to Hell Tour and over the years has remained a live track in AC/DC's repertoire, rotating back into the set for some tours as recent as the October 7, 2023 Power Trip festival show and during the 2024 Power Up European Tour.

"Get it Hot"

"Get it Hot" is a short, but grooving party rocker that stands out for its straightforward, high-energy approach to rock music, and its lyrics encapsulate a spirit of rebellion and carefree living. "Get it Hot" kicks off with a sudden drum hit and immediately begins the energetic rhythm, tight, and propulsive groove, and catchy verses of the song. The track essentially revolves around living life to the fullest, the thrill of partying, and the sheer joy of being young and unburdened with twists of sexual encounters in the verses of the song. The lyrics convey a sense of anticipation and excitement for a night out of partying, with a female companion, reminiscent of past adventures and fun times. "Goin' bend you like a G string, conduct you like a choir, so get your body in the right place, we'll set the world on fire" sings Bon in the second verse of the song, obviously referring to a passionate encounter, and underlining a laidback, almost carefree approach to life. The emphasis on no one playing slow or sentimental music ("Nobody's playing Manilow, nobody's playing soul") sets the tone for an evening dedicated to the raw energy and simplicity of rock 'n' roll. The song itself almost, in essence, creates a party atmosphere that encapsulates the essence of AC/DC's live performances. Overall, "Get It Hot" is a straightforward celebration of having a good time, characterized by the classic rock elements of excitement, physicality, and the unapologetic pursuit of enjoyment and living life to the fullest.

"If You Want Blood (You've Got It)"

AC/DC decided to compose a song with the title of the previous year's live album, likely already in the works since the year before but not completed yet. The demo version can be heard on *Volts*, which is part of the 1997 *Bonfire* box set. The inspiration for the song's (and previous live album's) title came from an incident witnessed by band members Angus and Malcolm Young, where a lead singer at a show exclaimed, "what do you want, fucking blood?!" as Malcolm recollected in an interview: "We remember seeing a band years ago, who were dying and the guy said 'what do you want, fucking blood?' To the audience, and it always stuck in our heads." The song begins with an aggressive guitar riff and unrelenting tempo that builds up commanding and powerful vocals. The song begins with a critique of the societal system, suggested by the lines "It's criminal, there ought to be a law." This implies a perception of injustice or unfairness in the world. The phrase "You get nothing for nothing" reinforces the idea that success and fulfillment often come at a cost. The chorus, with its repetition of "Blood on the streets, blood on the rocks, blood in the gutter, every last drop," employs the metaphor of blood to represent sacrifice, effort, and the gritty aspects of life's struggles. The line "Feeling like a Christian, locked in a cage, thrown to the lions, on the second page" evokes the idea of being under scrutiny or attack, akin to a gladiator or martyr facing challenges or persecution. The song's raw and straightforward approach reflects AC/DC's characteristic style and uses metaphorical expressions of challenges faced in the pursuit of one's goals or in the face of societal pressures. "If You Want Blood" served as the opening track for AC/DC's Power Trip performance in October 2023 as well as during the Power Up European Tour throughout 2024.

"Love Hungry Man"

The majority of the themes on *Highway to Hell* involve passion, sex, and desire, and "Love Hungry Man" is no exception. The track uses vivid and suggestive language to convey themes of intense physical desire and passion. In a 1998 interview, Angus referred to the song as "the result of being written after a night of bad pizza," expressing his disappointment with the resulting track. The song opens with the line "You're the one I've waited for," immediately establishing its theme of deep-seated obsession. Complete with AC/DC's witty and almost mischievous lyricism, the track is essentially about cunnilingus on his female lover. The song does not explicitly use metaphors for oral sex, but rather employs a general metaphor of hunger and appetite to describe the narrator's strong sexual desire. The longing is immediate and intense, focusing solely on physical attraction rather than emotional connection or personal details, as highlighted by "I don't know what your name is, I don't know what your game is." The chorus, "Cause I'm a love hungry man," reinforces the idea of being driven by a powerful, almost insatiable need for physical intimacy. The phrase "All I wanna do, is make a meal outta you" further emphasizes this metaphor of hunger and appetite, linking the concept of physical hunger directly to sexual desire. The song features a much more upfront bassline than most AC/DC tracks, which establishes a real foot-stomping groove to the song that fits so very nicely into the fold of the overall album. The vivid imagery and clever wordplay create a poetic yet provocative narrative, with lines like "Oh baby, you're such a treat, and you know, a man's got to eat," showcasing Bon's wittiness. "Love Hungry Man" is characteristic of AC/DC's style, which often includes bold and unapologetic explorations of raw and straightforward sexual themes.

"Night Prowler"

"Night Prowler," the closing track on the album stands as a testament to Bon Scott's masterful vocal abilities and dynamic range with his ability to evoke a wide range of emotions through his powerful and iconic voice. The song starts off with a deep breath into the microphone before the first guitar chord is struck. "Night Prowler" creates an eerie and suspenseful atmosphere that is perfectly complemented by Bon Scott's vocal prowess, which shines as likely Bon's finest vocal performance on record. The song's narrative is built around the imagery of a typical eerie night—a full moon, a distant dog barking, a baby crying, and a rat in the alley—setting a sinister and unsettling scene. The use of phrases like "a chill runs down your spine" and "someone walks across your grave" intensifies this atmosphere, suggesting a presence that is both threatening and stealthy. The song's slow and deliberate pacing, coupled with its sparse instrumentation, builds a suspenseful and unsettling ambiance. Bon's evocative delivery, filled with whispered nuances and spine-tingling inflections, adds an extra layer of darkness to the track, immersing listeners in the story of a mysterious prowler lurking in the night. The line "And you don't feel the steel, till it's hanging out your back" further adds to the sense of unforeseen danger and betrayal. From the whispered, low-register verses to the intense and climactic high notes, Bon effortlessly navigates the song's dynamic range. His ability to shift between soft and sinister tones to powerful and soaring vocal deliveries adds a haunting quality to the track, enhancing its chilling atmosphere. The chorus, "I'm your night prowler, asleep in the day, Night prowler, get out of my way," introduces the titular character, the Night Prowler, who is depicted as a menacing figure that becomes active at night. This character is portrayed as someone who invades personal spaces and privacy, creating a sense of fear and vulnerability ("As I slip into your room"). The imagery of the prowler breaking down doors and crawling across floors emphasizes the invasive and terrifying nature of this character. The song was written about a "peeping tom," apparently from some story about a pervert looking in bedroom windows to get a glimpse of naked women before running off. In 1985, however, AC/DC received bad press over the song as the serial killer, Richard Ramirez, who claimed to be an AC/DC fan, was dubbed the "night stalker" and the press instantly correlated the track with the killer. Interestingly, the song ends with the phrase "Shazbot, nanu nanu," which was Robin Williams' catchphrase as Mork from the sitcom *Mork & Mindy*. This unexpected and somewhat whimsical inclusion contrasts starkly with the rest of the song's dark and ominous tone and Bon must have been a big fan of the sitcom.

Interesting Facts

The Australian version of *Highway to Hell* features the same photo of the band, but completely overlayed with flames and with the neck of a bass guitar at the bottom illustrating a road with the album title beneath it. A version of the album released in East Germany in 1981 also featured a different album cover—a large AC/DC logo and the album title on a black background with a glowing red horizon at the bottom. The track listing for all versions of *Highway to Hell* were the same worldwide.

In 1982, an AC/DC film titled *Let There Be Rock* was released in theaters across North America. The film featured a live concert along with band interviews and backstage footage. The footage in the movie was filmed during the band's Highway to Hell Tour, primarily featuring footage from their concerts (day and evening shows) in Paris, France, from December 9, 1979. The movie was also released on video and eventually reissued on DVD. For AC/DC's fiftieth-anniversary marketing campaign in 2024, a special LP edition of the album was issued on orange blend vinyl.

7

Back in Black

Release date:	July 25, 1980 (U.K.)
	July 25, 1980 (U.S.)
Current edition:	Sony/Columbia, CD, LP
Personnel:	Brian Johnson, lead vocals
	Angus Young, lead guitar
	Malcolm Young, rhythm guitar
	Cliff Williams, bass guitar
	Phil Rudd, drums
Duration:	42:11
Recorded at:	Compass Point Studios, Nassau, Bahamas, April–May 1980
Produced by:	Robert John "Mutt" Lange
Chart position:	#1 Australian Albums
	#1 U.K. Albums
	#4 U.S. *Billboard* 200

Notable info: This is the first AC/DC album with Brian Johnson on lead vocals. *Back in Black* surpassed 27 million albums sold in the USA as of August 2024 and over 60 million worldwide, making it the biggest-selling rock album of all time globally and the second biggest-selling album of all time of any music genre. *Back in Black* is certified 25x platinum in the USA (double diamond), 12x platinum in Australia, with various multi-platinum, platinum, and gold certifications in multiple countries.

AC/DC's iconic seventh studio album, *Back in Black*, defied the impossible. Not only did the band decide to continue on without their singer and frontman, Bon Scott, who tragically died in February 1980 on the cusp of finally reaching the mainstream success they so longed to reach, but they became the biggest rock band in the world by the following year. *Back in Black*, produced under the guidance of Robert John "Mutt" Lange, marked a significant evolution for AC/DC. It is remembered as a cohesive experience, perfectly balancing its forty-two-minute runtime without any filler tracks. The album's artwork also pays homage to Bon, reflecting the band's grief and respect for their late frontman. *Back in Black* emerged from the ashes of tragedy to become a monumental testament to the band's resilience and enduring influence. The challenge that faced AC/DC was the daunting decision of carrying on without their charismatic lead singer. In a stroke of fate, the band enlisted Brian Johnson as Bon's successor, and the result was the creation of an album that would redefine the parameters of hard rock. Brian Johnson stepped in as the new singer, not as a replacement or an imitator, but as a new member who sang his own style and did things his own way, and his style was the perfect one-in-a-million discovery that AC/DC needed to be successful. Angus Young recalls: "For us at the time, we had lost our singer Bon Scott, and for us as a band it was our tribute to him. So, we felt you know if we came up with a title that summed it all up, and Back in Black seemed to be a good title, and we also felt we want the cover in black. It was more respect. When you're in mourning, you wear black, so that was our tribute to him." The album's power-packed lineup includes hits like "You Shook Me All Night Long," "Hells Bells," and "Shoot to Thrill," each track contributing to the album's status as a monumental force in rock 'n' roll history. The opening track, "Hells Bells," sets a somber yet powerful tone, reflecting the band's transition after Bon Scott's passing. Songs like "Shoot to Thrill" and "What Do You Do for Money Honey" offer energetic riffs and catchy choruses. The title track, "Back in Black," is known for its iconic guitar riff and serves as a tribute to Bon. "You Shook Me All Night Long," one of the album's most famous songs, combines hard rock with a more commercial radio-friendly edge. "Have a Drink on Me" and "Shake a Leg" continue the album's theme of high-energy rock. The album concludes with "Rock and Roll Ain't Noise Pollution," an anthemic song that celebrates the essence of rock music. *Back in Black* remains a defining album in AC/DC's discography and a benchmark in the history of rock music. *Back in Black* to date has become the best-selling rock album of all time and the second best-selling album of all time of any music genre globally. The album, a commercial success, has surpassed well over 60 million copies worldwide, and is widely regarded as one of the best rock albums of all time. The album is also the third best-selling album in the United States, selling over 27 million albums to date, certified double diamond by the RIAA. Each track showcases AC/DC's signature sound, blending powerhouse rhythms and guitar riffs with compelling and powerful vocals. In summary, *Back in Black* is not just a tribute to Bon Scott but a landmark in rock history. It showcases AC/DC's ability to turn grief into a powerful, enduring legacy, solidifying their status as the greatest hard rock band of all time.

"Hells Bells"

"Hells Bells," the opening track on *Back in Black*, is marked by the slow, ominous tolling of a 2,000-pound bronze bell, adding a solemn and dramatic tone to its introduction. This bell was specifically manufactured for the song by John Taylor & Co. Bellfounders in Loughborough, and its sound was recorded using Ronnie Lane's (Small Faces, The Faces, Ronnie Lane's Slim Chance) mobile studio inside the bell foundry. The tolling bells, shrouded in haunting reverb, create an eerie ambiance that sends shivers down the spine. The slow and deliberate pacing builds anticipation, akin to a foreboding storm on the horizon. The song's lyrics and overall theme serve as a tribute to Bon Scott, who tragically passed away just a few months earlier. Bon was known for his wild lifestyle, often described as "raising hell," a phrase that resonates throughout the song. The lyrics open with a portrayal of immense energy and impending doom, encapsulating feelings of grief, anger, and a strong determination to carry on despite the loss of their frontman and lead singer: "I'm rolling thunder, pouring rain, I'm coming on like a hurricane..." The mood and overall theme of the song can be felt throughout the track, with Brian Johnson screeching like a banshee, conveying his sentiments of both anger and sorrow. Brian's voice channels both raw energy and mournful resilience, a delicate balance between melodic hooks and guttural cries. The term "Hells Bells" itself is not just a title but an expression that conveys anger or shock. It also conjures images of the underworld and the act of raising hell, fitting the song's intense and powerful energy. "Hells Bells" holds significant positions in various notable music rankings, such as being ranked sixth in *The Guardian*'s list of the forty greatest AC/DC songs in 2020 and seventh in *Kerrang!*'s list of the twenty greatest AC/DC songs in 2021. The song stands as a profound testament to the band's ability to transform grief and adversity into a powerful and enduring musical creation, which also began the start of a new era for AC/DC. The band would travel on tour with the one-ton bell, which would be lowered from the stage truss and struck with a large mallet by Brian. The original bell was eventually retired and hung in Malcolm Young's house in Australia, and a newer, lighter version has been used in its place since, which Brian would swing from as it was lowered to the stage during the performance of the song. "Hells Bells" would serve as the opening track during AC/DC's Back in Black and For Those About to Rock Tours and has remained a staple in AC/DC's live set to this day.

"Shoot to Thrill"

"Shoot to Thrill" opens with an iconic, unmistakable AC/DC riff that epitomizes the essence of hard rock. Brian Johnson's raspy and commanding voice cuts through the relentless instrumentation, capturing the spirit of the song's title. Brian's vocal delivery is filled with intensity and conviction, which adds an extra layer of dynamism to the track. His ability to convey the song's rebellious and electrifying spirit showcases his talent as a frontman and his seamless integration into the band. There are multiple interpretations of the song's meaning. One interpretation suggests the song is about the experiences of heavily medicated British women in the late 1970s and early 1980s, who would frequent clubs and bars seeking excitement and extra-marital encounters: "Shoot to thrill, play to kill, too many women, with too many pills." This interpretation aligns with Brian Johnson's lyrical inspiration, as he recalled an article about a neighborhood pusher selling narcotics to bored, lonely, and depressed housewives in London suburbs. Another interpretation is more direct, portraying the song as a cautionary tale with the singer warning potential lovers about the dangers of confronting him. The lyrics suggest a man who is unafraid to "shoot to thrill," making it clear that he is someone to be wary of, yet also irresistibly intriguing. The trademark double-entendre-style lyrics fans were already familiar with are evident in this track, which could also be referring to climax during said sexual encounters. Angus Young, the lead guitarist, drew inspiration for the song's musical breakdown from the climactic trio gun-battle in Sergio Leone's classic western, *The Good, the Bad and the Ugly*. This sequence, occurring after the main solo, mirrors the slow, quiet build-up of tension in Morricone's "Il Triello," leading to a thunderous, cataclysmic finale. This musical homage adds a cinematic quality to the song, enhancing its intense and dramatic atmosphere. The track was used as part of the soundtrack for the motion picture film *Iron Man 2* in 2010, which was also released as a soundtrack album by AC/DC and has become one of AC/DC's most infamous songs to date, remaining in their live set lists for forty-three years.

"What Do You Do for Money Honey"

Fairly a straightforward meaning from the title alone, "What Do You Do for Money Honey" presents a vivid picture of a woman who is relentlessly ambitious and willing to do anything for money and pleasure and the consequences that come along with that lifestyle. This woman, depicted in the song, is characterized as working in bars, riding in cars, and living in a posh apartment, always in pursuit of financial and material gain, an otherwise high-end prostitute. The lyrics, which include lines like "You're working in bars, riding in cars, never gonna give it for free," and "Honey, what do you do for money?" emphasize the theme of materialism and the lengths to which people might go to secure wealth and luxury. AC/DC's ability to weave a narrative with double-entendres and catchy phrases adds an extra layer of intrigue to the song. The song's structure allows for each band member to shine, with moments for Malcolm Young's rhythm guitar to add texture and depth, while Brian Johnson's vocals soar above the instrumentation. The interplay between the instruments and vocals adds depth and layers to the song, which blend both aggression and melody during this track. AC/DC's devil-may-care attitude, as seen in this song, was a signature element of their music, a testament to their songwriting prowess and their ability to create songs that stand the test of time. As the third track on *Back in Black* (side A for those of us who listened to it since day one on vinyl), which follows the powerful opener "Hells Bells" and the intense "Shoot to Thrill," "What Do You Do for Money Honey" plugs in perfectly into the album, flowing seamlessly along, continuing the album's rhythmic drive.

"Given the Dog a Bone"

Much like 1977's "Go Down" from *Let There Be Rock*, we have another AC/DC track about oral sex. "Given the Dog a Bone" is a vivid portrayal of raw desire and physical intimacy, encapsulated in the metaphor of the title itself "Givin' the dog a bone." This metaphor serves as a direct expression of carnal pleasure, reflecting the primal and instinctual aspects of sexual desire. The lyrics, suggestive and confident, are characteristic of AC/DC's explicit and rebellious nature, aligning with their reputation for creating music that pushes societal boundaries during the mid- to late 1970s and the beginning of the 1980s: "Oh she's blowin' me crazy, til my ammunition is dry". The repetition of the catchy guitar riff throughout the song serves as a unifying element, creating a foundation that drives the song forward. AC/DC's clever wordplay and innuendos are on full display, injecting a playful and mischievous vibe into the track. The lyrics serve as a reflection of the band's unapologetic attitude and carefree, rock 'n' roll spirit, embodying the spirit of rock 'n' roll rebellion and indulgence without reservation. The song garnered mixed reviews; some critics complained at the time that it was too explicit. The track has found its way back into AC/DC's live set list once again, as it was recently performed live at the Power Trip festival in Indio, California, in October 2023.

"Let Me Put My Love into You"

Like many AC/DC songs, "Let Me Put My Love into You," the closing track on side one, is a straightforward representation of a sexual encounter, laced with suggestive imagery and passionate language, hinting at the desire for physical and intimate connection. The line "let me cut your cake with my knife" is a notable metaphor for sexual penetration. The song's lyrics walk the line between metaphor and explicitness, allowing the listener to interpret and engage with the song on their own terms: "Don't you worry, don't you fight, don't you struggle, cause it's your turn tonight." Brian Johnson's raspy and powerful voice amplifies the sensual nature of the song, his vocal delivery captures the essence of desire, making each line resonate with the intensity of desire portrayed in the lyrics.

"Back in Black"

"Back in Black," the title track from the album, stands as a monumental tribute to the band's former lead singer, Bon Scott, the overall theme of both the album and the album cover. The song, notable for its instantly recognizable guitar riff, was crafted as a positive celebration of Bon's life, avoiding any morbid tones. Brian Johnson, along with founding members Angus and Malcolm Young, intended to create a rock anthem that honored the memory of Bon, while encapsulating his life's edge and resilience through lines like "Nine lives, cats' eyes, abusing every one of them and running wild." The opening guitar riff of "Back in Black" is instantly recognizable and has become one of the most iconic in rock music. Angus Young's masterful guitar work creates a riff that is both catchy and powerful, setting the tone for the entire song. Brian's ability to channel the spirit of AC/DC and convey raw emotion through his vocals is showcased during this track, making the song even more impactful. "Back in Black" peaked at #37 on the *Billboard* Hot 100, contributing to the album's sales of over 50 million copies worldwide. Its influence extended beyond the music industry, featuring in popular culture, such as in the soundtrack for Marvel's *Iron Man 2* motion picture movie in 2010. The song's appeal is universal, hailed for its no-nonsense, powerful riff, and it has been lauded by various publications, including being ranked #4 on VH1's list of the 40 Greatest Metal Songs. Its inclusion in countless movie soundtracks, sports events, and rock playlists attests to its enduring popularity and its status as a rock anthem that stands the test of time. "Back in Black" remains a symbol of AC/DC's legacy and their ability to create music that resonates with fans across the globe.

"You Shook Me All Night Long"

"You Shook Me All Night" marked the band's first single with Brian Johnson as the lead vocalist, following the tragic death of Bon Scott earlier that year. The song explores themes of fast living and romantic encounters through the metaphor of cars and speed, a topic close to Brian Johnson's heart as a car enthusiast. The opening line of the first verse, "She was a fast machine, she kept her motor clean," set the tone for the song, reflecting the excitement and allure of both cars and women. This metaphor is a common thread in AC/DC's work, capturing the high-energy, straightforward rock ethos the band is known for and holding true to their trademark double-entendre lyrics. With its clever wordplay and imagery, the song paints a vivid picture of a memorable night of excitement and desire. Despite AC/DC's stance regarding the song lyrics and many of the other tracks from *Back in Black*, there have been long-standing claims from people outside of the band, some who were close to Bon, that some parts of the lyrics were actually written by Bon. However, those claims have only surmounted to speculation and have appeared in a handful of unofficial biographies written about the band. The band members, specifically Angus and Malcolm Young and Brian Johnson, have always stated that Bon did not write any of the songs. The guitar riff is yet another iconic and memorable riff from the album, set in the key of G major and following a G-C-D chord progression during the main verse and riff. "You Shook Me All Night Long" has achieved significant acclaim over the years. It was placed at #10 on VH1's list of the 100 Greatest Songs of the 80s and #1 on VH1's Top Ten AC/DC Songs. *Guitar World* ranked it at #80 on their 100 Greatest Guitar Solos list, and in 2021, *Rolling Stone* placed it at #287 on their Top 500 Greatest Songs of All Time. The song is also a staple at AC/DC concerts, rarely excluded from the setlist, and has seen four live versions officially released, the track has essentially become one of the biggest anthems in rock music to date.

"Have a Drink on Me"

"Have a Drink on Me" is an ode to drinking and the escapism provided by alcohol, imbued with the characteristic energy and straightforward approach that AC/DC is known for. Yet another tribute to their late singer, Bon Scott, "Have a Drink on Me" is an ode to their fallen brother. Bon's presence and influence are felt throughout the album, and this song, in particular, seems to reflect his spirit and the way he lived his life. Bon's death from acute alcohol poisoning in February 1980 had a profound impact on the band, and *Back in Black* as a whole was a tribute to him. "Whiskey, gin and brandy, with a glass

I'm pretty handy, I'm trying to walk a straight line, on sour mash and cheap wine." The album's all-black cover was a sign of mourning for Bon, chosen by the band to honor their late singer. The song has an aggressive, almost angry tone in which the somber expression of the loss of their singer resounds throughout. The song's lyrics, laced with typical AC/DC-style innuendos and straightforward rock language, convey a message of living in the moment and enjoying life's pleasures without worrying about the consequences. Lines like "Don't worry about tomorrow, take it today ... forget about the check, we'll get Hell to pay" encapsulate this carefree attitude. Much like the line "forget about the hearse, 'cos I'll never die" in the title track, the song preaches an unstoppable determination to forge forward.

"Shake a Leg"

"Shake a Leg" is a fast-paced rocker from the album that instantly kicks off with the raw energy of a boogie-blues infused riff. Malcolm and Angus Young set the pace along with the thunderous rhythm section of Phil Rudd and Cliff Williams, whose interplay with Brian Johnson's soaring vocals compliments the music perfectly. Brian's range in this track is incredible, making it probably one of the most difficult AC/DC songs to sing accurately. Its lyrics paint a picture of an independent individual who resists conformity and societal expectations and one who embraces a carefree lifestyle. The song's rebellious theme resonated particularly with the youth, who identified with the desire for independence and breaking free from societal formalities and rules: "Keepin' out of trouble, with eyes in the back of my face, kickin' ass in the class and they tell me I'm a damn disgrace." Of course, what would an AC/DC song be without metaphors and wordplay. "Shake a Leg" is no exception once again, complete with metaphoric references to masturbation "Oh shake a leg, shake your head." The track certainly showcases Angus Young's blistering guitar solos, a testament to his status as one of rock's most iconic guitarists

"Rock and Roll Ain't Noise Pollution"

The tenth and final track on *Back in Black*, "Rock and Roll Ain't Noise Pollution" stands as a defiant anthem celebrating the enduring spirit and cultural significance of rock music. The song emerged as a response to societal and governmental critiques of rock music being too loud or disruptive. Specifically, it was a reaction to complaints about noise pollution and the regulations against loud music in public spaces, such as the controversy surrounding London's Marquee Club and laws restricting the volume of music after certain hours. The band's rhythm guitarist, Malcolm Young, was inspired to write this song as a form of retaliation, emphasizing the unstoppable nature of rock 'n' roll. The song's lyrics, infused with a strong sense of defiance and rebellion, address the critics and naysayers of rock music directly. It challenges the notion that rock music is merely "noise pollution," asserting instead its value and significance. This theme resonates in the broader context of the cultural and artistic importance of rock music, in particular hard rock, which has often been under scrutiny or dismissed by critics and authorities. The song's message is clear: rock music is not just noise but a vital form of expression and an enduring cultural phenomenon that is eternal. The song's lyrics challenge those who dismiss rock music, asserting its enduring impact and significance. The track's creation was somewhat spontaneous, with Angus and Malcolm Young composing it in about fifteen minutes at the suggestion of their record label and management, who felt that one more song was needed for the album. The song opens with a memorable guitar riff that sets the tone for the rest of the track, as Brian sings during the intro "Hey there, all you middle men, throw away your fancy clothes, and while you're out there sittin' on a fence, so get off your ass and come down here, 'cause rock 'n' roll ain't no riddle, man, to me, it makes good, good sense" with a confident and defiant growl as the song kicks off. The song achieved significant recognition, as it was the fourth single released from the album in November 1980 and reached #15 on the UK singles chart, making it the highest charting song from the album. "Rock and Roll Ain't Noise Pollution" is not just a song, it is a statement—one which resonates the importance and significance of rock music to this day. The song's defiance and celebration of rock's power remain as potent today as they were upon its release. Its enduring popularity is a testament to the universal appeal of rock 'n' roll and the enduring impact and influence that AC/DC has had on the genre.

Interesting Facts

In January 2024, the official "Back in Black" video surpassed 1 billion views on YouTube. On the original versions of the album, the track "Given the Dog a Bone" is spelled this way, with the word "Given" on the album but was later changed to "Givin'." For AC/DC's fiftieth-anniversary marketing campaign in 2024, a special LP edition of the album was issued on black and white blended vinyl. As of August 2024, *Back in Black* was certified by the RIAA for 27 million copies sold in the USA, making it the third best selling album of all time in the United States.

8

For Those About to Rock (We Salute You)

Release date:	November 21, 1981 (U.K.)
	November 21, 1981 (U.S.)
Current edition:	Sony/Columbia, CD, LP
Personnel:	Brian Johnson, lead vocals
	Angus Young, lead guitar
	Malcolm Young, rhythm guitar
	Cliff Williams, bass guitar
	Phil Rudd, drums
Duration:	40:10
Recorded at:	Mobile One, H.I.S., Paris, France, May–September 1981
Produced by:	Robert John "Mutt' Lange
Chart position:	#3 Australian Albums
	#1 U.S. *Billboard* 200

Notable info: AC/DC's first #1 album on the *Billboard* charts in the USA. *For Those About to Rock (We Salute You)* is certified 4x platinum in the USA, 5x platinum in Australia, with multiple platinum and gold certifications in other countries.

Released on November 23, 1981, AC/DC's eighth studio album, *For Those About to Rock (We Salute You)*, emerged amid challenges, both in the studio and on the global stage. The album marked the follow-up to the massively successful *Back in Black* and faced the formidable task of living up to its predecessor's monumental success. Once again produced by the meticulous Robert John "Mutt" Lange, the recording process for *For Those About to Rock* proved to be arduous. The band, known for their relentless work ethic, found themselves confronting the demanding production methods of Lange, who was infamous for his perfectionism. The intense studio sessions and long hours took a toll on the band members, as they strived for the sonic excellence that had become synonymous with their name. Meticulous attention to detail and pursuit of sonic perfection led to a challenging and, at times, exhausting creative process. The result, however, was an album that showcased AC/DC's unyielding dedication to their craft. The title track, "For Those About to Rock (We Salute You)," became an instant classic and an anthem that resonated with fans worldwide. The song's thunderous cannons and powerful riffage epitomized the raw energy and spirit of AC/DC. The album also featured tracks like "Let's Get It Up," "Put the Finger on You," and "Inject the Venom," each contributing to the album's reputation as a powerhouse of rock music. The album quickly went platinum in the United States and catapulted to #1 on the *Billboard* charts after its release, solidifying AC/DC as the world's biggest rock band at the time. The success of the album, however, fell short of its predecessor's. This coupled with the record company's decision at the time to release *Dirty Deeds Done Dirt Cheap* in North America in March of the same year added confusion among the newer fan base as to who the lead singer was in the band as AC/DC was trying to establish Brian as their new singer. The album sales, although successful, suffered from the poorly timed decision on Atlantic Records' part to issue *Dirty Deeds Done Dirt Cheap*.

"For Those About to Rock (We Salute You)"

Perhaps another of the greatest rock 'n' roll anthems ever written, the title track from AC/DC's monumental 1981 album *For Those About to Rock (We Salute You)* joins the ranks of several other anthemic masterpieces in AC/DC's arsenal. As Angus Young was a big fan of history, its title and central lyric were inspired by the ancient Roman salute "*Ave, Caesar, morituri te salutant*" ("Hail, Caesar, those who are about to die salute you"). The song's genesis is tied to an inspiration from British poet and classicist Robert Graves, particularly a twist on a line by him about Roman gladiators. Angus and Malcolm Young crafted this song, deriving a key idea from a historic reference to the Colosseum and the fate of gladiators. Angus recalled in an interview:

> ... the title in itself comes from ... there was a book once written about the Roman empire at the time. Of course, the title was For Those About to Die, we salute you. We've been fooling around with this idea in the rehearsal room and this little guitar intro thing going and we had this very moody beginning, and it just kinda reminded me of that Roman thing, you know, the guy with the ... doing his fist over his arm and he's got his sword up, you know and tell the emperor For Those About to Die, we salute you and I just thought it would be a good title for a rock album.

The title and chorus concept emerged from this historical backdrop, blending with the song's musical elements to form a powerful rock anthem. The song and lyrics are a tribute to the enduring power of rock music and the bond between the band and their fans, symbolizing unity, rebellion, and camaraderie. With lines such as "Hail hail to the good times, 'cause rock has got the right of way, we ain't no legend, ain't no cause, we're just livin' for today" is such a powerful line in the first verse, which succinctly defines the meaning of the track. Brian Johnson's delivery is both commanding and infectious, further solidifying his place as a remarkable frontman and his contribution to the band's legacy. A unique element of the song are the cannon blasts, symbolizing the power and impact of rock music. The inspiration for these blasts came from a very different source: the televised wedding of Princess Diana. While recording the song, the band heard the cannons from the wedding on TV and decided to incorporate a similar effect into their music. This serendipitous occurrence led to the iconic inclusion of cannon blasts in the song, enhancing its dramatic and explosive nature and to this day remains as the standard closing track in AC/DC's live sets, complete with firing cannons during the encore performance. "For Those About to Rock (We Salute You)" has influenced the rock music scene significantly, solidifying AC/DC's place among the greatest rock bands and inspiring countless musicians for decades. The song's legacy is in its ability to unite rock enthusiasts, reminding them of the timeless power of rock music. Its influence extends to popular culture, featuring in movies, TV shows, sports events, and video games, making it a symbol of rock's enduring appeal. The explosive energy that surges through the crowd during the song's climactic finale is a testament to the enduring power of AC/DC's music.

"Put the Finger on You"

"Put the Finger on You" is a high-energy track that is fueled by driving guitar riffs and a rocking groove. The song exemplifies the band's characteristic style of hard rock with sexually charged lyrics. The title itself is a play on words, suggesting both accusation and sexual innuendo. Lyrically, the song employs straightforward and provocative language, typical of AC/DC's approach to songwriting. The lyrics can be interpreted as describing a flirtatious and possibly risqué interaction between a man and a woman. The man, presumably the narrator of the song, expresses a strong, almost aggressive sexual interest in the woman. The phrase "put the finger on you" can be understood as singling someone out or identifying them as the object of one's desire or attention. The metaphor of "putting a finger on someone" in this context refers to touching fingers as a sign of affection or intimacy, much aligned with the typical and expected innuendo of AC/DC's lyric writing. The man expresses a strong, almost aggressive sexual interest in the woman: "Yes, I've got fire in my fingertips, radiating onto you, I can't control, can't even hold it." "Put the Finger on You" depicts a narrative of desire and pursuit, with Brian Johnson expressing a deep and overwhelming attraction that defies control. Angus once spoke of the song: "That's basically a gangster like line they do in the movies.... We're not putting the finger on anyone in particular. It's always been the other fucking way around." AC/DC's songs often contain themes of masculinity, sexual prowess, and bold, unapologetic pursuit of pleasure. In the context of their broader discography, "Put the Finger on You" aligns with their typical portrayal of sexual themes in a direct and unambiguous manner. The song's energy and straightforward lyrics reflect the band's raw, high-energy rock style, which is central to their appeal and success. "Put the Finger on You" was included in the live set during the For Those About to Rock Tour; however, it has not been performed live again since.

"Let's Get it Up"

"Let's Get it Up," the first single released from the *For Those About to Rock (We Salute You)* album, is an up-tempo hard rock anthem with lyrics themed around a night of partying and sexual foreplay. It achieved commercial success, reaching the Top 25 in several countries and the Top 10 in Australia. The song's lyrical content is unabashedly bold, characterized by the band's iconic raw energy and edgy themes: "Loose lips, sink ships, so come aboard for a pleasure trip." Lead singer Brian Johnson described the track as "Filth, pure filth," an acknowledgment of the band's often provocative and unapologetic style; Angus stated: "You can take it one of two ways, meaning musically up, or the girls in the back room." This portrayal aligns with AC/DC's reputation for creating music that is direct, spirited, and rebellious, with disregard for critics or record company executives' opinions. Angus Young's guitar work in the song is particularly noteworthy. Kurt Loder, in his review of the song, highlighted Angus Young's "serpentine solo," which reflects his blues roots. This guitar solo adds a distinctive layer to the track, merging the band's signature hard rock sound with deeper musical influences. *Record World* described "Let's Get It Up" as a "cracking rocker with its celebratory chorus," highlighting its infectious and high-energy nature. The song's narrative invites the listener to join in a journey of pleasure, urging them to take control of their desires and embrace risk-taking. This message is encapsulated in the chorus and various verses, where Brian persuades his woman to embark on an adventurous experience together.

"Inject the Venom"

Perhaps one of AC/DC's heavier songs, "Inject the Venom" is a track that explores darker themes, particularly surrounding themes of revenge, power, and the consequences of wrongdoing. The lyrics present an uncompromising stance against those perceived as "bad," with a refusal to show leniency or forgiveness. This sense of aggression and retaliation is embodied in the chorus, which repeatedly commands to "inject the venom," symbolizing a form of justice delivered against those who have caused harm or pain. The narrative portrays a character betrayed or taken advantage of, seeking revenge through powerful and vengeful actions. The song is powered by an aggressive guitar riff with interplay between the riff and Brian Johnson's ferocious-sounding vocals. The lyrics are marked by a strong and aggressive tone, emphasizing themes of retribution and justice. The repeated lines, "No mercy for the bad if they want it, no mercy for the bad if they plead, no mercy for the bad if they need it, no mercy from me," set a tone of unyielding retribution. This absence of mercy for the "bad" reflects a harsh stance on punishment and justice, characteristic of many hard rock and heavy metal songs of that era. The use of "inject the venom" as a metaphor suggests administering a final, decisive blow to an adversary. It symbolizes a form of retribution that is both metaphorically poisonous and final. The lyrics "Inject your venom, it'll be your last attack" imply that this act of revenge will be conclusive and destructive. Brian Johnson once described the song "It's a power thing, like 'For Those About to Rock'." The song also explores themes of power and aggression, common in AC/DC's music. The lines "Got no heart, no—feel no pain, take your soul and—leave a stain" suggest a merciless and unfeeling approach to dealing with adversaries, indicating a complete lack of empathy or remorse. Overall, "Inject the Venom" encapsulates AC/DC's hard-hitting approach to themes of revenge and justice, set against the backdrop of their signature high-energy rock sound. The song's aggressive lyrics and powerful instrumentation create a sense of relentless force and determination, embodying the band's raw, unapologetic style.

"Snowballed"

"Snowballed," which was released as the B-side on the "Let's Get it Up" single, is a track that delves into themes of deception, manipulation, and the chaotic nature of fame and the music industry. The song's lyrics, delivered with the powerful vocals of Brian Johnson, shift between reality and metaphorical imagery to capture a life spiraling out of control, akin to a snowball rolling down a hill, gathering momentum and power. While AC/DC has not explicitly disclosed the exact source, it is believed that the song draws upon the chaotic nature of fame and the music industry, encapsulating the pressures and challenges faced by the band during their rise to success. This interpretation is supported by the band's statements in interviews and the song's ambiguous lyrics, which allow for individual interpretations, including societal manipulation and deceit, as well as reflections on the band's journey through fame's highs and lows. It could be assumed that it is about one of their former managers, with whom they broke ties with after much deception and theft was discovered about the culprit: "Dragged down to the bottom, screamin' for air, the shark must get his share." The song's themes of deception, resilience, and relentless pursuit of success resonate universally, reflecting the struggles individuals may face in their personal or professional lives. Angus described the meaning behind the track as "you've been conned, fooled again and we figured we'd been tricked enough in our time, so we came up with that." "Snowballed" delves into scenarios where the narrator finds themselves in unfavorable situations, such as a financial downfall or being overwhelmed in a hostile environment. The chorus emphasizes the feeling of being "snowballed," which means being deceived or tricked, suggesting that the narrator has been fooled and taken advantage of. This cautionary tale highlights the need to be cautious and aware of one's surroundings to avoid falling prey to manipulative forces.

"Evil Walks"

Musically, "Evil Walks" starts off with an ominous guitar riff that sets the stage for the track's dark and sinister theme. "Evil Walks" is a song that delves into the themes of manipulation, toxicity, and the malevolent influence of the woman described in the song. The lyrics use a range of vivid imagery and metaphors to paint a picture of a woman who embodies darkness and evil. This woman is described as having a "black shadow hanging over your shoulder" and "green eyes couldn't get any colder," suggesting a lack of empathy and a menacing presence. The chorus emphasizes the all-pervading nature of this evil woman, stating that she "walks behind you," "sleeps beside you," and "talks around you." This indicates that this sinister woman is always present, influencing and impacting every aspect of her victims' lives. The metaphor of a black widow spider is also used to symbolize deceit and treachery, with the lyrics describing the spider as weaving "evil notions" and spinning "dark secrets" in its web, ensnaring and entrapping its victims. The song also carries a tone of sarcasm and awareness, as seen in lines like "I sometimes wonder where you park your broom," implying that the narrator is aware of the manipulations and deceptions of the malevolent individual. The bridge of the song, with lines like "C'mon weave your web" and references to the "black widow," reinforces the theme of manipulation and the destructive nature of the woman described in the song, likely inspired by a relationship gone wrong. Given AC/DC's style and typical subject matter, the song likely is not meant to be taken literally but rather plays on the band's recurring themes of relationships, sexual encounters, and typical rock 'n' roll lifestyle.

"C.O.D."

"C.O.D." was the B-side for the "For Those About to Rock" promo single and interestingly was the very first song I heard from the album prior to its commercial release, as the radio station I was listening to at the time played it on the air to debut the "new AC/DC song" rather than the title track, which was the actual single. The song delves into themes of temptation, self-destructive behavior, and the consequences of one's actions. The song uses various metaphors and wordplay related to indulgence and sinful desires. The title "C.O.D." is an acronym for "care of the devil," symbolizing one's willingness to succumb to dark urges and desires. The lyrics portray desperation and reckless behavior, driven by instinctual desires, and depict a reliance on instant gratification and material excess. The song metaphorically suggests pushing boundaries and engaging in dangerous behavior without considering the consequences. It emphasizes the internal struggle with the devil representing inner demons and dark desires. The bridge highlights the cycle of temptation and its consequences, suggesting that the more one gives in to their desires, the stronger and more insatiable those desires become. "That call of a dog, cry of a bitch, the sign of a sinner's the size of his itch." Overall, "C.O.D." serves as a cautionary tale about the consequences of indulging in sinful desires and the struggle to resist temptations, symbolizing the curse of love and the high price of actions.

"Breaking the Rules"

"Breaking the Rules" is a powerful track that encapsulates themes of rebellion and nonconformity, and it is not the first time AC/DC have written a song to speak out against authority. The lyrics paint a picture of individuals who are seen as outcasts or rebels in society, those who are often marginalized or looked down upon. It vividly describes a lifestyle that is on the edge, characterized by hard living and an unwillingness to adhere to societal norms. Key phrases like "black sheep and a renegade" and "living like trash, a society rash" suggest a defiance against the established order. The song also criticizes the rigidity of rules and regulations in lines like "They got regulation ties, regulation shoes, those regulation fools with their regulation rules." This is a call for breaking free from societal constraints and doing things one's own way, as emphasized in the line "No rebellion, not today, I'm going to do things my own way, every day and every way." Overall, "Breaking the Rules" embodies a spirit of defiance and individuality, encouraging listeners to challenge norms and live life on their own terms. This theme resonates with the broader ethos of rock music as a genre that often celebrates nonconformity and rebellion.

"Night of the Long Knives"

"Night of the Long Knives" is a powerful song that blends metaphorical lyrics with a hard-hitting musical composition. The song's title and lyrics reference a specific historical event, particularly the Night of the Long Knives in the purge that took place in Nazi Germany on June 30, 1934. However, AC/DC's use of this imagery is more symbolic than literal, serving as a metaphor for betrayal, distrust, and the unpredictable nature of power struggles. Angus Young, a self-proclaimed fan of history, created the concept for this song, which showcases a different side of the band's songwriting approach. The lyrics pose questions about loyalty and betrayal, asking "Who's your leader, who's your man? Who will help you fill your hand? Who's your friend and who's your foe? Who's your Judas, you don't know?" These lines reflect a sense of uncertainty and paranoia, suggesting a scenario where alliances are unclear and trust is scarce. The refrain "Night of the long knives" further emphasizes the theme of sudden and violent resolution to hidden tensions and conflicts. Musically, the song is described as one of the album's heaviest moments, characterized by a pounding rhythm and aggressive boogie infused guitar riffs. It is noted for its dynamic shifts, which keep listeners engaged throughout the track.

"Night of the Long Knives" can be interpreted as a cautionary tale about the deceptive nature of power and the dangers of betrayal. The song serves as a reminder to be cautious about who we trust and to be aware of potential hidden agendas.

"Spellbound"

"Spellbound," the closing track on the album, is a mesmerizing and enigmatic track that captivates listeners with its haunting atmosphere and hypnotic rhythm. The song begins with a fantastic, slow-paced guitar riff—first from Angus and then joined by Malcolm. Brian's vocals are dynamic and complement the music, creating the atmosphere and tone of the track. The song's lyrics depict a series of unfortunate events and situations, symbolized by metaphors such as car crashes and reckless driving, to convey a sense of danger and unease: "Blinded by a bright beam, shattered by the windscreen, stunned by the whiplash, I'm a victim of a bad crash." This imagery paints a vivid picture of being caught in a destructive cycle, where one's actions or circumstances continuously lead to negative outcomes. After assessing the lyrics more thoroughly, I do believe that the inspiration for the track is an incident involving a car or motorcycle accident. The song explores feelings of being blindsided, shattered, and stunned, suggesting a loss of control and the inability to escape a negative situation. The repetition of phrases like "spinning 'round and 'round" emphasizes the feeling of being trapped in chaos and unable to break free. Brian Johnson's throaty vocals add depth to the song, enhancing the sense of despair and hopelessness in the lyrics. "You know I can do nothing right, I never sleep at night, can't even start a fight" sets a tone for self-pity and despair, which is further enforced with the chorus "Spellbound, my world keeps tumbling down". "Spellbound" is a brilliant sounding track and is often cited as a fan favorite from the album despite being a "deep cut."

Interesting Facts

The vinyl LP version of the album released in Spain in 1981 and featured a reverse-colored sleeve (black background with gold AC/DC logo, title, and cannon), which is now a rarity and collectible among fans. All standard versions of the vinyl LP were issued in a gatefold album cover with a live photo of the band performing during the Back in Black Tour.

9

Flick of the Switch

Release date:	August 19, 1983 (U.K.)
	August 19, 1983 (U.S.)
Current edition:	Sony/Columbia, CD, LP
Personnel:	Brian Johnson, lead vocals
	Angus Young, lead guitar
	Malcolm Young, rhythm guitar
	Cliff Williams, bass guitar
	Phil Rudd, drums
Recorded at:	Compass Point Studios, Nassau, Bahamas, April–May 1983
Produced by:	AC/DC
Chart position:	#3 Australian Albums
	#4 U.K. Albums
	#15 U.S. *Billboard* 200

Notable info: Phil Rudd was fired from the band before the album was finalized; however, his drum tracks were already completed and used for the album. This was the first self-produced AC/DC album. *Flick of the Switch* is certified platinum in the USA, 3x platinum in Australia, with gold certifications in other countries.

After the bands experience recording *For Those About to Rock (We Salute You)*, the decision was made to depart from the grandeur of their previous productions and to produce the album themselves. The extremely long and redundant recording sessions while working with "Mutt" Lange in Paris to record *For Those About to Rock* had taken its toll, and the band were not keen on returning to the studio with him again at this point. *Flick of the Switch* reflected a conscious decision by AC/DC to return to their roots, delivering a raw and unbridled dose of rock 'n' roll. The decision to self-produce marked a return to the hands-on approach that had characterized their earlier works. The result was a sound that, while perhaps less polished, exuded an authenticity and grit that resonated with fans craving the raw power of AC/DC. The album features the classic AC/DC sound with prominent guitar riffs, solid backbeats, and Brian Johnson's raspy vocals. The lyrics often deal with themes of defiance, power, and the rock 'n' roll lifestyle. The title track, "Flick of the Switch," epitomizes the album's ethos, featuring Angus Young's blistering guitar riffs and Brian Johnson's signature vocals, with a raw, stripped-down sound that the band was after during these recording sessions. The album as a whole is a testament to the band's commitment to the core elements of their sound—raucous guitars, pounding drums, and unabashed energy. Tracks like "Nervous Shakedown" and "Guns for Hire" showcase the band's ability to craft straightforward, no-nonsense rockers. In the midst of production and completion of the album, Phil Rudd was abruptly fired from the band, rumored to be related to long-time substance abuse, which had started taking its toll. Phil's drum tracks were completed for the album. Procul Harum drummer B. J. Wilson was hired in the event that additional drum tracks were needed, but this was not needed. After over 700 auditions, Simon Wright was hired as the new AC/DC drummer shortly after and in time for the tour. Simon also appears in the promotional videos for the songs from the album. Although the album did not fare as well on the charts or in album sales as the previous releases, it was still successful, and the band went on to tour the world to prove that they were still the kings of rock music. Over the years, however, the album has garnered a dedicated fan base appreciative of its unvarnished approach, and some often cite it as "Brian's Powerage."

"Rising Power"

"Rising Power," the opening track, is a song that captures the essence of the band's signature hard rock sound. The title signifies a rise to prominence, a surge of energy, and an unstoppable force; it is also a nod to AC/DC's electrifying sound of power, raw energy, and high-voltage rock. The song starts with a portrayal of a hard city life and an anticipation for an exhilarating encounter, suggesting a longing for escape and excitement. The chorus emphasizes a sense of liberation and defiance, with lines like "Rising power, we'll raise the night" and "Rising power, we'll wake the dead." This repeated refrain symbolizes a challenge to the status quo and to authority in general, a common theme that is found throughout *Flick of the Switch*. The inspiration for "Rising Power" likely came from AC/DC's own experiences as a band. They aimed to create a powerful anthem that would not only energize their fans but also reflect their journey through the music industry. The song can be interpreted in various ways, with some seeing it as a call to fight against societal oppression, while others view it as a metaphor for overcoming personal obstacles and rising above adversity. *Flick of the Switch* itself is noted for its themes of outlaw bravado and sexual innuendo, elements that were characteristic of AC/DC's music and appealed strongly to their fan base. With its themes of explosive force and dominance, "Rising Power" fits squarely within this context, reflecting the band's consistent embrace of high-energy rock music. This track, like much of AC/DC's work, is not just about the music itself but about the attitude and ethos it represents—a celebration of raw power, resilience, and the spirit of rock music.

"This House is on Fire"

"This House is on Fire" is a song that vividly encapsulates themes of uncontrollable energy, intense passion, and sexual attraction to a woman. The lyrics are crafted to convey the tumultuous nature of a fiery love affair, using the metaphor of a burning house to depict the relationship's intensity and its consuming nature. The song's lyrics describe a person who is both seductive and captivating, with lines like "Yonder she walks, hitting 1-0-3, a little tongue-in-cheek, hot personality" suggesting a confident and alluring presence. The chorus, "This house is on fire, and my flame is gonna burn in you," further paints the picture of a relationship engulfed in the flames of desire, highlighting the powerful impact of this passion on the individuals involved. The fiery imagery used throughout the song symbolizes not just the intensity of the love affair but the metaphoric use of fire and flames to establish the extreme attraction to the woman described in the song. The repeated line "This house is on fire" could be interpreted as a metaphor for a situation or relationship that is out of control, consumed by an intense, possibly destructive energy. The imagery of fire and burning is often used in rock music to symbolize powerful emotions or transformative experiences. In the context of this song, it might suggest a passionate, possibly tumultuous relationship, or perhaps the uncontainable energy and excitement that AC/DC's music itself generates. Furthermore, the song's title and chorus could also be seen as a reflection of the band's own status at the time. Coming off the massive success of their previous albums, AC/DC was a band at the peak of their powers, burning brightly in the rock music landscape. "This House is on Fire" can be seen as both a literal description of their fiery music and a metaphorical statement about their place in the world of rock 'n' roll—a band so full of energy and power that they seem to set the world around them ablaze.

"Flick of the Switch"

"Flick of the Switch," the title track from the album, is a vibrant showcase of the band's raw and energetic rock style. The song maintains a driving pace that never lets up, propelled by its hard-hitting riffs and aggressive rhythm, which is complimented by Brian Johnson's gritty and raspy voice. The lyrics describe a passionate and electrifying love affair, where the woman involved is portrayed as both seductive and potentially destructive. The song opens with descriptions of this woman as a "she devil" and "evil," indicating her captivating yet dangerous nature. Phrases like "suicidal voltage line" and "signals outta distress" suggest the exhilarating yet perilous aspects of being with her, hinting at both the allure and the risk involved in the relationship The chorus, with lines like "With a flick of the switch, she's gonna blow you sky high" and "Flash the eye, electrify," suggest a theme of explosive, uncontrollable energy, akin to the sudden release of power one might imagine flipping a switch would unleash. The "flick of the switch" metaphor symbolizes her ability to dramatically alter the dynamics of the relationship, indicating that her actions can lead to intense and potentially overwhelming experiences, but not without AC/DC's metaphoric use of orgasm. This imagery of electricity and power conveys the song's theme of a volatile and chaotic connection that is as electrifying as it is unstable.The song further explores the idea of a relationship that is both addictive and damaging. The repeated line "with a flick of the switch, she gonna give you pain, she gonna blow your brain" highlights the destructive nature of this love affair. It suggests a relationship that is exhilarating yet fraught with pain and mental turmoil, with the final line "She gonna put the light out on you" symbolizing a potentially devastating end to the relationship. Musically, "Flick of the Switch" follows AC/DC's trademark style of high-energy rock, characterized by Angus and Malcolm Young's iconic riffs. The song's solo section amplifies this electric energy, underlining the power and intensity of the track and overall vibe of the album. In the context of AC/DC's discography, "Flick of the Switch" can be seen as an embodiment of the band's straightforward, no-frills approach to rock music, capturing the essence of their sound: raw, powerful, and direct. The song's energetic rhythm and straightforward lyrics reflect the band's commitment to the fundamentals of rock music and AC/DC's trademark sound that fans have loved since the beginning.

"Nervous Shakedown"

"Nervous Shakedown" was the third single from *Flick of the Switch* and was also a regular live track played during the tour. Another track that follows suit and carries the band's signature hard rock sound and lyrical style. It would appear that the song title draws its inspiration from The Rolling Stones "Nervous Breakdown," similar to how "Highway to Hell" was likely a play on Led Zeppelin's "Stairway to Heaven." The lyrics depict a scene that can be interpreted as a confrontation with authority or a tense, high-pressure situation, conveyed through a narrative of being stopped, challenged, and threatened with imprisonment. Phrases like "'Freeze', said the man cruisin' the beat, 'you get your hands up and spread your feet'" and "It's a dirty lie, it's a shakedown" illustrate a scenario of being wrongfully accused or caught in a situation of power abuse. This portrayal of a "nervous shakedown" can be seen as a metaphor for the kind of intense, confrontational scenarios that are often a theme in rock music, particularly in the hard rock genre. AC/DC drew inspiration for "Nervous Shakedown" from their own experiences and observations of the pressures and anxieties prevalent in a fast-paced society. The song reflects a universal feeling of being overwhelmed and restless during this confrontation and an innermost feeling of rebellion against it. These intense instrumentals mirror the song's theme, emphasizing the urgency and unease portrayed in the lyrics. It aligns with the rock and blues-inspired style that the band is renowned for, adding a layer of introspection and thematic depth to their music. The song's depiction of a high-pressure confrontation, set to the band's hard-hitting rock sound, captures the essence of AC/DC's music: confrontational, energetic, and unapologetically bold.

"Landslide"

"Landslide" is a fast-paced, high-energy rocker, which closes side A of the album. The song is yet another from *Flick of the Switch* that encapsulates themes of rebellion and individualism. The lyrics tell the story of a young man who is nonconformist and faces opposition from his family, yet remains undeterred in his quest to forge his own path. His family's reactions, ranging from scolding to frustration, highlight the conflict between his rebellious spirit and societal expectations. Despite these challenges, he sees his life as an exciting, albeit sometimes nightmarish, adventure. The chorus of the song describes him as a "landslide," a metaphor for an unstoppable force of nature. This imagery reinforces his powerful, confident demeanor and his refusal to be defeated. He is depicted as someone who constantly strives to win and surpass his previous accomplishments, embodying the spirit of a "breaker" and a "maker" who breaks barriers and creates his own destiny. The song also touches on themes of defiance against traditional values and religious restrictions, emphasizing his determination to carve out his own path, which at the time during the mid-'80s was a "hot topic" of typical traditional value-oriented parents and families versus the sudden surge of hard rock and metal fans worldwide. Long hair, denim and leather, alleged devil-worshipping, drugs and alcohol, and sex infatuations with the youth was the new thing that parents were dealing with, special thanks to hard rock and heavy metal music at the time. Funnily enough, none of these allegations were so worrisome to have caused such a stir, because in the end the fans of the music of the '80s, such as AC/DC fans, have become some of the most respected and professional adults to date. The lyrics of "Landslide" provide a glimpse into AC/DC's thoughts on life's challenges and uncertainties. "Landslide" could be interpreted as a metaphorical journey through life's ups and downs, representing the obstacles encountered and the perseverance needed to overcome them. The lines "Now momma he ain't no toy, never ever get his share, get his stack in a gunnysack, still be room for air" suggest a sense of defiance and resilience. This character, despite being underestimated or overlooked ("never ever get his share"), maintains a sense of freedom and unyielding spirit ("still be room for air"). The phrase "This boy is lost, it's a rockin' double dare, he's out to scare" could indicate a rebellious nature, someone who challenges norms and expectations. "Landslide" could be seen as an embodiment of the rebellious and powerful spirit of rock music itself. The character depicted in the song, with his defiant and overwhelming presence, could be a metaphor for the impact of rock music—how it shakes up the status quo, breaks barriers, and creates new paths. This aligns with AC/DC's own reputation in the rock world, known for their high-energy performances and impactful music. In essence, "Landslide" is a song that conveys the themes of power, rebellion, and resilience. The imagery and metaphors used in the lyrics, combined with AC/DC's energetic and forceful musical style, create a vivid portrayal of a character or force that is as unstoppable and transformative as a landslide, mirroring the band's own impact in the world of rock music. The song's relentless riffage and driving rhythm section create a powerful sonic foundation that immerses the listener in a wall of sound. The Young brothers' intricate guitar interplay and dynamic solos showcase their virtuosity and their ability to generate a massive, earth-shaking sound.

"Guns for Hire"

"Guns for Hire," the first single released from *Flick of the Switch* and featured as the opening track on side 2 of the album, is a powerful rock anthem that explores themes of rebellion, individuality, and the desire for freedom—a very common theme among the tracks from this album.

This track not only kicks off the B-side of the album but also served as the electrifying opener during the corresponding Flick of the Switch Tour. The song portrays a rebellious and adventurous persona, emphasizing a determination to live life on his own terms. The song's lyrics present a character who describes himself as "a real entertainer, a mischief maker, a lover of no fixed abode," suggesting a free-spirited, rebellious persona. This character is depicted as living outside the boundaries of conventional society, embodying the spirit of rock and roll's defiance and non-conformity. The repeated chorus "I got guns for hire, shoot you with desire" is particularly evocative. On one level, the metaphor of "guns for hire" can be seen as a representation of the character's readiness to challenge and confront, embodying a sense of danger and unpredictability. On another level, the phrase "shoot you with desire" introduces a layer of sexual innuendo, a common element in AC/DC's lyrics, where the "gun" serves as a metaphor for male genitalia. This intertwining of themes of power, danger, and sexuality is characteristic of the band's lyrical style, adding depth and intensity to their music. Furthermore, the character in the song describes himself as "a wanted poster, a needed man, wanted right across the land," which reinforces the idea of an outlaw figure, celebrated and desired yet simultaneously on the fringes of society. This portrayal aligns with the band's own image as rock icons who embraced the outsider status and pushed the boundaries of the rock genre. This imagery portrays the narrator as a smooth operator and a dominant force, leaving a lasting impact on everyone he encounters, especially the women he goes to bed with. In summary, "Guns for Hire" is a celebration of individuality, rebellion, and a lust for life. The metaphoric use of "guns" and the portrayal of a roguish, larger-than-life character reflect the band's ability to combine hard-hitting rock music with vivid, evocative storytelling.

"Deep in the Hole"

"Deep in the Hole" delves into themes of internal struggle and personal demons. The song portrays a vivid picture of a person entrapped in their own vices, battling the darkness that can consume anyone at some point in their lives. The lyrics depict this as a metaphorical representation of the internal conflict between good and evil, self-control, and temptation, resonating with the universal human experience of succumbing to destructive behavior and the relentless struggle to overcome it. The music, coupled with Brian Johnson's gritty vocals, creates a powerful portrayal of emotional turmoil in the song. The song encapsulates the battle against the inner darkness, urging listeners to strive for redemption. "Deep in the Hole" expresses the urgency to break free from the clutches of self-destruction and pursue a better path. Like many AC/DC tracks, this track's lyrics are marked by their straightforward and hard-hitting style. The repeated phrase "Deep in the hole" suggests a sense of being trapped or overwhelmed. This could be a metaphor for various situations, such as being in a difficult relationship, facing personal challenges, or the outright direct metaphor of sexual intercourse. Imagery of being deep in a hole conveys a feeling of inescapability and depth of the situation. This song delves deep into themes of inner struggle and the challenges posed by a world rife with decadence and temptation. AC/DC masterfully paints a vivid picture of a person ensnared in their own vices, battling the demons that haunt them. The lyrics convey a metaphorical representation of the darkness that can engulf anyone, highlighting a constant internal conflict between good and evil, self-control, and temptation. The song serves as a reminder that, even in the darkest moments, there is hope and the possibility of redemption. It resonates on a personal level, offering solace to those trapped in their own dilemmas and reminding them that they are not alone in their journey towards the light

"Bedlam in Belgium"

"Bedlam in Belgium" tells the gripping tale of the band's chaotic 1977 performance during the Let There Be Rock Tour, which led to arrests and a cancellation of the show. During the tour, an incident occurred during the band's appearance in Kontich, Belgium, where a near-riot broke out as police tried to shut down the show after the band allegedly ignored a strict curfew. This event not only sets the backdrop for the song but also gives it a palpable sense of authenticity and urgency. The portrayal of a band defying authority and continuing to play despite the escalating situation reflects AC/DC's rebellious spirit and their commitment to their music and fans. The lyrics paint a vivid picture of the mayhem and frenzy that unfolded, recounting the band's struggle to navigate through the turmoil and capturing the pandemonium and electrifying energy of that chaotic night. Furthermore, the song describes a scene of tumult and confrontation, with lines like "In Belgium, it was bedlam, getting ready, stayed on the stage, cops in a rage, Crowd yelled for more, it was war, war, war," painting a picture of a wild and uncontrollable environment. The song's portrayal of a wild, unruly concert where the "law got the drop on me" resonates with the band's image as non-conformists and trailblazers in the rock music world. This theme of defiance against authority and the establishment is a recurring motif in AC/DC's music, in particular on *Flick of the Switch*, and is powerfully encapsulated in this song.

"Badlands"

"Badlands" portrays a character who is a "pistol packin' man," suggesting a tough, no-nonsense persona. This character is in search of a woman who understands his lifestyle, embodying a sense of independence and defiance. Musically, the overall vibe of the track encapsulates the theme of the track, giving the listener a sense of an almost "Wild West" imagery. Throughout the song, the lyrics emphasize a wild and free existence, with lines like "I ride it hard, I ride it high" and "Make love to you till you reach for the sky." This imagery conveys a sense of living life to the fullest without constraints. The repeated mentions of the "badlands" in the chorus reinforce the theme of a rugged and untamed life. The song's narrative paints the protagonist as an outlaw and a bandit, a person who lives on the edge and is unfazed by danger. Phrases like "I got A. 45 that'll make you fry" and "In the badlands, looking for a woman, in the bad lands, as bad as me" suggest a life lived outside the law, in the metaphorical "badlands" where rules don't apply. This setting reflects the song's themes of living on the edge and embracing a lifestyle outside of conventional boundaries. The lines "My shooter loaded, come on girl, I'm gonna give you a thrill" suggest a combination of danger and excitement, characteristics often associated with the allure of the badlands. Moreover, the song's themes are in line with the overall character of *Flick of the Switch*, which is known for its emphasis on outlaw bravado and sexual innuendo, as seen in other tracks like "Guns for Hire" and "Rising Power." "Badlands" offers a glimpse into a world of rogue adventures and unbridled passion.

"Brain Shake"

"Brain Shake," the final track from the album, by the title itself suggests a sense of intense impact or disturbance, perhaps metaphorically speaking to the effect of the music or the state of mind the song aims to induce. It can also be a hat tip to the "headbanger" domination of the music industry during the 1980s or perhaps as a tribute to Angus' own onstage antics of non-stop frantic head bobbing. The lyrics convey a vivid image of rock 'n' roll lifestyle, filled with exhilaration and intensity. The song opens with "Alright hold tight, I really wanna ball tonight," setting a scene of anticipation for a night of wild enjoyment. The phrase "on a bender no space defender" suggests a desire to let loose without restraint, a common theme in rock music reflecting freedom and rebellion. The repeated encounters with a "black widow" and the phrase "Fee fi fum smell the blood of rock 'n' roll" evoke a sense of danger and excitement inherent in rock music and lifestyle. The "black widow" metaphor could symbolize a dangerous but irresistible woman, or more broadly, the seductive and perilous nature of the rock 'n' roll world. The chorus, "Brain shake, brain shake, brain shake," suggests an overwhelming experience that shakes one to the core, possibly referring to the mind-altering impact of intense music, or the disorienting effects of a wild lifestyle. The line "For mercy's sake" implies a sense of desperation or being overwhelmed, while "All I could take" and "You can't fake" reinforce the authenticity and rawness of the experience. "Brain Shake," like much of AC/DC's work, celebrates the high-energy, carefree spirit of rock 'n' roll, with a focus on living in the moment and embracing the wilder side of life.

Interesting Facts

The single for "Nervous Shakedown" featured a picture sleeve depicting a live shot of Angus, mirrored three times to depict motion. The same image was later used for the '74 *Jailbreak* EP released the following year.

10

Fly on the Wall

Release date:	June 28, 1985 (U.K.) June 28, 1985 (U.S.)
Current edition:	Sony/Columbia, CD, LP
Personnel:	Brian Johnson, lead vocals Angus Young, lead guitar Malcolm Young, rhythm guitar Cliff Williams, bass guitar Simon Wright, drums
Duration:	40:30
Recorded at:	Mountain Studios, Montreux, Switzerland, October 1984–February 1985
Produced by:	Angus Young & Malcolm Young
Chart position:	#4 Australian Albums #7 U.K. Albums #32 U.S. *Billboard* 200

Notable info: This is the first AC/DC album to feature Simon Wright on drums. *Fly on the Wall* is certified platinum in the USA, 3x platinum in Australia, with gold and silver certifications in other countries.

AC/DC's tenth studio album, *Fly on the Wall,* released June 28, 1985, was recorded in Montreux, Switzerland, and is the first album to feature new drummer Simon Wright, who replaced Phil Rudd after the release of *Flick of the Switch* in 1983. At a time when glam metal and MTV were dominating the airwaves, AC/DC remained resolute in their commitment to their signature sound, eschewing trends and staying true to their roots. Produced by the band themselves and engineered by Tony Platt, *Fly on the Wall* is characterized by its stripped-down, no-frills approach. The title track, "Fly on the Wall," sets the tone for the album, featuring a relentless rhythm and gritty lyrics. The album's overall sound reflects the band's

"Can I Sit Next to You, Girl"/"Rockin' in the Parlour" 7-inch vinyl single, Australia, 1974 (Albert Productions AP-10551), and "Can I Sit Next to You, Girl"/"Rockin' in the Parlour" 7-inch vinyl single, New Zealand, 1974 (Polydor 2069 051). (*Bill Voccia Collection*)

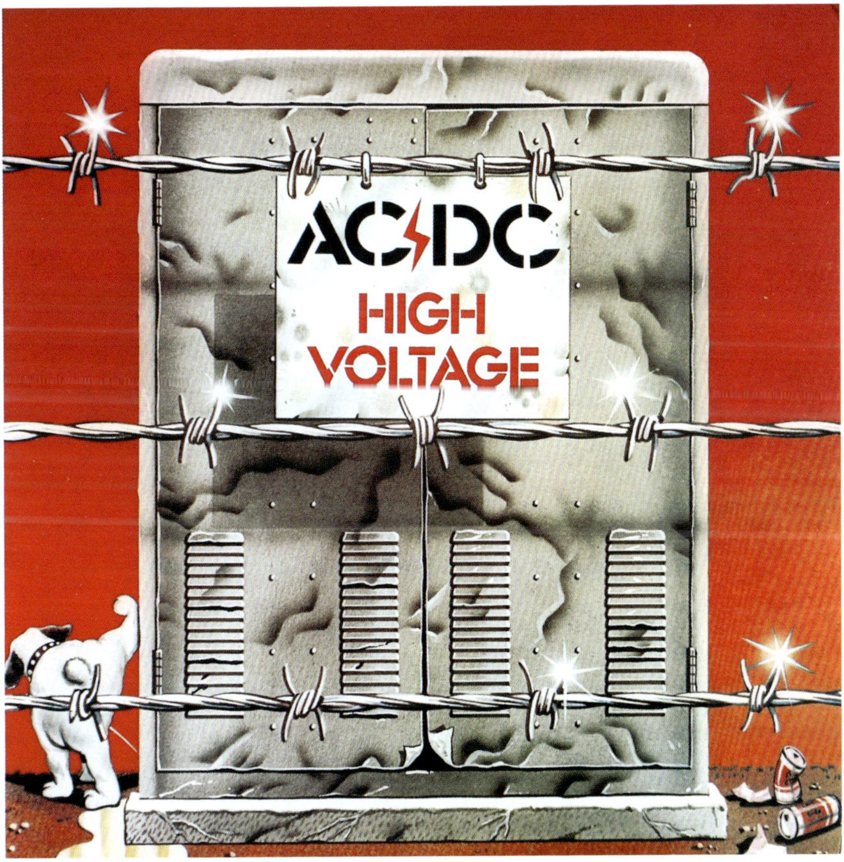

"High Voltage" LP, Australia (Albert/EMI APLP.009). (*Bill Voccia Collection*)

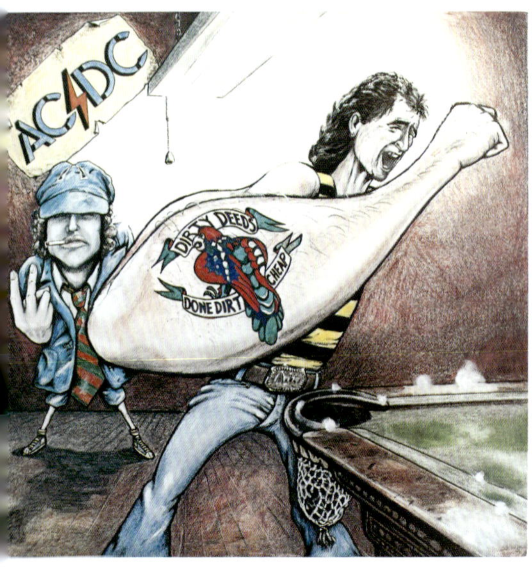
AC/DC
DIRTY DEEDS
DONE DIRT
CHEAP

APLP.0
AC/DC
DIRTY DEEDS DONE DIRT CHEAP
side one
1. DIRTY DEEDS DONE DIRT CHEAP
2. AIN'T NO FUN
(waiting 'round to be a millionaire)
3. THERE'S GONNA BE SOME ROCKIN'
4. PROBLEM CHILD
side two
1. SQUEALER
2. BIG BALLS
3. R.I.P. (rock in peace)
4. RIDE ON
5. JAILBREAK
All titles written by: ANGUS YOUNG, BON SCOTT & MALCOLM YOUNG
Produced by VANDA & YOUNG
Recorded at ALBERT STUDIOS, Sydney, Australia
AC DC are: BON SCOTT, ANGUS YOUNG, MALCOLM YOUNG, PHIL RUDD & MARK EVANS
Management: MICHAEL BROWNING
Cover Concept & Design: KETTLE ART PRODUCTIONS
ALBERT PRODUCTIONS

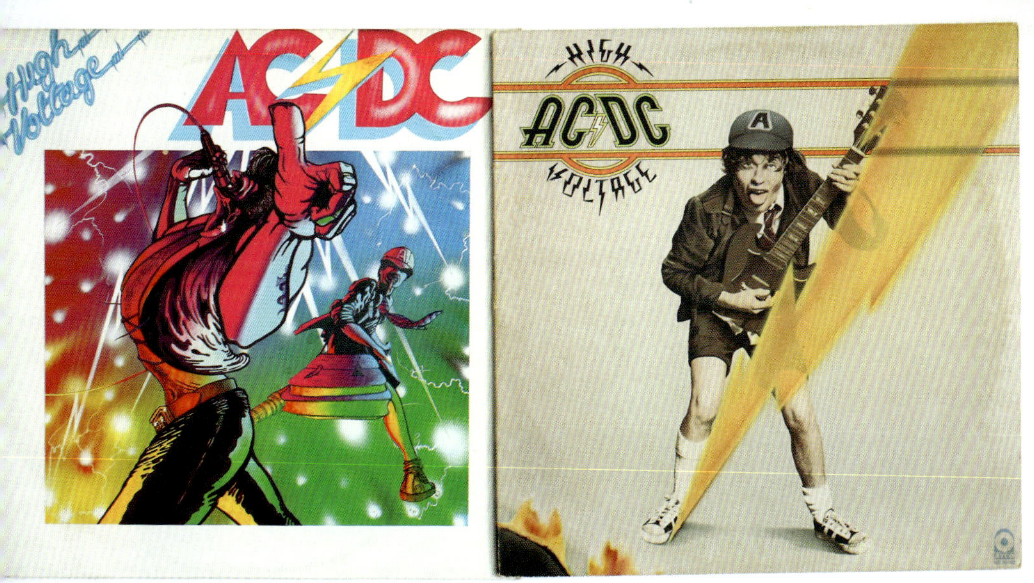

"High Voltage" LP, U.K. (Atlantic K 50257), and "High Voltage" LP, U.S.A. (Atco SD 36-142). (*Bill Voccia Collection*)

Opposite above: "T.N.T." LP, Australia (Albert/EMI APLP.016). (*Bill Voccia Collection*)

Opposite below left: "Dirty Deeds Done Dirt Cheap" LP, Australia (Albert/EMI APLP.020). (*Bill Voccia Collection*)

Opposite below right: "Dirty Deeds Done Dirt Cheap" LP (back cover), Australia (Albert/EMI APLP.020). (*Bill Voccia Collection*)

"Let There Be Rock" LP, Australia (Albert/EMI APLP.022). (*Bill Voccia Collection*)

ALBERT PRODUCTIONS
J. Albert & Son Pty Ltd Locked Bag 4000 Neutral Bay NSW 2089 Australia

DATE 02/07/1977 FILE No APLP 022 REEL No 1 Of 1
PRODUCER & COMPANY Albert Productions SPEED 15 IPS [ ] MONOAURAL [X] STEREO
ARTIST AC / DC [ ] 3 TRACKS [ ] 4 TRACKS [ ] 8 TRACKS
TITLE Let There Be Rock STUDIO STEREO MASTER TAPE

TAKE	TITLE	TIME	COMENT
	SIDE ONE		
1	Go Down	5:17	Angus Young, Malcolm Young y Bon Scott
2	Dog Eat Dog	3:30	"
3	Let There Be Rock	6:02	"
4	Bad Boy Boogie	4:18	
	SIDE TWO		
1	Overdose	5:47	Angus Young, Malcolm Young y Bon Scott
2	~~Crabsody In Blue~~ PROBLEM CHILD	4:39	"
3	Hell Ain't A Bad Place To Be	4:12	"
4	Whole Lotta Rosie	4:47	"

PRODUCER / Harry Vanda & George Young

J. Albert & Son Pty Ltd Locked Bag 4000 Neutral Bay NSW 2089 Australia Sydney. N.S.W.

"Let There Be Rock" master reel, Australia (Albert APLP022). (*Bill Voccia Collection*)

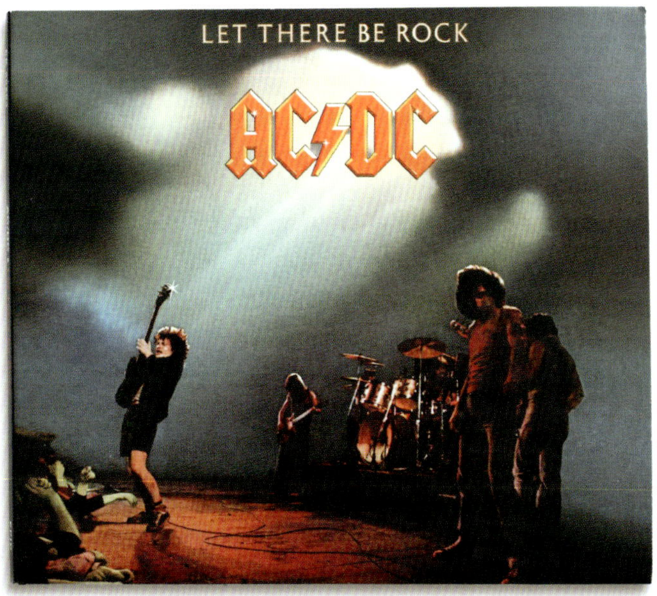

"Let There Be Rock" CD, U.S.A., promotional copy (Epic EK 80203). (*Bill Voccia Collection*)

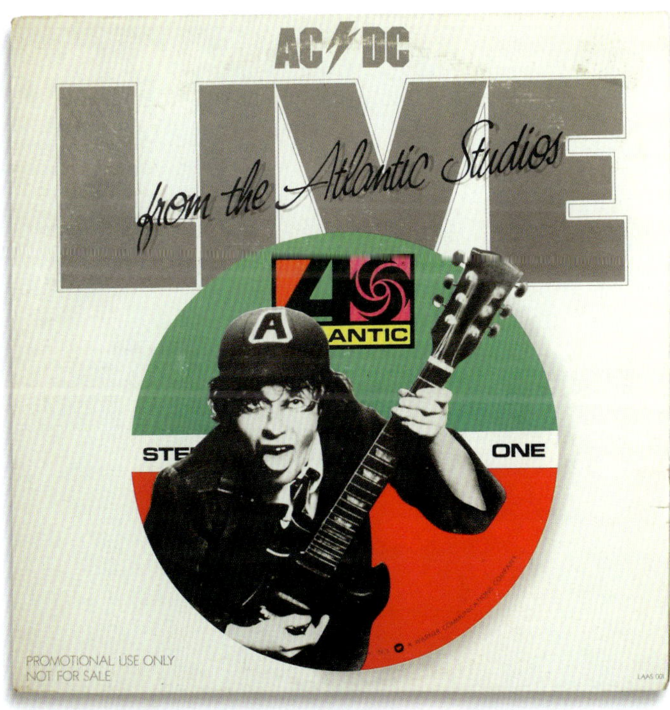

"Live From the Atlantic Studios" LP, U.S.A., promotional only (Atlantic LAAS 001). (*Bill Voccia Collection*)

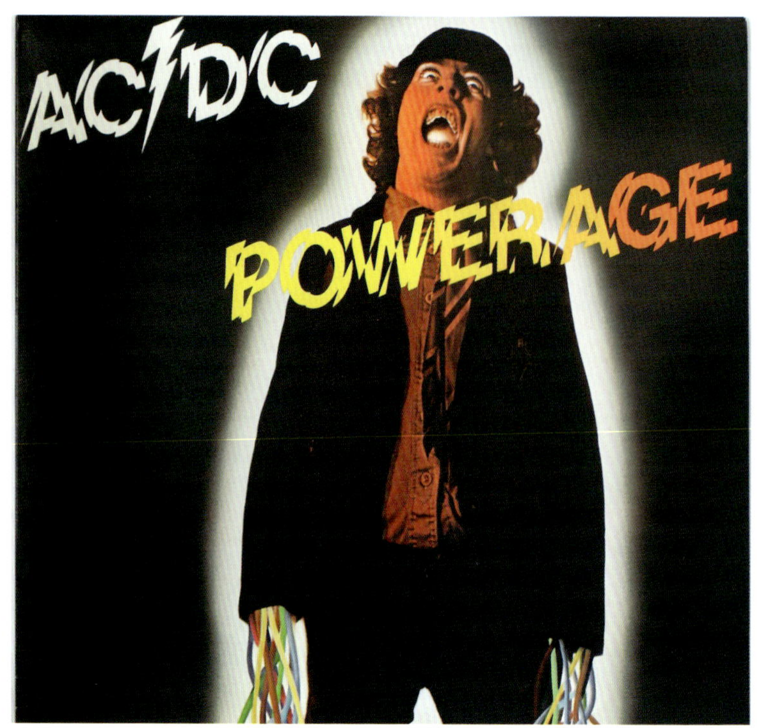

"Powerage" LP, Australia (Albert/EMI APLP.030). (*Bill Voccia Collection*)

"If You Want Blood (You've Got It)" U.S.A. (Atlantic SD 19212). (*Bill Voccia Collection*)

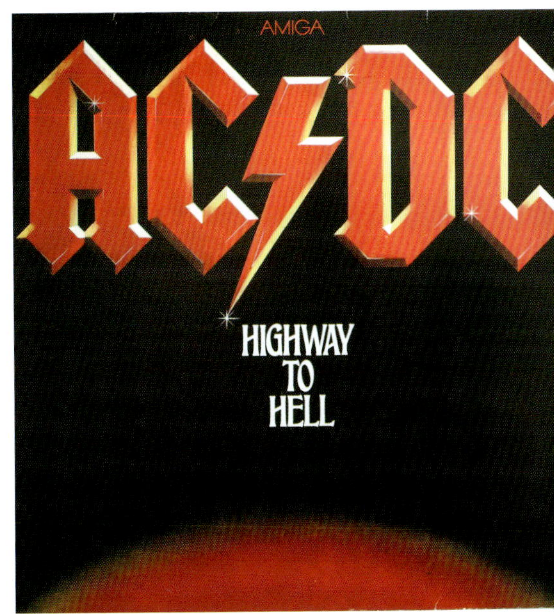

Above left: "Highway to Hell" Australia (Albert/EMI APLP.040). (*Bill Voccia Collection*)

Above right: "Highway to Hell" German Democratic Republic (AMIGA 8 55 838). (*Bill Voccia Collection*)

"Back in Black" CD, U.S.A., promotional copy (Epic EK 80207). (*Bill Voccia Collection*)

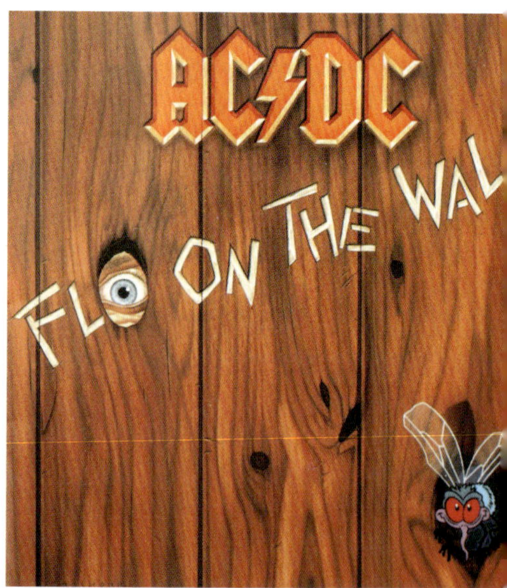

Above left: "For Those About to Rock We Salute You" LP, Spain (reverse color sleeve) (Atlantic s 90.471). (*Bill Voccia Collection*)

Above right: "Fly on the Wall" CD, U.S.A., promotional copy (Epic EK 80210). (*Bill Voccia Collection*)

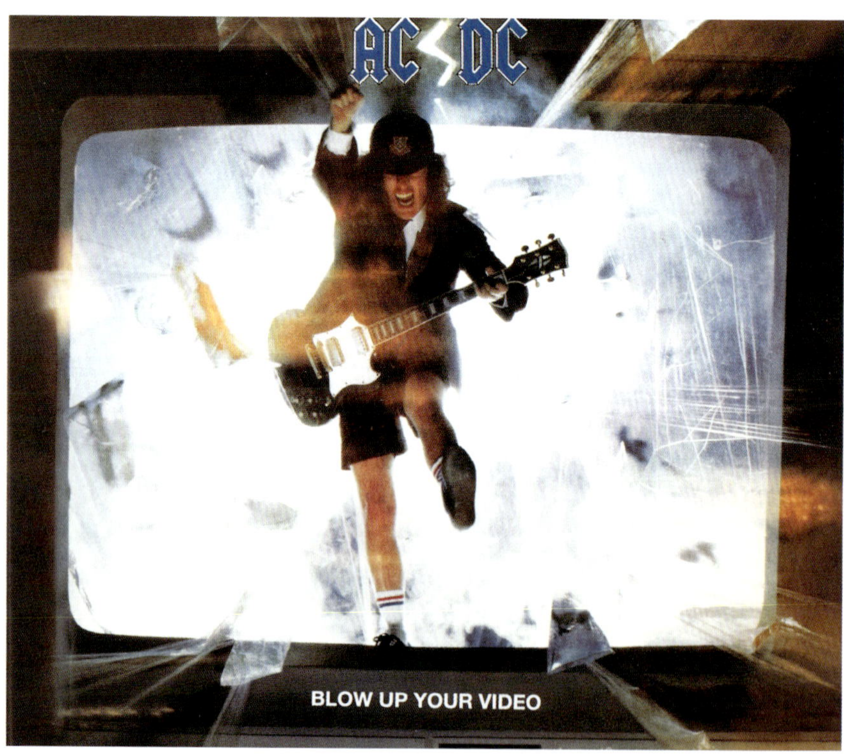

"Blow Up Your Video" CD, U.S.A., promotional copy (Epic EK 80212). (*Bill Voccia Collection*)

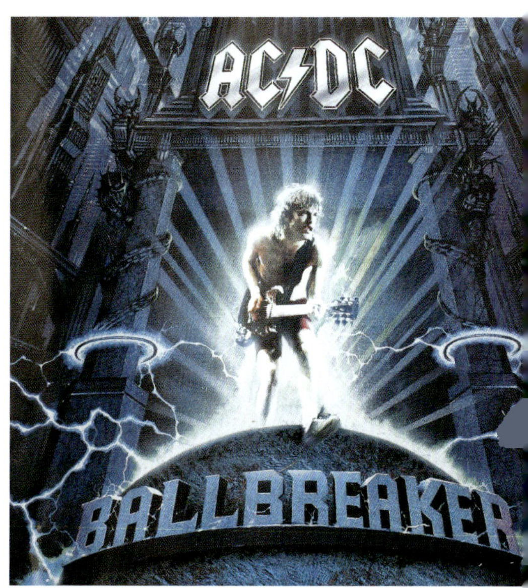

Above left: "The Razors Edge" CD, U.S.A. (Atco D 13379). (*Bill Voccia Collection*)

Above right: "Ballbreaker" CD, U.S.A. (EastWest 61780-2). (*Bill Voccia Collection*)

"Stiff Upper Lip" CD, U.S.A. (EastWest 62494-2). (*Bill Voccia Collection*)

Above left: "Black Ice" deluxe edition CD, U.S.A. (Columbia 88697 38376 2). (*Bill Voccia Collection*)

Above right: "Power UP" CD, U.S.A., limited deluxe box (with built-in speaker and illuminated logo) (Columbia 19439744472). (*Bill Voccia Collection*)

Left: Bonfire CD box set, U.S.A. (EastWest 62119-2). (*Bill Voccia Collection*)

Opposite above: Volts CD, U.S.A. (from *Bonfire* box set) (EastWest 62119-2). (*Bill Voccia Collection*)

Opposite below: Backtracks collector's edition deluxe box set, U.S.A., contains three CDs, two DVDs, a vinyl LP, and a booklet housed in a working 1-watt guitar amplifier (Columbia 88697540982). (*Bill Voccia Collection*)

AC/DC
VOLTS

AC/DC

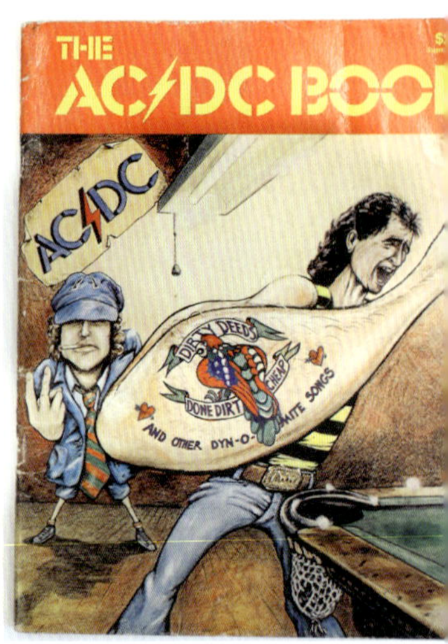

Above left: A 1976 Australian tour program (*left*) and the 1976 *Dirty Deeds Done Dirt Cheap* autumn U.K. tour program (*right*). (*Bill Voccia Collection*)

Above right: The AC/DC Book, Australian song book, 1976 (Albert AL2781C). (*Bill Voccia Collection*)

Sheet music for "Dirty Deeds Done Dirt Cheap" Australia, 1976 (Albert Publications AL2413T) (*left*); "Problem Child" U.S.A., 1977 (Edward B. Marks Music Corporation MS 1884) (*center*); and "It's a Long Way to the Top (If You Wanna Rock 'n' Roll)" Australia, 1976 (Albert Publications AL2047P) (*right*). (*Bill Voccia Collection*)

Above left: 7-inch vinyl singles: "High Voltage Rock 'n' Roll"/"Soul Stripper" Germany, 1976 (Atlantic ATL 10 772) (*top left*); "High Voltage/Live Wire" U.K., 1976 (Atlantic K10860) (*top right*); "High Voltage"/"It's a Long Way to the Top (If You Wanna Rock 'n' Roll)" Portugal, 1977 (Atlantic N-S-28-177) (*bottom left*); and "It's a Long Way to The Top (If You Wanna Rock 'n' Roll)" Germany, 1976 (Atlantic ATL 10 859) (*bottom right*). (*Bill Voccia Collection*)

Above right: Maxi single "Grab a Hold of This One!", "Dirty Deeds Done Dirt Cheap"/"Big Balls"/"The Jack" 7-inch single, U.K., 1977 (Atlantic K 10899). (*Bill Voccia Collection*)

Vinyl singles: "Rock 'n' Roll Damnation"/"Sin City" U.K., 1980 (Atlantic K 11142), 7-inch single (*left*); "Rock 'n' Roll Damnation"/"Sin City" U.K., 1978 (Atlantic K 11142) 12-inch single (*center*); "Rock 'n' Roll Damnation"/"Sin City" Germany, 1978 (Atlantic ATL 11 142) 7-inch single (*top right*); and "Rock 'n' Roll Damnation"/"Kicked in the Teeth" Netherlands, 1978 (Atlantic ATL 11.193) (*bottom right*). (*Bill Voccia Collection*)

7-inch vinyl singles: "Highway to Hell"/"If You Want Blood (You've Got It)" Germany, 1979 (Atlantic 11 321) (*left*); "Girls Got Rhythm"/"Get it Hot" Netherlands, 1979 (Atlantic 11.401) (*center*); "Girls Got Rhythm"/"T.N.T." Germany, 1979 (Atlantic 11 411) (*right*). (*Bill Voccia Collection*)

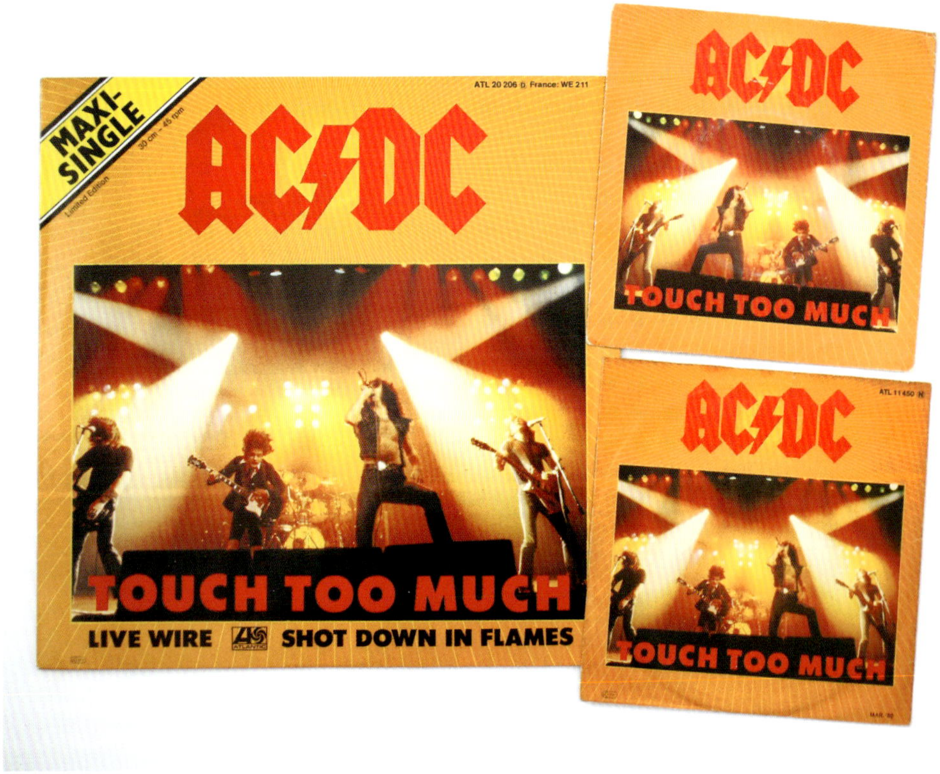

Vinyl singles: "Touch Too Much"/"Live Wire"/"Shot Down in Flames" 12-inch maxi single, France, 1980 (Atlantic ATL 20 206) (*left*); "Touch Too Much"/"Live Wire"/"Shot Down in Flames" 7-inch single, U.K., 1980 (Atlantic K 11435) (*top right*); "Touch Too Much"/"Live Wire" 7-inch single, Germany, 1980 (ATL 11 450) (*bottom right*). (*Bill Voccia Collection*)

7-inch vinyl singles, Japan: "Rock 'n' Roll Damnation"/"Sin City" 1978 (Atlantic PS-311A) (*top left*); "Highway to Hell"/"If You Want Blood (You've Got It)" 1979 (Atlantic P-464A) (*top right*); "Touch Too Much"/"Walk All Over You" 1980 (Atlantic PS-544A) (*bottom left*); and "Whole Lotta Rosie"/"Hell Ain't a Bad Place to Be" 1980 (Atlantic PS-372A) (*bottom right*). (*Bill Voccia Collection*)

7-inch vinyl singles, Japan: "For Those About to Rock (We Salute You)"/"T.N.T." 1982 (Atlantic P-1649) (*left*); "Danger"/"Back in Business" 1985 (Atlantic P-1991) (*top center*); "Shake Your Foundations"/"Send for the Man" 1985 (Atlantic P-2038) (*bottom center*); "You Shook Me All Night Long"/"Back in Black" 1980 (Atlantic P-631A) (*top right*); and "Who Made Who"/"Guns for Hire" 1986 (Atlantic P-2134) (*bottom right*). (*Bill Voccia Collection*)

Vinyl singles: "You Shook Me All Night Long"/"Have a Drink on Me" 7-inch single, Spain, 1980 (Atlantic 45-2014/Hispavox 45-2014) (*top right*); "Hells Bells"/"What Do You Do For Money Honey" 7-inch single, Germany, 1980 (Atlantic ATL 11 650) (*bottom right*); AC/DC "Rock and Roll Ain't Noise Pollution"/"Hells Bells" 12-inch single, including original button, U.K., 1980 (Atlantic K11630T)) (*center*); "You Shook Me All Night Long"/"Have a Drink on Me" 7-inch single, France, 1980 (Atlantic 11 600) (*top right*); and "Hells Bells"/"What Do You Do For Money Honey" 7-inch single, France, 1980 (Atlantic 11 650) (*bottom right*). (*Bill Voccia Collection*)

"Let's Get It Up"/"Snowballed" 7-inch vinyl single, U.S.A., 1981 (Atlantic 3894). (*Bill Voccia Collection*)

Above left: 4-inch reel to reel albums: "For Those About to Rock (We Salute You)" U.S.A., 1983 (Atlantic 1R1 7351, Columbia House edition); "Flick of the Switch" U.S.A., 1983 (Atlantic 1R1 7603, Columbia House edition); and "Dirty Deeds Done Dirt Cheap" U.S.A., 1983 (Atlantic 1R1 7276, Columbia House edition). (*Bill Voccia Collection*)

Above right: Original *Let There Be Rock: The Movie* theater ticket stubs, various theaters, U.S.A., 1982. (*Bill Voccia Collection*)

Various AC/DC radio station promotional stickers. (*Bill Voccia Collection*)

Above left: 7-inch vinyl singles: "Danger"/"Back in Business" U.S.A., 1985 (Atlantic 7-89532) (*top left*); "Danger"/"Hell or High Water" Australia, 1985 (Albert/EMI AP1554) (*top right*); "Shake Your Foundations"/"Stand Up" U.K., 1986 (Atlantic A9474) (*bottom left*); and "Sink the Pink"/"Shake Your Foundations" Spain, 1985 (Atlantic S 789512-7) (*bottom right*). (*Bill Voccia Collection*)

Above right: "Shake Your Foundations"/"Stand Up" 7-inch vinyl-shaped picture disc, U.K., 1986 (Atlantic A9474P). (*Bill Voccia Collection*)

"Danger"/"Back in Business" 7-inch vinyl-shaped picture disc, U.K., 1985 (Atlantic A9532P). (*Bill Voccia Collection*)

"Who Made Who" (special collector's mix)/"Guns for Hire" 12-inch vinyl single, U.K., 1986 (Atlantic A9425T). (*Bill Voccia Collection*)

"The Razors Edge" 12-inch, four-track promo sampler EP, red vinyl, U.K., 1990: "Thunderstruck"/"Fire Your Guns"/"Money Talks"/ "Mistress For Christmas" (Atco SAM 693). (*Bill Voccia Collection*)

3-inch CD mini-singles: "Money Talks"/"Borrowed Time" Japan, 1991 (Atco AMDY-5040) (*top left*); "That's the Way I Wanna Rock 'n' Roll"/"Kissin' Dynamite" Japan, 1988 (Atlantic 10SW-49) (*bottom left*); and "Thunderstruck"/ "Fire Your Guns" Japan, 1990 (Atco AMDY-5031) (*right*). (*Bill Voccia Collection*)

"The Razors Edge" era singles: "Are You Ready"/"Got You by the Balls" 7-inch vinyl single, limited edition w/patch, U.K., 1991 (Atco B8830X) (*top right*); "Rock Your Heart Out"/"Shot of Love" CD single, Australia (Albert Productions 657559 2) (*bottom left*); "Mistress for Christmas" promotional-only CD, U.S.A., 1990 (Atco PRCD 3639-2) (*second from bottom left*); "Are You Ready" promotional-only CD, U.S.A., 1991 (Atco PRCD 3746-2) (*top middle*); "Are You Ready"/"Got You by the Balls" 7-inch vinyl single, limited and numbered, U.K., 1991 (Atco B8830W) (*bottom middle*); "Thunderstruck"/ "Fire Your Guns" 7-inch vinyl single, Australia, 1990 (Albert Productions 656319 7) (*top right*); "Money Talks" promotional-only CD, U.S.A., 1990 (Atco PRCD 3661-2) (*second from bottom right*); and "Thunderstruck"/"Fire Your Guns" CD single, Europe, 1990 (Atco 7567098907-7) (*bottom right*). (*Bill Voccia Collection*)

"Big Gun"/"Back in Black" (live)/"For Those About to Rock (We Salute You)" (live)12-inch maxi single, U.K., 1993 (Atco B 8396 T) (*left*); "Big Gun"/"Back in Black" (live)/"For Those About to Rock (We Salute You)" (live) CD maxi single, U.K., 1993 (Atco B 8396) (*top right*); and "Big Gun"/"Back in Black" (live)/"For Those About to Rock (We Salute You)" (live) CD single, Australia, 1993 (Albert 6594382) (*bottom right*). (*Bill Voccia Collection*)

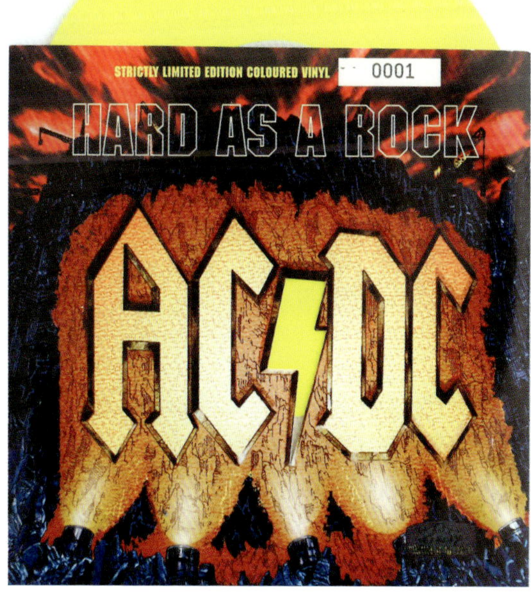

"Hard as a Rock"/"Caught with your Pants Down" limited edition vinyl 7-inch single, yellow vinyl (number 0001), U.K., 1995 (EastWest A4368X). (*Bill Voccia Collection*)

"Hard as a Rock"/"Caught with your Pants Down" CD single, slipcase, France, 1995 (EastWest 7559 64368-9) (*top left*); "The Furor" promotional-only CD single, France, 1996 (EastWest PRCD 278) (*top middle*); "Hail Caesar"/"Whiskey on the Rocks"/ "Whole Lotta Rosie" (live) CD single, includes guitar pick, Europe, 1995 (EastWest 7559 66051-2) (*top right*); "Ballbreaker" New Zealand Tour EP, four-track CD maxi single, New Zealand, 1996 (Albert Productions 8832712) (*bottom left*); and "Ballbreaker" Australian Tour EP, four-track CD maxim single, Australia, 1996 (Albert Productions 8831632) (*bottom right*). (*Bill Voccia Collection*)

"Money Talks" singles: "Money Talks"/"Down on the Borderline" 7-inch vinyl single, Australia, 1990 (Albert Productions 656500 7) (*left*); "Money Talks"/"Mistress for Christmas"/"Borrowed Time" 12-inch vinyl picture disc, U.K., 1990 (Atco B 8886 TP) (center); and "Money Talks"/"Borrowed Time" 7-inch vinyl single, U.K., 1990 (Atco B8886T) (*right*). (*Bill Voccia Collection*)

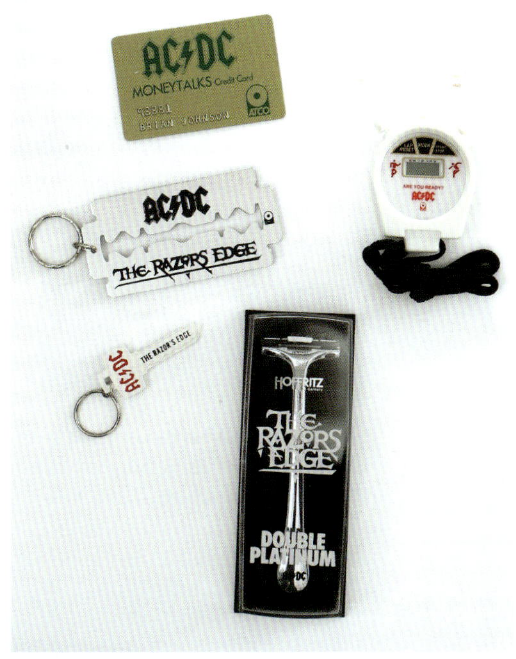

Right: "The Razors Edge"-era promotional-only items, Atco Records: Brian Johnson "Money Talks" credit card, "The Razors Edge" mirrored key chain, "Are You Ready" key, "Are You Ready" stopwatch, "The Razors Edge" "double platinum" Hoffritz razor. (*Bill Voccia Collection*)

Below: "Money Talks" promotional-only money/swag bag (contains Angus Dollars), Atco records 1990. (*Bill Voccia Collection*)

"Safe in New York City"/"Cyberspace"/"Back in Black" (live) CD single, Germany, 2000 (Elektra 7559-67072-2) (*left*), and "Satellite Blues"/"Let There Be Rock" (live) CD single, Australia, 2001 (Albert Productions 7243 8 89840 2 7) (*right*). (*Bill Voccia Collection*)

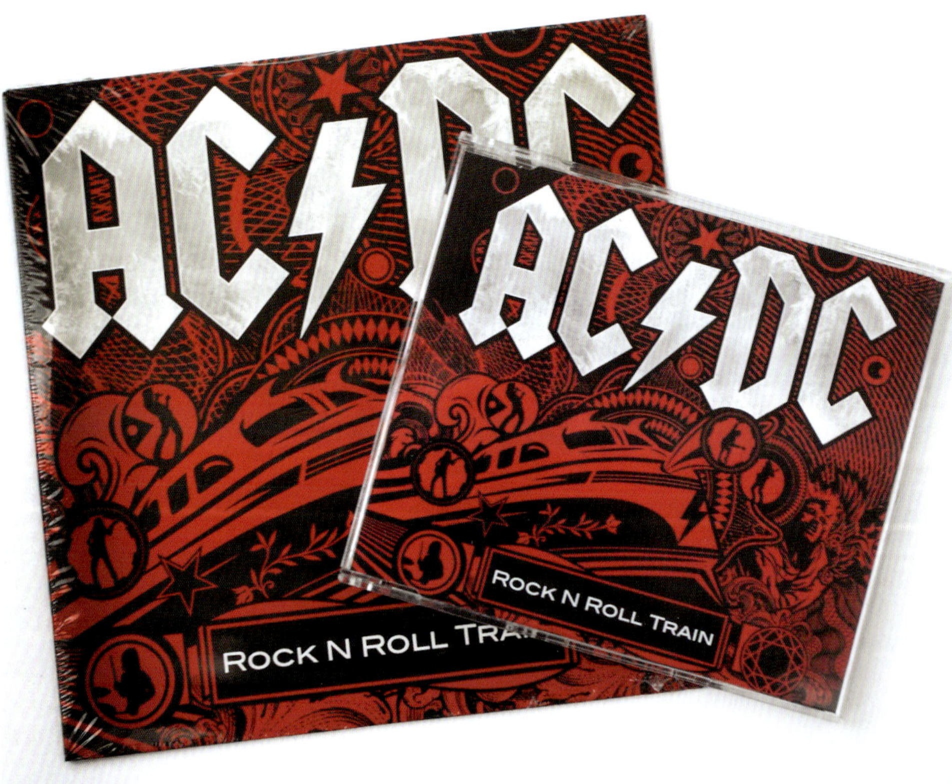

"Rock 'N' Roll Train"/"War Machine" 7-inch vinyl single, U.S.A. (Columbia 88697 383617) (*left*), and "Rock 'N' Roll Train" promotional-only CD single, U.S.A. (Columbia 88697 38372 2) (*right*). (*Bill Voccia Collection*)

determination to resist the gloss and glamour that characterized much of the rock music of the era. In an age where music videos and image played a crucial role in an artist's success, AC/DC kept their focus squarely on the music. Despite the prevalent glam metal scene and MTV's influence, AC/DC's authenticity shone through. The band's refusal to conform to the prevailing trends showcased their commitment to their own brand of rock 'n' roll. Tracks like "Shake Your Foundations" and "Sink the Pink" maintain the classic AC/DC groove, proving that the band could weather the storm of evolving musical landscapes while staying true to their roots. The album overall did not receive as much critical praise as previous AC/DC recordings, not that critics have ever really been that forthcoming. Retrospective reviews also tended to be negative, with some critiques stating that the band seemed to be trying too hard to fit into the changing music landscape dominated by hair metal and thrash metal. However, the album has been described as misunderstood and underrated, retaining raw and solid components typical of AC/DC's classics, like colorful solos and great backup vocals. AC/DC decided to self-produce the album, with production duties being handled by Angus and Malcolm Young. Many fans complain to this day that the biggest deficit for an otherwise great album was the somewhat lackluster resulting production. Brian's vocals seem buried in the already muddied sounding mix—quite opposite from the previous three releases.

"Fly on the Wall"

"Fly on the Wall," the title track, kicks off the album. It is a hard-hitting, straightforward, and gritty rock song that summarizes AC/DC's trademark sound. The song served as the opener throughout the Fly on the Wall Tour and begins with an aggressive riff that is unmistakably AC/DC. The title itself is themed around the concept of surveillance and invasion of privacy. This theme is encapsulated in the song's title, which refers to a hidden observer, symbolizing the lack of privacy and the feeling of constantly being watched, whether by authorities, media, or society itself. Lyrically, the song tells more of a tale of being in an entrapped situation, perhaps a distraught relationship, with lines during chorus such as "I was trapped like a fly on the wall, I was caged like a zoo animal, no escape from the fate that you make, you're a snake, I've had all I can take…" Overall, the song is a strong track from the album and features all of the aspects that define AC/DC's sound.

"Shake Your Foundations"

"Shake Your Foundations" is a song about embracing a carefree attitude and enjoying oneself, a common theme in many AC/DC songs over the years. The lyrics depict a lively scene in a bar, where everyone is encouraged to let loose and have a great time. The phrase "shake your foundations" is a metaphor for breaking free from societal norms and expectations, but it can also convey the power and energy of AC/DC's high-voltage style loud rock music, which essentially "shakes the foundations" of the ground of the building you are in (as demonstrated during the ending scene of the promotional video for the song). The song conveys the excitement and energy of the environment, highlighting the physicality and intensity of the experience with lines like "shake it to the floor." It also touches on a theme of romantic encounter, suggesting a moment of passion and liberation from inhibitions. The chorus of "Shake Your Foundations" is an anthemic call to action "Aye Aye Oh! shake your foundations, Aye Aye Oh! shake it to the floor." Brian Johnson's gritty vocals deliver a memorable and catchy refrain that invites participation. Overall, the song centers on embracing one's desires, living in the moment, and defying conventions, urging listeners to let go of their worries and immerse themselves in the joy of life

"First Blood"

"First Blood," much like many AC/DC songs, is centered around themes of physical intimacy and sexual satisfaction. The song expresses a sense of urgency and longing for physical touch, with lyrics that emphasize the desire for a sexually submissive partner. "Got a screaming feeling, need a little loving healing, want some of that stuff, 'cause I like a hot touch" during the opening verse describes the strong desire for physical intimacy. Angus told *Guitar* magazine (December 1985): "I know one song immediately is 'First Blood' [every album has one or two songs that kids related to and always remember]. I have this thing when I'm stage where if I can put one foot in front of the other, it's got that energy thing. This song has it." The chorus, featuring the phrase "first blood," suggests a yearning for dominance, further emphasized by repeated references to "bad dog," indicating a submissive inclination in the partner. Overall, "First Blood" is suggestive of the quest for a partner who aligns with their dominant desires, offering the physical satisfaction they seek.

"Danger"

"Danger," the first single from *Fly on the Wall*, is a slow-paced track that honestly surprised me when I first heard it as the track that was selected as the lead-off album single. The usual energy and in-your-face wall of sound that I had grown accustomed to seemed to be severely lacking and Brian's vocals were lost in the mix. The song gradually grew on me; however, it still is not one of my top picks from the AC/DC catalog. The track captures the rebel spirit that the band is known for. The song presents a world filled with danger at every turn, challenging societal norms. The lyrics celebrate the thrill of taking risks, living life on the edge, and rejecting the mundane, carrying a tone of caution and recklessness. The song begins with a warning against talking to strangers who smile, suggesting a sense of paranoia or mistrust. This is emphasized by the repeated lines "Keep away from the danger," which serves as a refrain throughout the song. The narrative then shifts to a scene where red lights are flashing, indicating danger or emergency, and the protagonist describes themselves as "bruised and broke and bandaged," likely from a night of heavy drinking. This imagery of self-inflicted harm through excessive alcohol consumption portrays a lifestyle of excess and disregard for personal safety. The chorus "Danger, danger, don't talk to strangers" is repeated multiple times, reinforcing the theme of danger associated with unknown people. This could be interpreted as a metaphor for the perils of the rock 'n' roll lifestyle, where encounters with strangers and potentially harmful situations are frequent. The song continues with the protagonist describing another round of drinking and the consequences of their actions, stating they were "just raising hell" and not intending harm. This reflects a common theme in rock music of rebellion and living on the edge, often with little regard for the consequences. Overall, "Danger" conveys a message of living dangerously and the potential consequences of such a lifestyle, while also depicting the allure and thrill that often accompany it

"Sink the Pink"

"Sink the Pink" showcases AC/DC's knack for crafting lyrics that balance cheeky innuendos with their own brand of rock 'n' roll poetry. The suggestive nature of the song's lyrics adds a playful and provocative edge. The clever wordplay provides an entertaining layer of storytelling that keeps listeners engaged. The lyrics encapsulate the band's typical hard rock attitude, combining elements of playfulness, rebelliousness, and a carefree approach to life. "Sink the Pink" features a memorable and anthemic chorus that is sure to resonate with fans, and one that portrays a scene of indulgence and revelry: "Sink the pink, it's all the fashion, drink the drink, it's old fashioned." The repetition of the phrase "sink the pink" suggests a focus on enjoyment and perhaps a hint of sexual innuendo, common in AC/DC's lyrics. The song's verses continue with this theme, using vivid imagery to describe a scene filled with high-energy and possibly risqué behavior. The lyrics depict a world engaging in various forms of excitement and danger, from interacting with alluring women to metaphorical references to playing with guns and fire. Throughout the song, there's an emphasis on living in the moment and seeking out thrilling experiences. The lines "Gimme water, gimme wine, gonna show you a good time" suggest a desire for both the simple and the luxurious, a metaphor for embracing all aspects of life. "Sink the Pink" is a catchy rocker that is essentially a rock 'n' roll party song and a standout track from the album.

"Playing with Girls"

This track is one of my favorites from *Fly on the Wall*; it has a great boogie-inspired guitar riff with an awesome groove. It opens side two of the album with Brian Johnson's raspy "Oooh ooh oooh" before the song explodes with a powerful blast of guitar and drums. The lyrics exhibit the band's signature style of bold and sexually charged rock 'n' roll. The song opens with the line, "Highball women that are hot to touch, legs do the talking spelling out the lust," immediately setting a tone of overt sexuality and desire. This is further emphasized with the imagery of "sugar daddies" and their apparent attractions, painting a picture of a hedonistic and indulgent scene. The chorus, "Playing with girls gonna get you hot, playing with guns gonna get you shot, playing with fire gonna heat you up, playing with me you're gonna get the lot," uses a series of metaphors to communicate the risks and excitement associated with various forms of thrill-seeking. The comparison of interacting with women to playing with guns and fire suggests a sense of danger and unpredictability in these encounters. This song, like many in AC/DC's catalog, embraces themes of masculinity, sexual conquest, and the rock and roll lifestyle. The lyrics reflect a swaggering confidence and a celebration of indulgence and pleasure-seeking behavior. The tone is unapologetically bold and aligns with the band's image as quintessential rock 'n' roll rebels.

"Stand Up"

"Stand Up" delivers a powerful message of resilience and determination wrapped in AC/DC's distinctive trademark sound. The track seems to celebrate the idea of taking charge and embracing the spotlight, both literally and metaphorically. The song encourages an attitude of confidence and assertiveness, resonating with AC/DC's typical themes of empowerment and boldness. The song opens with an energetic call to action, "Put on the headset, get on the stage, out on the midnight escapade." This immediately sets the tone for a night of adventure and possibly defiance. The lines, "I didn't wanna steal your thunder I wouldn't wanna play your game, making all the headlines, getting on the front page," suggest a desire to stand out and make an impact, yet without overshadowing others or engaging in someone else's agenda. This reflects a sense of individualism and confidence. The chorus, "Stand up, stand up and take it, stand up, stand up and make it, stand up, stand up and face it," is a powerful and repetitive directive encouraging resilience, proactivity, and courage. This could be interpreted as a metaphor for facing life's challenges head-on and seizing control of one's destiny.

"Hell or High Water"

"Hell or High Water" starts off with the unmistakable trademark AC/DC guitar sound, showcasing Angus and Malcolm's signature style. The song wastes no time in propelling forward, with the rhythm section of Malcolm Young's rhythmic guitar and Cliff Williams' thunderous bass laying a solid foundation. The lyrics of the track reflect the band's characteristic hard rock energy and straightforward, rebellious style. The song, like many in AC/DC's catalog, features themes of defiance, resilience, and a kind of reckless bravado. The repeated chorus line "Come hell or high water" is an idiom meaning to persevere no matter how difficult the circumstances. This phrase, used as the song's hook, encapsulates the band's often unyielding and tenacious attitude. The lyrics also make references to fighting on the main street, breathing your last breath, and hot loving, indicating a blend of danger, romance, and a carefree approach to life's challenges. Moreover, the song includes phrases like "mama don' told me, papa don' scold me," suggesting a rebellious youth going against parental guidance or societal expectations. This aligns with the band's image of non-conformity and living on the edge. The repetitive nature of the chorus, emphasizing "hell hell hell give em hell," drives the point of defiance and resilience. Overall, "Hell or High Water" exemplifies AC/DC's signature sound and themes: a combination of high-energy rock music, defiant lyrics, and an unapologetic embrace of a wild, rebellious lifestyle. The song's straightforward structure, relentless rhythm, and anthemic chorus make it a classic representation of the band's enduring appeal in the rock genre.

"Back in Business"

This song grooves right from the beginning with a great guitar riff that opens the track. "Back in Business" is another example from the album that showcases AC/DC's signature style of straightforward, high-energy rock music. The lyrics of this song are a classic example of AC/DC's themes of rebellion, resilience, and an unapologetic, larger-than-life attitude, much like the themes of other songs from the album. The song starts with a metaphor of being like a "cannonball going down the track," setting the tone for something unstoppable and powerful. This imagery is consistent with the band's usual representation of raw power and unstoppable force. The lines "Need good loving but I want it back" and "I was born in trouble, they gave up on me" reflect a defiant, rebellious character, often found in AC/DC's lyrics, portraying someone who is misunderstood and undervalued by society. The gang-like vocals of the chorus, "Back in business again," repeated multiple times throughout the song, signifies a return to form, possibly after a setback or a period of absence. This could be interpreted as a metaphor for the band itself, always coming back strong regardless of the challenges they face. It's a declaration of their enduring presence in the rock scene. The song also includes lines like "Teacher preaching what not to be," suggesting a rejection of conventional norms and authority. This aligns with the band's image of non-conformity and living outside societal expectations. "Back in Business" is a song that embodies AC/DC's essence—a blend of high-octane rock music, rebellious and defiant lyrics, and a spirit of resilience. The song's straightforward structure and anthemic chorus make it a classic representation of the band's style and appeal in the rock genre.

"Send for the Man"

"Send for the Man," the tenth and final track on *Fly on the Wall*, serves as a dynamic and energetic conclusion to the album's rock-infused journey. The lyrics of the song, much like those we have seen with other tracks on this record, are a quintessential example of the band's straightforward, hard rock style, characterized by bold, assertive themes and a sense of rebelliousness. The song opens with provocative questions: "Do you want love? Dirty dirty love? Do you want lust? Just a little lust?" These lines immediately set a tone of raw, unapologetic sexual desire, which is a recurring theme in many AC/DC songs. The band often explores themes of lust, love, and the darker sides of human desire in their lyrics, usually in a direct and unabashed manner. The chorus, "Send for the man," is repeated several times, creating an anthemic and commanding presence. This phrase could be interpreted as a call to action or a declaration of the singer's readiness to fulfill the desires mentioned in the opening lines. The song portrays the protagonist as someone who is confident, almost cocky, in their abilities to satisfy these desires, further emphasized by the lines "You want a bad reputation, you wanna better your score, I got the qualifications, I can open any door." The lyrics also include phrases like "Keep away from that decadent Dan, send for the man, he won't give a damn," suggesting a preference for a more straightforward, no-nonsense approach in contrast to someone more pretentious or superficial. "Send for the Man" showcases AC/DC's typical blend of high-energy rock music with lyrics that are bold, rebellious, and steeped in themes of desire and defiance. The song's straightforward structure, powerful rhythm, and anthemic chorus are characteristic of the band's enduring appeal in the rock genre.

Interesting Facts

AC/DC released a five-track video package the same year *Fly on the Wall*, which featured five promotional music videos from the album that play through a sequence and feature an animated fly (from the album cover) throughout. The videos included "Fly on the Wall," "Danger," "Sink the Pink," "Stand Up," and "Shake Your Foundations." The videos were later reissued on AC/DC's *Family Jewels* DVD released in 2005.

11

Who Made Who

Release date:	May 26, 1986 (U.K.)
	May 26, 1986 (U.S.)
Current edition:	Sony/Columbia, CD, LP
Personnel:	Brian Johnson, lead vocals
	Angus Young, lead guitar
	Malcolm Young, rhythm guitar
	Cliff Williams, bass guitar
	Simon Wright, drums
	Phil Rudd, drums (on all previously released tracks)
	Bon Scott, lead vocals ("Ride On")
	Mark Evans, bass guitar ("Ride On")
Duration:	37:50
Recorded at:	Compass Point Studios, Nassau, Bahamas, December 1985 (Tracks 1, 3, 8)
Produced by:	Harry Vanda & George Young
Chart position:	#4 Australian Albums
	#16 U.K. Albums
	#33 U.S. *Billboard* 200

Notable info: This is a soundtrack album for the motion picture *Maximum Overdrive*. The album contains only three new tracks; the remaining tracks are from previous releases. *Who Made Who* is certified 5x platinum in the USA, 5x platinum in Australia, with platinum and gold certifications in other countries.

Who Made Who is a soundtrack album released in 1986, which was written and recorded for the motion picture film *Maximum Overdrive*. *Maximum Overdrive* is a horror film, starring Emilio Estevez, based on the short story *Trucks* by Stephen King. The overall theme of the movie is about a sudden situation where all machines are given a life of their own, the focus being on tractor trailers, which hunt down their victims, who are trapped inside of a small, remote diner. The album contained only three new AC/DC tracks, the title track and two instrumentals "D.T." and "Chase the Ace." The remaining songs from the album were chosen between the band and Stephen King himself, which consisted of previously released AC/DC songs taken from *Back in Black*, *For Those About to Rock (We Salute You)*, *Fly on the Wall*, and *Dirty Deeds Done Dirt Cheap*. A longer, extended mix version of the song was released and available as a 12-inch vinyl maxi single and would later become available as part of the 2009 *Backtracks* box set. Although the song "Shake Your Foundations" appeared on the album, which was taken from *Fly on the Wall*, the version released on *Who Made Who* is a different mix.

"Who Made Who"

"Who Made Who" was the title track for the soundtrack of the film *Maximum Overdrive*. It is a standout song that captures the essence of AC/DC's signature sound. It was the first time that the band was tasked with penning a song specifically for a movie and the final result was a clever song crafted to the theme of the film. The song beings with drummer Simon Wright's steady beat and Cliff Williams' driving basslines, who are then joined by Malcolm Young's rhythmic prowess to create a rockin' groove that propels the song forward. "Who Made Who" stands out for its exploration of the theme where machines, trucks, gadgets, and devices created by mankind gain autonomy and start to dominate, reflecting the movie's premise of machines coming to life and turning hostile towards people. The lyrics delve into this concept of technological control and autonomy, posing questions about the creation and the creator. It is a fascinating play on the idea that the creations of humanity, intended to serve and assist, could potentially turn against their creators. This theme resonates with broader philosophical questions about the relationship between humans and their creations, whether they be machines, technology, or even societal systems. From a musical standpoint, "Who Made Who" aligns with AC/DC's signature hard rock genre. The track showcases the band's characteristic sound, marked by driving guitar riffs and a steady rhythm section, complemented by Brian Johnson's distinct vocal style. This song, like many in AC/DC's catalog, captures the energy and raw power that the band is renowned for, making it not just a thematic fit for a film about rebellious machines, but also a representation of the band's enduring sound and style. "Who Made Who" serves as a perfect companion to the high-octane action of the movie and it effectively complements the on-screen mayhem of the horror film. Its driving energy and anthemic nature make it a standout among the other tracks on the soundtrack, solidifying its status as a rock classic. Moreover, "Who Made Who" has become a fan-favorite in AC/DC's discography, standing as a testament to the band's ability to create enduring and timeless rock anthems. The track returned to AC/DC's live set during The Razors Edge Tour 1990–91 and a live version of the song is available on the *AC/DC Live* album released in 1992.

"D.T."

"D.T.," an acronym for Delerium Tremens, is an instrumental song from the album, a rare occasion for AC/DC, who had never released an instrumental on an album previously. "Fling Thing" was the only other prior instrumental recording that the band released, but it was only available as the B-side to the "Jailbreak" 7-inch single (Australia and U.K. only). The song does a great job in complementing the visuals and narrative of the film, setting a somber tone and suspenseful atmosphere, especially during the mid-section of the track. The track's ebb and flow, marked by subtle shifts in tempo and intensity, create a sense of suspense and anticipation.

"Chase the Ace"

"Chase the Ace" aptly captures the sense of impending danger and the unpredictable nature of the story's mechanized monsters. Another instrumental from the album, "Chase the Ace" begins with a driving beat and chugging riff that perfectly captures the visuals of a chase scene. The track builds in intensity, starting with a catchy riff and building intensity, which then progresses through various moments, all the while maintaining a sense of urgency and momentum. "Chase the Ace" seamlessly fits into the overall landscape of the *Who Made Who* soundtrack album. It serves as an instrumental interlude between vocal-driven tracks, providing a moment of instrumental brilliance and showcasing AC/DC's musical dexterity as a band.

Interesting Facts

The band was originally approached by Stephen King, who happens to be a huge fan of AC/DC, to ask them to write a score for his upcoming, self-directed film. AC/DC went into the studio and recorded several instrumental musical pieces, much of which can be heard throughout the film. It wasn't until later that the original request morphed into an entire soundtrack album, along with the new song "Who Made Who." An extended mix version of "Who Made Who" was released as a special 12-inch vinyl single and later reissued as part of the AC/DC *Backtracks* box set in 2009. The extended mix version runs 4:50, whereas the album version runs 3:27.

12

Blow Up Your Video

Release date:	January 18, 1988 (U.K.)
	January 18, 1988 (U.S.)
Current edition:	Sony/Columbia CD, LP
Personnel:	Brian Johnson, lead vocals
	Angus Young, lead guitar
	Malcolm Young, rhythm guitar
	Cliff Williams, bass guitar
	Simon Wright, drums
Duration:	42:48
Recorded at:	Miravel Studios, Correns, France, August–September 1987
Produced by:	Harry Vanda & George Young
Chart position:	#2 Australian Albums
	#2 U.K. Albums
	#12 U.S. *Billboard* 200

Notable info: This is the final AC/DC album to feature Simon Wright on drums, who left to join the band Dio the following year. This is the final album to feature Brian Johnson's lyrics, with subsequent songs primarily written by Angus and Malcolm Young. *Blow Up Your Video* is certified platinum in the USA, 3x platinum in Australia, with platinum and gold certifications in other countries.

Blow Up Your Video saw long-time producers Harry Vanda and George Young return for production, adding a layer of familial and musical synergy to the album. As the 1980s progressed, the rock scene underwent various transformations, and the band found themselves adapting to the evolving landscape while staying true to their core identity. The result: another album featuring AC/DC's unmistakable, signature sound. Tracks such as "Heatseeker," the first single off the album, exemplifies the album's hard-hitting nature, featuring relentless rhythm and high energy. Songs like "That's the Way I Wanna Rock 'n' Roll" and "Meanstreak" further showcase AC/DC's hard-hitting style, with lyrics that emphasize themes of rebellion, raw energy, and an unapologetic embrace of rock 'n' roll lifestyle, underscoring their resilience in the face of a shifting musical landscape of the general music scene itself. In the late 1980s, the glam metal and "hair" metal scenes dominated the charts, and MTV continued to exert a significant influence on the music industry. Despite these trends, AC/DC maintained their sonic integrity, steering clear of the flashy aesthetics and commercial compromises that characterized many of their contemporaries. The title of the album, *Blow Up Your Video*, was AC/DC's answer to the current scene, which they were clearly not fans of. As Malcolm Young recalled in an interview: "Well, that was MTV again, the big budgets, and you know, they wouldn't play us really, you know, because we weren't MTV friendly. And it was all around, in the rock music who got dressed up again with the satin and all the crap that went with it. So, it was just sort of us just tryin' to say screw MTV ... and let's get back to some rock 'n roll again." As AC/DC navigated the challenges of a shifting industry, the band's determination to blow up their own sonic boundaries rather than succumb to external pressures of management and industry once again affirmed their enduring legacy and longevity in the world of rock 'n' roll as the world's biggest rock band. The middle tracks, including "Go Zone" and "Kissin' Dynamite," maintain the album's momentum. These songs are infused with suggestive and playful lyrics, a hallmark of AC/DC's songwriting. "Kissin' Dynamite," in particular, stands out for its vivid imagery and metaphorical language, capturing the spirit of risk and adventure. "Nick of Time" and "Some Sin for Nuthin'" explore themes of urgency and moral ambiguity, respectively. "Nick of Time" presents a narrative of high-stakes escapism, while "Some Sin for Nuthin'" offers a cynical view of human motivations, critiquing the often-selfish reasons behind people's actions. The album concludes with "Ruff Stuff," "Two's Up," and "This Means War," each adding unique elements to the album's narrative. "Ruff Stuff" is a celebration of the band's rough and raw musical style, "Two's Up" delves into themes of intimacy and adventure, and "This Means War" serves as a powerful and confrontational closing statement. *Blow Up Your Video* stands as a testament to AC/DC's enduring appeal. It captures the band's ability to blend straightforward, powerful music with themes that resonate with their audience—from rebellion and defiance to the more playful and risqué aspects of rock 'n' roll. This album not only reflects AC/DC's musical identity but also contributes significantly to the landscape of late 1980s rock music. The lyrics often deal with themes of rock 'n' roll, personal freedom, and playful mischief. Although the album did not achieve the same level of critical acclaim as some of the band's earlier works, it was a commercial success and helped maintain the band's popularity in the late 1980s. *Blow Up Your Video* marked the last time Brian Johnson contributed as a lyricist/songwriter, with subsequent songs primarily written by the Young brothers.

"Heatseeker"

"Heatseeker," the opening track and first single released from the album, is a song that contributed to AC/DC's resurgence in popularity following a period of relatively disappointing commercial success. The song's lyrics, like many of AC/DC's tracks, are filled with high-energy, dynamic imagery, and sexual references. Lines such as "I'm a heatseeker, burnin' up the town" and "I wanna see you get up, see the whites of your eyes" convey a sense of relentless pursuit and intensity. The lyrics metaphorically describe someone or something as a "heatseeker," suggesting someone who is out to fulfill their sexual desires. This could also be interpreted as a metaphor for the band's own approach to their music and performances—energetic, unrelenting, and impactful. The lyrics frequently refer to power and motion, with phrases like "turn up the heat," "fire up the coal," "keep that motor turning," and "keep those tires burning." These automotive and mechanical metaphors are often used in rock music to symbolize raw power and relentless energy, both key components of AC/DC's musical style, which could also likely have been inspired by Brian Johnson's love for racing and race cars. The song's significance was not just limited to its place in the album but extended to AC/DC's live performances. "Heatseeker" was often the opening song in the North American leg of the tour. This set the tone for the concerts, starting them off with a burst of energy and excitement, as emphasized by a heatseeking missile pod rising up onto the stage during the song's performance that Angus would jump out from to the crowd's approval. The live version of the song, featured on the *AC/DC Live* album released in 1992, is about twice the tempo, which I find makes the song that much more powerful and alive than the original studio version.

"That's the Way I Wanna Rock 'n' Roll"

"That's the Way I Wanna Rock 'n' Roll," the second song from the album and also the second single is a track that reflects the band's preference for live performances and their emphasis on authentic, energetic rock 'n' roll, contrasting with the increasingly automated and remote-controlled nature of modern entertainment. The song's lyrics convey a strong, rebellious attitude towards contemporary media and a desire to return to the roots of rock music. With lines like "Blow up my video, shut down my radio, told boss man where to go, turned off my brain control," the song expresses a desire to break free from the constraints and influences of mainstream media and entertainment, embodying the band's raw, unfiltered approach to music and overall theme of the album title itself. The track is an overall statement of the desire to return to true rock 'n' roll in its purest form and to discard the costumes, makeup, and glamor that was essentially asphyxiating the music industry by the later part of the 1980s. "That's the Way I Wanna Rock 'n' Roll" was released in various packaging on vinyl (12-inch and 7-inch) and CD formats, which was backed with "Kissin' Dynamite." Some versions also included a non-album B-side, "Borrowed Time."

"Meanstreak"

"Meanstreak" kicks off with a catchy guitar riff and groove anchored by drummer Simon Wright and bassist Cliff Williams, laying a solid foundation for the rest of the band to build upon. The song's lyrics, filled with imagery of danger and a lust for adventure, evoke a sense of liberation and defiance. The lyrics suggest a persona that embraces an untamed, unapologetic nature, contrasting with societal norms and expectations. The song identifies someone who refuses to be molded or taught, indicating a resistance to conformity. This is exemplified by lines like "I'm the perfect culture vulture in the face of poverty" and "I'm the guy they just can't teach." The repeated use of "Meanstreak" in the lyrics emphasizes the self-pride in their own rebellious identity. The reference to "kicking the castle that's been built up on the beach" suggests a willingness to challenge and disrupt established structures or expectations. This theme of nonconformity and defiance is a common thread in many AC/DC songs ever since their early days, reflecting the band's overall image as icons of rebellious rock 'n' roll. Brian Johnson's vocal performance captures the rebellious spirit of the song, exuding confidence and attitude that match the song's aggressive tone.

"Go Zone"

"Go Zone" kicks off with a pulsating beat, courtesy of drummer Simon Wright and bassist Cliff Williams. The lyrics are characteristic of AC/DC's usual style, known for its often sexually suggestive themes. The song appears to be about seeking excitement and pleasure, emphasizing a carefree and rebellious attitude. The opening lines, "Want some relaxation need to get some r n r, that's rest and recreation, don't need no vacation, I don't have to go that far," suggest a desire for a break from the routine, but not necessarily in the form of a traditional vacation. Instead, the song implies seeking relaxation through more immediate, possibly hedonistic means. Phrases like "Don't need no private eye forget the FBI, 'cos when the beaver sing, let me out I'm closin' in" seem to play with the theme of seeking pleasure while evading authority or societal norms. The reference to "beaver" is likely a double-entendre, typical of AC/DC's lyrical style, which often includes playful or cheeky innuendos. The chorus, "In the go zone, ready to fly, In the go zone, standin' up high, In the go zone, down on the block, In the go zone, ready to rock," reinforces the theme of being in a state of readiness for action or excitement. The "go zone" could be interpreted as a mental or physical state where one is ready to embrace fun and excitement without reservations. The line "Gotta have my candy gotta have my sugar sweet, I wanna give you a treat" further emphasizes the theme of indulgence and pleasure-seeking. This is consistent with many of AC/DC's songs, which often celebrate the joys of living in the moment and embracing life's pleasures. "Go Zone" aligns with AC/DC's usual themes of living life to the fullest, embracing excitement, and a certain degree of rebelliousness against conventional norms. The song's energy and lyrics fit well within the band's larger discography, which often celebrates the rock 'n' roll lifestyle. "Go Zone" is also the B-side to the "Heatseeker" single.

"Kissin' Dynamite"

"Kissin' Dynamite" is a song that tells a tale of fiery desire, reckless abandon, and the electrifying power of love. The repeated phrase "Feel like kissin' dynamite" serves as a powerful metaphor for engaging in thrilling, potentially dangerous experiences. This theme is a common one in AC/DC's music, which often celebrates living on the edge and embracing high-risk, high-reward situations. The lyrics "Like the thunder in the mountain, Like the lightning in the sky, Like the eye of a tornado, she watch it all go by" further enhance this imagery, depicting a scenario that is as exhilarating as it is perilous. The song embodies the spirit of rock 'n' roll as a medium that's not just about the music, but also about a lifestyle that defies convention and embraces the wilder, more unpredictable aspects of life. The reference to a woman who "comes for recreation" and "plays her games at night," who wants to "work on her vocation" and "set the world alight," suggests a figure who is both captivating and formidable.

This portrayal is aligned with the band's frequent depiction of women as powerful and enigmatic figures in their songs. "Kissin' Dynamite" is a song that resonates with the themes of adventure, danger, and the unpredictable thrill of life, embodying the spirit of rock music as envisioned by AC/DC. It is also the B-side to the "That's the Way I Wanna Rock 'n' Roll" single.

"Nick of Time"

Like many AC/DC tracks, particularly those from the last few albums, "Nick of Time" embodies themes of urgency and living on the edge. The song conveys a sense of being pursued or under pressure, as evidenced by lyrics like "Lynch mob on your tail, think they were searchin' for the holy grail" and "Everybody tryin' to find you guilty, make you wanna tow the line." These lines suggest a narrative of being chased or judged, possibly by society or authority figures. The chorus "Saved by, saved in the nick in time" implies a last-minute rescue or escape, emphasizing the thrill and adrenaline of narrowly avoiding disaster. This aligns with AC/DC's recurring theme of living dangerously and embracing moments of high tension and excitement. The lyrics tell a tale of perseverance and seizing the moment, embodying the spirit of taking chances and embracing life's challenges head-on. The song also touches on themes of defiance and resilience against adversity. In the song, Brian sings about a situation of fighting against forces trying to pin him down or make him conform, as indicated by the line "I didn't figure on them anyway." This rebellious attitude is a hallmark of AC/DC's music, reflecting their commitment to individuality and resistance to being controlled or subdued. "Nick of Time" is a track which showcases AC/DC's classic rock sound and their penchant for storytelling that revolves around high-stakes scenarios, defiance, and last-minute salvations.

"Some Sin for Nuthin'"

"Some Sin for Nuthin'" is a devilish track that explores themes greed, temptation, and the futility of sinning for unworthy causes. The clever wordplay and cheeky references add a layer of intrigue and playfulness to the song, painting a vivid picture of a world where rules are meant to be broken. The chorus, "Some sin for gold, some sin for shame, some sin for cash, some sin for gain, some sin for wine, some sin for pain," lists various motivations behind people's actions, especially those that are morally questionable or outright wrong. This enumeration of different kinds of "sins" represents the various vices and temptations that people succumb to, whether for material gain, personal pleasure, or other reasons. The line "But I ain't gonna be the fool who's gonna have to sin for nothing" suggests a conscious decision to avoid making mistakes or committing wrongful acts without a significant reason. It reflects a philosophy of not getting involved in dubious activities unless there's a compelling reason to do so, possibly hinting at a sense of wisdom or learning from past experiences. The reference to "Nero evil mind, He was born way before his time" alludes to the Roman Emperor Nero, known for his tyrannical rule, connecting historical tyranny to contemporary themes of power and corruption. The song seems to criticize those who manipulate or exploit others for personal gain, as suggested by the lines "You gotta lay down the rules, push up the price, turn on the heat put you on ice." The song presents a cynical view of human motivations and behaviors, emphasizing the often selfish and destructive reasons behind people's actions. It fits within AC/DC's broader musical themes of critiquing societal norms and behaviors through the lens of hard rock music.

"Ruff Stuff"

The song "Ruff Stuff" is an embodiment of AC/DC's classic hard rock sound and their typical themes of raw energy and unapologetic boldness. The lyrics, "If ya don't want ruff stuff, don't wantcha face round here," set a defiant and confrontational tone, suggesting an environment or attitude where only the tough and resilient are welcome. This aligns with AC/DC's reputation for creating music that is straightforward, powerful, and unrefined in its appeal to rock 'n' roll sensibilities. The lines "I like 'em big and I like 'em small, and if you ask me to take an oath, I would take them all," exemplify the band's use of sexual innuendos. This could be interpreted as a metaphor for the band's music and persona, which is versatile, encompassing a range of styles and influences, yet consistently maintains a hard-edged rock identity. The repetition of "Gimme that ruff stuff" throughout the song serves as a rallying cry, reinforcing the theme of embracing the more rugged and unrestrained aspects of life and music. This phrase could be seen as a metaphor for the band's own music—direct, powerful, and without pretense, reflecting their straightforward approach to rock music.

"Two's Up"

Like many tracks on this album and from AC/DC's discography in general, "Two's Up" is another track that encapsulates the band's signature blend of high energy and suggestive themes. Despite not receiving the same level of recognition as some of AC/DC's more famous tracks, "Two's Up" is an underrated gem that deserves more attention The lyrics "Like the way you slip, there ain't nothing like a two's up, that's the way it is, two's up, that's what I wanna hear" set a tone of raw and direct expression, characteristic of the band's straightforward approach to rock music. The song's chorus, "And it's a two's up, Gonna be two's up, we're gonna have a two's up," uses the phrase "two's up" as a metaphor, likely suggesting a situation involving two people in a close, perhaps intimate or adventurous, encounter. This interpretation aligns with the band's frequent use of double-entendres and playful, yet risqué language in their lyrics. Lines like "Gimme head gimme tails, gimme double up an' comin' over on the rails" further emphasize the song's theme of intense and passionate experiences. The use of gambling metaphors ("Gimme head gimme tails") might also signify taking risks and living on the edge, themes prevalent in many AC/DC songs. Overall, "Two's Up" reflects AC/DC's typical style, where the music is not just about the sound but also about embodying a certain attitude and lifestyle.

"This Means War"

The Closing track on *Blow Up Your Video*, "This Means War" serves as the ultimate climax, with its fast-paced torrent of energy. Lyrically, the song conveys a strong message of confrontation and conflict, as indicated by its title and the repeated declaration in the lyrics, "This Means War!" The intensity and straightforwardness of this phrase captures the essence of the song's theme—an unambiguous declaration of a battle-like situation. The lyrics "Do you know what it means, do you know what it means, do you know what it means, this means war!" challenge the listener, emphasizing the seriousness and the inevitability of the conflict being described. This could be a metaphor for personal struggles, societal conflicts, or the confrontational aspects of human nature. The line "Where's the 7th Cavalry" invokes historical imagery, perhaps alluding to the famous military unit known for its role in the American Indian Wars, adding a sense of urgency and historical weight to the song's theme. AC/DC's style often includes songs with strong, aggressive themes, and "This Means War" fits this pattern. The song combines their signature high-energy rock sound with lyrics that speak to themes of struggle, resistance, and the inherent conflicts in life, encapsulated by the stark and powerful declaration of war in the chorus. "This Means War" also serves as an anthem of unyielding resolve, embodying AC/DC's unwavering spirit and determination. The lyrics depict a metaphorical battle cry, urging listeners to stand firm in the face of adversity and never back down.

Interesting Facts

During the U.S. leg of the Blow Up Your Video Tour, Malcolm Young decided to check into rehab to battle his ongoing problem with alcohol. Malcolm's nephew, Stevie Young, would sub on rhythm guitar for him during that portion of the tour.

13

The Razors Edge

Release date:	September 24, 1990 (U.K.)
	September 24, 1990 (U.S.)
Current edition:	Sony/ Columbia, CD, LP
Personnel:	Brian Johnson, lead vocals
	Angus Young, lead guitar
	Malcolm Young, rhythm guitar
	Cliff Williams, bass guitar
	Chris Slade, drums
Duration:	46:29
Recorded at:	Windmill Lane Studios, Dublin, Ireland, and Little Mountain Studios, Vancouver, BC, Canada, 1990
Produced by:	Bruce Fairbairn
Chart position:	#3 Australian Albums
	#15 U.K. Albums
	#2 U.S. *Billboard* 200

Notable info: This is the first and only studio AC/DC album to feature Chris Slade on drums. This is the first AC/DC album since 1980 to not include Brian Johnson as a co-songwriter. *The Razors Edge* is certified 5x platinum in the USA, 5x platinum in Australia, 5x platinum in Canada, 2x platinum in Germany, 2x platinum in Switzerland, with multiple platinum and gold certifications in other countries.

AC/DC's *The Razors Edge*, their twelfth studio album, is often heralded as a triumphant return for the band. Coming on the heels of a period of relative quiet for the band, the album marked a significant resurgence in AC/DC's popularity, featuring hits like "Thunderstruck," "Are You Ready," and "Moneytalks," and reinforced their status as one of the preeminent forces in rock music. Produced by Bruce Fairbairn, *The Razors Edge* showcased AC/DC's ability to adapt to the changing musical landscape of the early '90s while retaining their timeless sound. The album featured an overall crisper production sound, where Brian's vocals were much more prominent than they were on the previous two releases. In my opinion, the album is AC/DC's most commercial-sounding release to date. *The Razors Edge* would also be the first and only album to feature then-new drummer Chris Slade, who joined the band to replace Simon Wright, who departed to join the band Dio in 1989. All of the songs on *The Razors Edge* are written by and credited to Angus and Malcolm Young, making it the first AC/DC album since joining in 1980 to not list Brian Johnson on the songwriting credits. Angus stated in an interview with *RIP* magazine in 1990: "Brian was just at home at this time, sorting out a few marital problems and legal problems. Me and Mal wrote the lyrics as well as the music this time, and that relieved a lot of pressure, 'cos it meant all he had to do was come in and sing." The standout anthem, "Thunderstruck," became an instant classic, with Angus Young's electrifying guitar riff and Brian Johnson's signature vocals capturing the essence of AC/DC's sonic brilliance. The song, in particular, resonated with fans and played a pivotal role in reintroducing AC/DC to a new generation of listeners. The success of "Thunderstruck" catapulted the album to commercial heights, and other tracks like "Moneytalks" and "Are You Ready" further solidified its impact. *The Razors Edge* became a chart-topping success, reasserting AC/DC's dominance at a time when the music scene was experiencing a slow and unfortunate shift toward grunge and alternative rock. AC/DC further fueled their success at the time by embarking on an immense global tour, further solidifying their reputation and endurance as the world's biggest rock band. The combination of a hit album and a relentless touring schedule not only revitalized the band but also brought them back into the mainstream spotlight. *The Razors Edge* achieved considerable commercial success, reaching #2 on the U.S. *Billboard* 200 and #4 on the UK Albums Chart. It earned multi-platinum certifications in several countries, including Australia, Canada, Germany, Switzerland, and the United States. To promote the album, the band undertook The Razors Edge World Tour from November 1990 to November 1991. Some performances from this tour were recorded for the 1992 live album titled *AC/DC Live*, considered one of the best live albums of the 1990s.

"Thunderstruck"

"Thunderstruck" kicks off with a thunderous and unmistakable guitar riff, courtesy of the one and only Angus Young. The opening sequence builds anticipation, steadily increasing in intensity until it explodes into a full-fledged storm of high-voltage rock 'n' roll. The relentless, driving rhythm section of bassist Cliff Williams and drummer Chris Slade sets the foundation, joined by Malcolm Young's solid rhythm. "Thunderstruck" was the first single released from *The Razors Edge* in 1990 and is a track that encapsulates the high-energy, electrifying essence of what AC/DC's music is all about. The song opens with a repeated invocation of "thunder," setting a tone of awe and power, akin to the overwhelming force of nature. The lyrics tell a story of exhilaration and wild experiences, symbolized by the recurring motif of thunder, akin to AC/DC's essence and overall theme of a band—high-voltage rock 'n' roll as it has been since the beginning. A moment of revelation is recounted in the song ("I was caught in the middle of a railroad track"), suggesting a point of no return, a transformative experience that's both thrilling and terrifying. The song's narrative moves through a series of high-octane experiences, from reckless escapades on the highway to encounters in Texas with "some dancers who gave a good time." This journey is not just physical but also metaphorical, indicating a life lived on the edge, full of risk and excitement. The phrase "Thunderstruck" itself implies being profoundly affected or changed by these experiences, akin to being struck by lightning—a sudden, intense, and unforgettable event. Musically, the song's pounding rhythm and the "sound of the drums, beating in my heart" mimic the heartbeat of the singer, intensifying the sense of adrenaline and excitement. The "thunder of guns" metaphorically "tears the me apart," symbolizing the powerful impact of these experiences on their psyche. The line "And I was shaking at the knees, could I come again please?" could indicate both fear and exhilaration, embodying the adrenaline rush and physical response to being deeply moved or affected, of course, with the expected subtle sexual overtones of AC/DC songs. The mention of "Went through to Texas, yeah Texas, and we had some fun" and interacting with "girls" and "dancers" indicates a journey filled with enjoyment and perhaps a bit of rebellious behavior. The repetition of the word "Thunderstruck" throughout the song not only serves as its central theme but also acts as a driving force, emphasizing the song's energetic and electrifying nature. "Thunderstruck" would become one of AC/DC's biggest hits and most iconic and loved fan favorites over the past few decades and is a song that re-established AC/DC's dominance in the world of rock music. The track has surpassed one billion views on YouTube as of 2021 and has been used in countless movies and sports events.

"Fire Your Guns"

"Fire Your Guns" is another example of AC/DC's signature style; it is a fast-paced rocker, combining raw energy with suggestive themes. Released as the B-side to the "Thunderstruck" single, the song was also performed live during The Razors Edge World Tour 1990–91. "Fire Your Guns" is about the electrifying thrill of attraction and the desire to embrace life's more exhilarating moments. It reflects AC/DC's enduring themes of high energy, sensuality, and a no-holds-barred approach to living life to the fullest. The lyrics are straightforward, characterized by their vivid imagery and high-energy expression, emphasizing physical attraction. The song opens with a description of a woman with captivating physical attributes: "She got eyes of blue, body curves, Legs that'll shake the earth." This line sets the stage for a song that is both visually evocative and sensually charged. The repeated use of the word "Fire" in various contexts throughout the song suggests a theme of intense, uncontrollable passion and energy. Phrases like "Fire when she's going down," "Fire then she make you drown," and "Fire then she blow you round" imply a sense of overwhelming passion and intensity, in a romantic or sexual context. The "fire" could symbolize the burning intensity of attraction or the overwhelming nature of the experience. The chorus, "Fire your guns!" repeated multiple times, serves as a metaphorical call to action or an expression of unbridled enthusiasm and excitement. It captures the essence of the song's theme of living life with passion and fervor. The line "Yeah you want some fun" ties back to AC/DC's overarching theme of seeking excitement and adventure, often in the context of rock and roll lifestyle. The song reflects the band's characteristic blend of rock 'n' roll bravado and simple, yet powerful lyrical motifs.

"Moneytalks"

"Moneytalks" was the second single released from *The Razors Edge*, issued in November 1990, and it would become AC/DC's highest charting single and first Top 40 hit on the *Billboard* Top 40 to date, peaking at #23 in the United States. The song would also be performed live during The Razors Edge World Tour, accompanied by a flurry of AC/DC "Angus" *faux* dollars that would be dropped from the rafters of venues during the shows. The lyrics are straightforward yet impactful, embodying the band's style of using simple, catchy phrases to convey deeper meanings. The track offers a candid commentary on the influence of money in society. The chorus "Come on come on listen to the Money talk, come on come on lovin' for the money" suggests the allure and seduction of money. It highlights how people are drawn to the promise of wealth, often prioritizing it above other values. In true AC/DC fashion, the song's delivery amplifies its message. The driving rhythm and catchy chorus make the song not only a critique but also an anthem that's easy to remember and sing along to. The phrase "Moneytalks, B.S. Walks" is a colloquial way of saying that money has the final say in most situations, overshadowing words or promises that aren't backed by financial power. Overall, "Moneytalks" uses AC/DC's typical hard rock energy to deliver a critique of materialism and the dominance of monetary power in society. The song combines catchy rhythms with a message about the sometimes-overwhelming influence of money, a theme that resonates with many listeners. Some interesting promotional items were issued with the album release, which included a "Moneytalks" money bag as well as individual "Moneytalks" credit cards, one for each of the band members. These items were extremely limited in numbers and are now highly collectible.

"The Razors Edge"

The title track from the album is a song rich in imagery and metaphor. The lyrics convey a sense of danger and urgency, using the motif of the "razor's edge" as a central symbol. The opening lines, "There's fighting on the left, and marching on the right," suggest a world divided by conflict and ideological extremes. This could be interpreted as a commentary on the political or social climate at the time, highlighting a world torn by differing opinions and strife. As stated by Angus Young in a 1990 interview with *RIP* magazine: "It's thinking about the moment just before a big storm when you look to the sky and see huge black clouds coming over, people used to say, here comes the Razors Edge and we thought that fitted quite well with what's happening in the world at the moment." Angus continued: "We're thinking about the ongoing thing between the Russian's and the Yanks. I mean, they've always been at loggerheads, but recently it died down a bit, and everything seems peaceful. But the world's never really been like that." The repeated lines "Here comes the razor's edge" serve as a warning of an approaching existential threat. The "razor's edge" could symbolize a critical turning point or a moment of intense peril where decisions have significant consequences. The razor's edge is a powerful metaphor for a precarious or critical situation. It implies a fine line between life and death, success and failure, or sanity and madness. The notion of being "cut to shreds" by the razor's edge suggests the potentially destructive outcome of living in such extreme conditions. The song captures the tension and uncertainty of its era, while also speaking to timeless themes of risk, moral ambiguity, and the human response to danger. "The Razors Edge" was another track from the album included in the live set during the 1990–91 world tour.

"Mistress for Christmas"

AC/DC's first and only Christmas song, "Mistress for Christmas" features lyrics that are both playful and suggestive, aligning with the band's reputation for crafting songs with a strong sense of humor and a touch of irreverence. The festive song was issued on a one track promotional only CD single depicting Angus Young standing next to a Santa Sack with a woman's nylon-covered legs sticking out. The lyrics of "Mistress for Christmas" maintain a playful tone, infusing humor and innuendo, and putting a rock spin on holiday traditions. The chorus, "Mistress for Christmas, you know what I'm talking about, Mistress for Christmas, they're gonna send me down, send me down, Mistress for Christmas, I want the woman in red at the bottom of my bed," is a cheeky request for a risqué Christmas gift. This reflects the band's characteristic blend of rock 'n' roll bravado with a lighthearted, slightly mischievous tone. The track employs a playful, slightly irreverent approach to songwriting. It combines AC/DC's signature hard rock sound with lighthearted lyrics, creating a festive song that stands out for its humor and boldness.

"Rock Your Heart Out"

"Rock Your Heart Out" is a straightforward, high-energy track that encapsulates the spirit of rock 'n' roll in its most elemental form. The lyrics reflect the energy and rebellious nature of the genre, encouraging listeners to embrace the moment and experience the raw power and freedom that comes with it. The lines "Got the devil in you, got the devil in me, play a dangerous tune, come on dance with thee" suggest a sense of unity in rebellion and the shared experience of enjoying something edgy or risky. This reflects a common theme in rock music, where the "devil" often symbolizes rebellion against conventional norms. The chorus, "Throw your fists up, shout your mouth off, beat the walls down, got to freak out, rock your little heart out," is a call to action, encouraging listeners to let loose and fully immerse themselves in the moment. It's about experiencing the music with every fiber of your being, embodying the physical and emotional release that rock music often provides. Another significant line, "Got everything you want, got everything you need, don't worry about the cost, just sell your soul to me," could be interpreted as a commentary on the seductive power of rock 'n' roll, suggesting that it offers everything one could desire at the expense of societal norms or expectations. The track offers a celebration of the genre of rock 'n' roll itself, encapsulating the spirit and energy that has defined rock music over the decades.

"Are You Ready"

"Are You Ready" was the third and final single released from *The Razors Edge*, issued in March 1991 on a few different 7-inch and 12-inch formats, CD, and cassette versions with different artwork depending on the region of release. The song is the opening track from side two of the album, and it embodies the band's signature sound and delivers an explosive dose of pure rock 'n' roll power. The song is an overall celebration of having a good time and living life to the fullest, a common theme throughout AC/DC's repertoire. The repeated anthemic chorus, "Are you ready for a good time, then get ready for the night line," serves as an anthem of sorts, calling on listeners to prepare themselves for an unforgettable experience. This call to action is a staple of AC/DC's music, often aiming to rouse and energize their audience. The lines "Who all need it, who all need it, you all breathe it, we all breathe it" suggest a universal craving for the thrill and escapism that rock music offers. This reflects the band's understanding of their music as not just entertainment but as a vital part of their fans' lives—something they "need" and "breathe." Overall, the song is about the collective experience of enjoying rock music, emphasizing the communal and exhilarating aspects of listening to and participating in a rock concert. "Are You Ready" encapsulates AC/DC's ethos of providing high-octane, spirited rock music that unites fans in a shared experience of excitement and joy. Overall, the track is about having a great time and a rock 'n' roll party song, complete with the AC/DC trademark sound and memorable chorus line.

"Got You by the Balls"

"Got You by the Balls" was released as the B-side to the "Are You Ready" single in 1991. It kicks off with an unmistakable AC/DC-style riff, and it is one of my favorite guitar riffs from the album. The song employs straightforward and suggestive lyrics, typical of the band's style, and it appears to be a commentary on power dynamics, particularly in the context of money and seduction. The opening lines, "Hey mister businessman, head of the company, are you looking for a lady, one who likes to please," set the tone for the song. It introduces a scenario where a powerful businessman is searching for companionship, possibly of a transactional nature. This sets up a narrative about power and control. The chorus, "She got you by the balls," repeated multiple times, is both literal and metaphorical. It suggests a woman holding power over a man, potentially turning the tables in a situation where the man is typically seen as the one in control. This could be interpreted as a commentary on the unexpected ways power can shift, especially when seduction and money are involved, such as a blackmail situation. The phrase "But she won't sacrifice, what you want tonight, she won't come across, unless there's money in her hand" further emphasizes the theme of transactional relationships and the idea that even powerful individuals can find themselves at a disadvantage in certain situations. The song reflects AC/DC's straightforward approach to songwriting, where they often tackle bold and provocative subjects with a touch of humor and irreverence.

"Shot of Love"

"Shot of Love" is another AC/DC track from *The Razors Edge* featuring lyrics characteristic of the band, combining themes of desire and passion with a straightforward, high-energy rock sound. The chorus, "Shot of love, shot of love, shot of love, make you bleed, shot of love," uses the metaphor of a "shot of love" to convey an intense, possibly overwhelming experience of passion or desire. This metaphor could be interpreted as suggesting that love or passion, like a shot, is something powerful and transformative, capable of deeply affecting one or of course the more direct metaphor of an orgasm. The line "A humpin' an' a pumpin', got you jumpin', shot of love" further emphasizes the physical and visceral nature of the song's theme. It reflects AC/DC's tendency to blend humor with suggestiveness, creating songs that are both playful and edgy. The repeated phrase "And I warn you it's the best shot of your life" implies that this experience is not only intense but also unparalleled—a once-in-a-lifetime kind of event. "Shot of Love" exemplifies AC/DC's skill in crafting songs that are direct, catchy, and embody the spirit of rock 'n' roll. The lyrics celebrate the raw, primal aspects of human emotion and experience, packaged in a high-energy musical style that is quintessentially AC/DC.

"Let's Make It"

"Let's Make It," like many other AC/DC tracks, is a song that celebrates enjoying life, particularly through the lens of a rock 'n' roll lifestyle. While it may be considered a lesser-energetic track compared to their usual offerings, it possesses a unique charm and a distinct groove that sets it apart. The song's lyrics encapsulate the band's typical themes of hedonism and living in the moment, seen throughout their discography. During the song, the repeated line "Let's make it, don't waste it, let's make it, come on and taste it" serves as an invitation to fully engage in the pleasures of life. This could be interpreted as a call to embrace opportunities, enjoy oneself, and make the most of every moment. The lyrics, "I'll be your ladies' man, If you give me the chance, we'll keep a jumpin' 'til the music run dry, and if we take a rest, we'll smoke some cigarettes, and start a smokin' goin' out of control," depict a scene of continuous celebration and indulgence. This reflects AC/DC's penchant for depicting a lifestyle that revolves around music, partying, and enjoying the company of others. The song's message is simple yet effective: life is for living, and it should be lived to the fullest, especially in the context of a party or concert setting. "Let's Make It" captures the essence of the rock 'n' roll ethos, where the focus is on immediate pleasure and the celebration of the here and now. The lyrics are a testament to the band's ability to create songs that are both fun and invigorating, encouraging listeners to embrace life's pleasures.

"Goodbye and Good Riddance to Bad Luck"

"Goodbye and Good Riddance to Bad Luck" features lyrics that convey themes of liberation and a fresh start. The song appears to be about breaking free from a period of misfortune and embracing a more positive future and turning adversity into triumph. It was perhaps written as a testament to some of the band's personal trials and tribulations over the years, including those that were health related—i.e. Malcolm's battle with alcohol in the late '80s and the loss of Bon Scott. The lines "Back out of jail and chasin' some floos', bad luck has changed, broken the chains" suggest a narrative of someone who has been through tough times (symbolized by "jail") and is now experiencing a change in fortune. The imagery of breaking chains is a powerful metaphor for liberation and the shedding of past burdens. The chorus, "Goodbye goodbye goodbye and good riddance to bad luck, goodbye and good riddance to bad luck," is a triumphant farewell to a period of adversity. It expresses a strong sense of relief and optimism, indicating a transition to better times. The lyrics also touch upon themes of desire and indulgence, as seen in "Wantin' what's coming all for the take, freedom for lovin' and lust for the taste." This could be interpreted as a return to the pursuit of pleasure and success, now unhampered by previous setbacks. Overall, the song is about overcoming adversity and moving forward with a sense of hope and renewed energy. "Goodbye and Good Riddance to Bad Luck" reflects AC/DC's ability to craft songs that are not only energetic and engaging but also carry a message of resilience and optimism.

"If You Dare"

"If You Dare" is the twelfth and closing track from *The Razors Edge*. It has a slightly different style to most of the other songs from their discography. The song lacks a guitar solo and is an otherwise straightforward, high-energy rocker; actually, it is one of my favorites from the entire album. The song features lyrics that are suggestive and playful, inviting a sense of adventure and spontaneity. The song is about taking risks and engaging in the thrill of the moment. The repeated invitation, "Honey do you love me, love me like you do, honey won't you come outside and play, if you dare," is both a romantic and a daring proposition. It suggests a challenge or a call to break free from the mundane and experience something exciting and possibly unconventional. The phrase "If you dare" is key to the song's theme; it implies a challenge to step outside of one's comfort zone, to take risks, and to engage in something thrilling. This could be interpreted in the context of a romantic relationship, where the invitation to "come outside and play" suggests a departure from the routine into something more adventurous. The lyrics are characteristic of AC/DC's style, which often includes themes of excitement, risk-taking, and the pursuit of pleasure. The song captures the essence of rock 'n' roll as not just a musical style but a way of life that embraces living boldly and without restraint. "If You Dare" is a song that combines the themes of love, adventure, and the classic rock 'n' roll spirit of living life on the edge. It embodies the band's philosophy of seizing the moment and enjoying life to its fullest, much like many of the songs from *The Razors Edge* and AC/DC's entire discography.

Interesting Facts

The song "Thunderstruck" was leveraged during the 2010 Stuxnet infection of the Iranian nuclear program, where the song would randomly play at maximum volume from multiple infected workstations in the middle of the night.

14

Ballbreaker

Release date:	September 22, 1995 (U.K.) September 26, 1995 (U.S.)
Current edition:	Sony/ Columbia, CD, LP
Personnel:	Brian Johnson, lead vocals Angus Young, lead guitar Malcolm Young, rhythm guitar Cliff Williams, bass guitar Phil Rudd, drums
Duration:	49:11
Recorded at:	Record Plant Studios, New York, New York, and Ocean Way Studios, Los Angeles, California, February–May 1995
Produced by:	Rick Rubin, Mike Fraser
Chart position:	#1 Australian Albums #6 U.K. Albums #4 U.S. *Billboard* 200

Notable info: This album marked the return of Phil Rudd on drums. *Ballbreaker* is certified 2x platinum in the USA, 3x platinum in Australia, with multiple platinum and gold certifications in other countries.

By the mid-1990s, AC/DC's *Ballbreaker* album arrived at a juncture where the music landscape had once again shifted; grunge and alternative rock was now dominating the airwaves. The album consists of eleven tracks, each exemplifying AC/DC's hard-hitting, blues-inspired rock sound. Undeterred, AC/DC delivered an album that blended their signature sound with a contemporary edge. Produced by Rick Rubin, *Ballbreaker* marked the significant return of drummer Phil Rudd and resulted in a solid, hard-rocking album that harked back to the band's roots. In an interview with Angus and Malcolm, they recalled with a lot of laughter: "Oh that one was with Mr. Rubin ... yea, he was a man that wasn't around too often." The album explores themes of rebelliousness, power, and the quintessential rock 'n' roll lifestyle. Throughout the album, the band's energy and raw power are on full display, making it a standout addition to AC/DC's discography. It is evident that the band's lyrical content had become much different by this time, although they have always attempted to maintain a similar tongue-in-check, double-entendre lyric style throughout their songs. The title track, "Ballbreaker," with its thunderous rhythm and signature guitar work of Angus and Malcolm Young, sets the tone for an album that refused to bow to passing trends. The track "Hard as a Rock," the first single from the album, became a standout anthem, showcasing the band's ability to craft memorable and enduring rock anthems. Despite the changing musical landscape and a prolonged absence from the studio, *Ballbreaker* demonstrated AC/DC's ability to adapt without compromising their essence. The album's success also lay in its return to a more straightforward production style, capturing the raw energy and spontaneity reminiscent of AC/DC's earlier classics. Songs like "Hail Caesar" and "Cover You in Oil" exuded the unbridled power that had endeared AC/DC to fans worldwide. *Ballbreaker* was well-received for its raw energy and was seen as a return to form for the band, gaining commercial success and positive reviews from critics. The album resonated with both loyal fans and a new generation, reaffirming AC/DC's status as a timeless force in rock music.

"Hard as a Rock"

The opening track and first single released from *Ballbreaker*, 'Hard as a Rock' is a powerful and direct metaphor that encapsulates the core essence of AC/DC's musical style and thematic content. The song actually originated back from 1986 during the *Who Made Who* recording sessions. It conveys a sense of unyielding strength and resilience, themes often found in their music. In typical AC/DC fashion, the metaphor is also a direct reference to male genitalia, though it could also be interpreted as a statement of the band's consistency and enduring presence in the rock music scene, especially considering the song was released in the mid-'90s, decades after AC/DC's formation. The sound of the overall track is pristine, capturing the essence of AC/DC's live energy while maintaining clarity and power. The guitars possess a sharpness that slices through the mix, while the drums pound with a thunderous groove. The lyrics also contain typical AC/DC sexual innuendo and wordplay, a common feature in their songs: "her bad behavior, will leave you standing proud, hard as a rock." These elements add a playful, yet edgy tone to the song, aligning with the band's rebellious and straightforward rock image. "Hard as a Rock" can be seen as a reflection of AC/DC's staying power and relevance in the rock genre. Despite the changing musical landscape of the '90s, with the emergence of grunge and alternative rock, AC/DC stayed true to their roots, and this song is a testament to that. It showcases the band's commitment to their distinctive style and their ability to continue producing high-energy rock music that resonates with their audience. "Hard as a Rock" is a quintessential AC/DC song, combining straightforward, impactful lyrics with high-energy music. It reflects the band's enduring presence in rock music and their ability to stay true to their signature style. The single was available on in different formats and special packages, including a limited edition, numbered, 7-inch single on yellow vinyl.

"Cover You in Oil"

This song has a fantastic groove right from the start. "Cover You in Oil," the second single released from *Ballbreaker*, is an excellent example of the band's distinctive style, characterized by its bold, unapologetic lyrics and driving rock sound. The band's chemistry shines through, as each instrument seamlessly complements the others, allowing Brian Johnson's vocals to add an extra layer of energy to the song. "I'll make her wet, gonna make her mine, she like it hard she like it slow, all right honey come on let's go … Cover you in oil, let me cover you in oil, I wanna cover you in oil" are lyrics that are emblematic of AC/DC's approach to songwriting, which often includes overtly sexual themes and innuendo. The phrase "Cover you in oil" can be interpreted as a metaphor for desire and physical attraction, staying true to the band's characteristic style of blending raw energy with suggestive themes. The direct and somewhat provocative language reflects the band's ethos of rock 'n' roll as a form of rebellion and liberation. AC/DC's music often emphasizes freedom of expression and pushing against societal norms, and this song is no exception. Moreover, the rhythmic and repetitive nature of the lyrics, particularly in the chorus, creates a catchy and memorable hook. This simplicity and repetitiveness are key elements of AC/DC's music, making their songs easily recognizable and accessible to a wide audience. Angus told *Guitar World*: "Well I always liked that double meaning thing. And I do like to do a bit of painting when I get some free time. I just thought it would be a good play on words.… People always think the worst, uh oh these guys are gonna cover everyone in hot oil, it's gonna be Sodom and Gomorrah!" "Cover You in Oil" showcases AC/DC's trademark style of hard-hitting rock music combined with bold and suggestive lyrics. The song encapsulates the band's ethos of freedom, rebellion, and straightforward rock 'n' roll, contributing to their lasting impact on the genre.

"The Furor"

"The Furor" is a song about embracing the role of a disruptor, challenging authority, and seeking to bring about change. Musically, AC/DC's signature hard rock sound reinforces the themes of the song, with driving rhythms and powerful guitar riffs, amplifying the sense of rebellion and intensity. The song conveys themes of rebellion, control, and challenging authority. "The Furor" does not delve into complex lyrical themes; instead, it embraces simplicity and a direct, no-nonsense approach. The lyrics touch upon themes of rebellion, chaos, and the exhilaration of living on the edge. The lyrics are filled with imagery of defiance and a desire to shake up the status quo. The song begins with "Here comes the furor, kick the dust, wipe the crime from the main street, await the coming of the Lord," suggesting a scenario of upheaval and cleansing. The term "furor" itself implies intense excitement or agitation, setting the tone for a song about causing a stir and making an impact. The lines "Hangin' round with them low down and dirty, bringin' order from the boss" and "Kicked around, messed about, get your hands dirty, on the killin' floor" depict a gritty, rough environment where the protagonist is involved in disruptive or rebellious activities. The song could possibly be referring to a figure within organized crime. The word "furor" itself can be interpreted in several ways. It might refer to a frenzied or passionate intensity, suggesting a wild, uncontrolled force; alternatively, it could be seen as a play on words, echoing the sound of "fury" but with a more personal, almost intimate connotation. The mention of the "killin' floor" adds a sense of danger and confrontation to these endeavors. The chorus, "I'm your furor, I'm your furor, baby," serves as a declaration of identifying as an agent of chaos and change. It suggests a confident and assertive attitude, embracing the role of being a provocateur or a catalyst for furor. The song's narrative also hints at a desire to escape and create something new, as shown in "Frame of mind, cross the line to a new state, I can shake the law, find a mine, gonna build me a new place, no knockin' door to door." This suggests a breakaway from conventional rules and the pursuit of personal freedom and autonomy. The lyrics convey a sense of defiance and a desire to shake up the established order, themes that are likely echoed in the band's energetic and forceful musical style.

"Boogie Man"

"Boogie Man" showcases the band's ability to infuse their signature rock 'n' roll sound with a bluesy flavor. The song's main riff is built upon bluesy chord progressions, injecting a raw and soulful energy into the mix. The lyrics of "Boogie Man" present a vivid portrayal of a character who embodies a mix of danger, seduction, and rebelliousness. The lines, "I'm the boogie man, yeah the boogie man. I like fine suits, smoke the best cigars. Like talkin' sex to women, girls in fast cars," establish this persona as someone who revels in luxury and a fast-paced, hedonistic lifestyle. The reference to being "under the bed ready to bite" plays into the traditional concept of the boogie man as a lurking, sinister figure, adding a layer of danger and mystery. It's clear that AC/DC uses the boogie man motif to explore themes of power, sensuality, and a certain rebellious defiance against societal norms. The song's persona revels in being an outsider and embraces a lifestyle that's both enviable and slightly dangerous. This aligns with AC/DC's broader content, which often includes a celebration of freedom, unbridled passion, and a non-conformist attitude. The song would be performed live during AC/DC's Ballbreaker World Tour, which included Angus' infamous striptease routine, which had previously been part of "Bad Boy Boogie," "Jailbreak," and "Baby Please Don't Go" in prior years.

"The Honey Roll"

"The Honey Roll" starts off with a boogie-inspired riff that transforms into a swaggering rhythm with a foot-tapping groove. The song showcases AC/DC's cheeky lyrical approach, focusing on themes of seduction and indulgence. "The Honey Roll," with its visceral and evocative lyrics, encapsulates the raw, unapologetic energy characteristic of AC/DC's style. The song's lighthearted and mischievous tone adds to its charm and makes it a delightfully fun addition to the band's discography. The songs opening lines, "Honey roll over and lettuce on top. Strap you to the bed and make you rock. Run it up the flag, send it on home. Push you to the wall and make you moan," set a tone that exemplifies a raw, unapologetic expression of sexuality. This theme of primal, unrestrained desire is a common thread in many of AC/DC's songs, reflecting their straightforward approach to rock music. The lyrics playfully flirt with innuendo and celebration of the rock 'n' roll lifestyle, painting a vivid picture of late-night escapades and enticing encounters. The lyrics employ direct, uncomplicated language, a hallmark of AC/DC's songwriting.

Phrases like "Run it up the flag, send it on home" and "Push you to the wall and make you moan" are less about nuanced storytelling and more about creating a visceral, sexual experience. This approach aligns with the band's overarching ethos of delivering straightforward, hard-hitting rock music. The song's lighthearted and mischievous tone adds to its charm and makes it a fun addition to AC/DC's catalog. The repeated chorus lines, "She's mine, take what I want, get what I need, don't take it all," emphasize a possessive and hedonistic attitude, resonating with the band's rebellious and carefree image. The song's structure, revolving around these bold, repetitive choruses, is designed to be catchy and memorable, making it a staple in live performances. "The Honey Roll" captures the essence of the band's appeal—a no-frills, electrifying brand of rock that focuses on the fundamental elements of rhythm, energy, and attitude.

"Burnin' Alive"

"Burnin' Alive" is a powerful track from *Ballbreaker* with a fantastic riff that starts off the song and builds up momentum. The song was inspired by the cult followers in Waco, Texas, who all died in a fire during a raid in 1993. "Burnin' Alive" is a song with lyrics that are intense and filled with vivid imagery, encapsulating themes of chaos, rebellion, and the inevitability of change or destruction. Quite different than most of the band's other songs lyrically, this song explores different themes than the typical AC/DC topics of sex, non-conformity, and living life to the fullest. The repeated lines, "Burnin' alive, burnin' alive, It's an all-out war, an all-out war, Burnin' alive, Burnin' alive," set a tone of relentless energy and a sense of being engulfed in a powerful force beyond control. This could be interpreted as a metaphor for personal struggles, societal upheaval, or even the raw energy of rock music itself. The clever lyrics, "No firewater or Novocain, no thunderstorm, no John Wayne, no kids to rock, nowhere to run, so watch out 'cause this place is gonna burn," suggest a situation devoid of relief or escape. The absence of "firewater" (alcohol) or "Novocain" (pain relief), combined with cultural icons like John Wayne, point to a setting where traditional means of solace or heroism are absent. This creates an atmosphere of impending doom and highlights a stark, unvarnished reality. Additionally, the mention of a "little town called Hope" and the line "And someday maybe it'll go up in smoke" introduces a sense of irony. The contrast of hope with the inevitability of destruction further intensifies the song's theme of unavoidable change and the transient nature of safety and stability. "Burnin' Alive" is representative of AC/DC's ability to create a powerful narrative through their music, combining high-energy rock with lyrics that evoke strong imagery and provoke thought about the nature of struggle, change, and the societal issues. While the song may not be as well-known as some of AC/DC's more commercially successful songs, "Burnin' Alive" is truly a hidden gem within their discography and one of my favorites from *Ballbreaker*.

"Hail Caesar"

"Hail Caesar," the third single released from *Ballbreaker*, is a song that showcases the band's ability to fuse their hard-hitting rock sound with historical themes. Inspired by Angus Young's interest in history, the song pays tribute to the mighty Roman empire and its iconic leader, Julius Caesar. The production captures the raw power of the band's performance, ensuring that each instrument has its place in the mix. The lyrics of "Hail Caesar" are rich in historical and metaphorical imagery, blending elements of ancient Roman culture with contemporary expressions of power and rebellion. The chorus, "All hail Caesar hail hail! All hail Caesar hail hail!" is a direct allusion to the Roman tradition of saluting the emperor, symbolizing the recognition and submission to a supreme authority. This refrain is interspersed with vivid scenes during the breakdown like "Swinging in the chariot, around and around we go, the senators rehearse the tale," which evoke the grandeur and spectacle of Roman political and military power. Furthermore, the song includes references to iconic figures and events, as in "He be the count of Monte Cristo, could be a quake any day, maybe somebody from Siam, Begin the era of a new rage." These lines draw on a range of historical and literary allusions, from Alexandre Dumas' adventurous character to seismic shifts (both literal and metaphorical), indicating sudden and significant changes in power dynamics or societal structures. The mention of "Siam" (modern-day Thailand) adds an element of global awareness, suggesting that change and revolution can arise from any corner of the world. The song's narrative also delves into themes of betrayal and the fickleness of fame and power: "Instead of sending to the lions, they cover him with praise, all hail Caesar ... down at the epicenter, things started heatin' up, rockin' on the Richter scale." This portrays a character who, instead of being thrown to the lions (a fate of many in Roman arenas), is celebrated, only to experience the volatile nature of such acclaim, akin to the unpredictable shaking of an earthquake. "Hail Caesar" is a powerful example of AC/DC's skill in weaving historical references into their music, using them to comment on modern themes of power, authority, and the ever-present potential for sudden, dramatic change in society. The song captures the essence of AC/DC's robust and rebellious spirit, paying homage to the past while speaking to contemporary issues. The song would also be performed live during the Ballbreaker World Tour.

"Love Bomb"

"Love Bomb" is a track characterized by AC/DC's high-energy, metaphorical language that combines themes of love and destruction in a typically bold and provocative manner. The song exemplifies AC/DC's signature style of blending rock 'n' roll music with bold and vivid lyrics that evoke strong, raw emotions and a sense of untamed spirit. The song is a celebration of sexuality, likened to a bomb's force, capturing the essence of passion in a uniquely energetic and powerful way and is yet another song with direct metaphors of the male anatomy. The lyrics, "crusin' the sky let's fly, blowin' all day and night, open your bays and drop those bombs away," further intensify this metaphor, suggesting a reckless, carefree dive into the throes of passion. The imagery of cruising the sky and dropping bombs could be seen as a representation of a high-octane, adventurous approach to love and relationships, typical of AC/DC's thematic style. The chorus, "Love bomb, love bomber, don't scare no bother, where the size doesn't matter, come long short or badder," employs the metaphor of a "love bomb" to express a powerful, explosive form of love or attraction or the more direct male sex organ reference. The tongue-in-check track is a fun and humorous addition to AC/DC's catalog, with the expected sexual innuendoes found throughout their discography.

"Caught with Your Pants Down"

"Caught With Your Pants Down," like many AC/DC tracks, celebrates a carefree and rebellious spirit, with an emphasis on the excitement and unpredictability of rock 'n' roll lifestyle. The track features a fast-paced riff and driving rhythm section. Brian Johnson's vocals are delivered with a devilish charm, perfectly capturing the cheeky and mischievous tone of the lyrics. The lyrics encapsulate a moment of unbridled passion and the thrill of living on the edge, consistent with the band's overarching themes of freedom, boldness, and living in the moment. The lyrics of "Caught with Your Pants Down" carry the band's characteristic style of bold and suggestive rock 'n' roll. The repeated chorus, "Caught with your pants down!" is a straightforward expression of being found in a compromising or unexpected situation, likely with a humorous or cheeky undertone. This phrase is commonly used to describe being caught off-guard, often in a somewhat embarrassing scenario, and the song seems to play with this idea in a playful and risqué manner. The lines "She take 'em down, down, down, she rip off her stockin's when the place start rockin'," suggest a scenario of uninhibited, perhaps impromptu passion. The imagery of a woman taking control ("She was a woman with a mission stick it in your face") and the energetic setting ("when the place started rockin'") portray a scene of spontaneous and wild behavior, which is a recurring theme in AC/DC's music.

"Whiskey on the Rocks"

"Whiskey on the Rocks," the B-side to the "Hail Caesar" single, paints a vivid picture of indulgence and revelry, centered around the theme of drinking whiskey. The song has a fantastic sounding signature guitar riff, showcasing masterful interplay between brothers Angus and Malcolm Young. Personally, the song is one of my favorites from the album. The song is a classic sounding AC/DC track that celebrates the joy of drinking and the freedom that comes with letting loose and enjoying the moment, reminiscent to "Have a Drink on Me" from *Back in Black* fifteen years prior. The song's focus on whiskey as a symbol of pleasure and indulgence is consistent with the band's broader themes of living life on one's own terms and embracing the raw, unfiltered experiences life has to offer. The lyrics of "Whiskey on the Rocks" paint a vivid picture of indulgence and revelry, centered around the theme of drinking whiskey. It's a celebration of letting loose and embracing the pleasures of life, with whiskey serving as the elixir of choice. The lines, "It's on the house mac it's whiskey galore, we drink a lot that demon drop, this one's on me, here's mud in your eye, whiskey on the rocks, a double or a shot, whiskey on the rocks, elixir from the top," depict a scene of uninhibited enjoyment and a carefree attitude towards life's pleasures. The repetition of the phrase "Whiskey on the rocks, a double or a shot," emphasizes the song's focus on drinking and the enjoyment it brings. This could be seen as a celebration of the simple pleasures in life, particularly those found in a glass of whiskey. The phrase "elixir from the top" suggests that the whiskey being consumed is of high quality, adding to the theme of indulgence and luxury. The casual tone and the encouragement to "throw seven sheets to the wind" further underline the song's theme of letting go of worries and immersing oneself in the moment. This sentiment is characteristic of AC/DC's music, which often revolves around themes of living life to the fullest, embracing the present, and enjoying the pleasures life has to offer without overthinking the consequences.

"Ballbreaker"

Another favorite track of mine, the hard-hitting title track and album closer, "Ballbreaker," is a tour de force of powerful hard rock that showcases the band's enduring ability to deliver relentless energy and gritty intensity. The song combines raw energy with vivid, provocative imagery, centering around themes of intense physical encounters and assertive, powerful femininity. The song was another from the album that was performed live during the Ballbreaker World Tour. The lyrics are characterized by a straightforward, unapologetic tone that is typical of the band's style. The song opens with "Breakin' balls, bangin' walls, work hard and tough, and I want some rough," immediately setting a tone of hard-hitting, no-holds-barred energy. The imagery is suggestive and aggressive, painting a picture of intense physicality and unrefined power. Throughout the song, there are references to a dominant female figure, as illustrated in lines like "She open her overcoat, livin' out her dreams, rippin' off my jeans." This character is portrayed as commanding and in control, challenging traditional gender roles and expectations. The repeated line "You are a ballbreaker" emphasizes this aspect, using the term "ballbreaker" to denote someone who is formidable and unyielding. The lyrics also convey a sense of exhilaration and danger in the interactions between the narrator and the female figure. Phrases like "Her hand went for my throat, as I began to choke" and "Honey shoot your load" suggest a raw, primal encounter that blurs the lines between pleasure and aggression. The chorus, repeated multiple times throughout the song, reinforces the central theme and the character's powerful presence. The simple, direct repetition of "Ballbreaker" serves as a chant-like tribute to the dominating force represented by the female character. Musically, the song features AC/DC's signature hard rock sound, with driving guitar riffs and a pounding rhythm section that complements the song's aggressive and energetic tone. "Ballbreaker" is a song about raw, unbridled encounters and a celebration of powerful femininity. It captures the essence of physicality, dominance, and the exhilarating interplay of power dynamics, all set against the backdrop of AC/DC's high-octane rock style. The song encapsulates the essence of AC/DC's unmistakable sound and is a testament to AC/DC's infinite endurance in rock music.

Interesting Facts

Marvel Comics contributed to the *Ballbreaker* inner sleeve artwork of the album.

15

Stiff Upper Lip

Release date:	February 28, 2000 (U.K.)
	February 28, 2000 (U.S.)
Current edition:	Sony/ Columbia, CD, LP
Personnel:	Brian Johnson, lead vocals
	Angus Young, lead guitar
	Malcolm Young, rhythm guitar
	Cliff Williams, bass guitar
	Phil Rudd, drums
Duration:	46:57
Recorded at:	The Warehouse Studios, Vancouver, BC, Canada
Produced by:	George Young
Chart position:	#3 Australian Albums
	#12 U.K. Albums
	#7 U.S. *Billboard* 200

Notable info: This was the final AC/DC album produced by George Young. *Stiff Upper Lip* is certified platinum in the USA, 3x platinum in Australia, with multiple platinum and gold certifications in other countries.

On 2000's *Stiff Upper Lip* album, AC/DC returns to their roots not only in their songwriting but with the return of producer and elder brother of Angus and Malcolm, George Young. Absent was Harry Vanda, George's long-time production partner, but the result was a very well-written, blues-driven hard rock release by AC/DC making it one of their strongest albums in over a decade. The creation of *Stiff Upper Lip* began in the summer of 1997 in London and the Netherlands, with Malcolm on guitar and Angus on drums. Initially, the band had plans to work with producer Bruce Fairbairn, known for his work on *The Razors Edge* and *AC/DC Live*, but after Fairbairn's death in May 1999, they turned to George Young to complete the album. It would be the final album produced by

George before his death in 2017. Recorded and mixed at Bryan Adams' Warehouse Studios in Vancouver, Canada, from September to November 1999, the album saw a total of twelve of the eighteen total songs recorded. Bassist Cliff Williams described it as an "easy-to-record album" with Malcolm and Angus having everything prepared. Brian Johnson stated it was "the best fun I ever had in the studio" and "got back to our roots." The album was noted for delving deeper into the band's blues roots and featured a notably clean sound. An interesting detail is that Malcolm takes a rare guitar solo on the track "Can't Stand Still," while Angus contributes backing vocals on "Hold Me Back." Released on February 28, 2000, *Stiff Upper Lip* marked a triumphant continuation of the band's rock 'n' roll legacy into a new millennium. Coming off the success of *Ballbreaker*, AC/DC, led by the indefatigable brothers Angus and Malcolm Young, returned with an album that not only sustained their iconic sound but also showcased a renewed vibrancy and enthusiasm. The title track, "Stiff Upper Lip," serves as a quintessential example of the album's spirit, boasting a catchy riff that immediately harks back to the band's heyday. The album's lyrical themes touch on familiar AC/DC territory—love, lust, and the highs and lows of life on the road. Tracks like "Meltdown" and "Can't Stop Rock 'n' Roll" showcase the band's enduring ability to craft anthems that are not only musically infectious but also lyrically relatable. The album cover is notably adorned with a bronze statue of Angus Young, a motif that was also used as a prop during their tours. The three main singles released from this album were "Stiff Upper Lip," "Safe in New York City," and "Satellite Blues." A special two-disc tour edition of the album was released in Australia, New Zealand, and Europe in January 2001, which included additional live tracks and videos. AC/DC's refusal to pander to passing trends and their unwavering commitment to their distinctive sound earned them both critical acclaim and commercial success. To me, the album serves as one of AC/DC's strongest Brian-era albums since *Flick of the Switch*.

"Stiff Upper Lip"

"Stiff Upper Lip," the title track of the album, captures the essence of AC/DC's sound, blending a really awesome sounding blues-infused guitar riff with a dynamic groove that kicks off the album. The song would also be the first single to be released, the title inspired by the phrase that is traditionally associated with a display of fortitude and unemotional demeanor in the face of adversity. However, in the context of the song, it takes on a more defiant and rebellious meaning, embodying the band's trademark attitude and style. Angus Young "there's always been a bit of humor, too. Even when we started, I used to always say, 'I've got bigger lips than Jagger and I've got bigger lips than Presley when I stick them out.'" The lyrics, characterized by a straightforward and rebellious tone, reflect themes of self-assuredness and unyielding boldness, which are staples in AC/DC's musical identity. Throughout the song, there's a consistent theme of confidence and assertiveness. The lyrics "I was born with a stiff, stiff upper lip" and "I keep a stiff upper lip" emphasize an inherent and unwavering strength. This could be interpreted as a metaphor for the band's own journey and stance in the music industry, known for their steadfast commitment to their style of hard rock. The song makes use of metaphors and imagery of being predatory and assertive, as seen in lines like "Like a dog, and I howl" and "I got the teeth that'll bite you." To me, this track is a standout song from AC/DC's discography, being not only my favorite on the album, but a song that is right up there with many of AC/DC's most fan-revered songs from the very beginning.

"Meltdown"

"Meltdown" is a song that, much like many other AC/DC tracks, explores themes of intense desire and the overwhelming power of attraction. The song uses the imagery of heat and fire to depict the escalating passion and urgency in a romantic or sexual encounter. Phrases like "Man it's gettin' hot hot hot" and "It's a meltdown" suggest a situation that is becoming increasingly intense and uncontrollable, mirroring the often-overwhelming nature of physical and emotional desire. The repetitive use of the word "meltdown" serves as a central metaphor, likening the emotional and physical responses to a loss of control, akin to a nuclear meltdown. Throughout the song, there's a sense of spontaneity, as reflected in lines like "Gotta get up and climb her" and "Stokin' up the fire," which further emphasize the urgency and unbridled nature of the feelings portrayed in the song. The track in general portrays passionate desire of a woman, using imagery of heat and fire to convey the intensity, which, lyrically, stays true to the majority of AC/DC's catalog. EastWest records (AC/DC's label at the time) issued a promotional five-track CD during the Stiff Upper Lip Tour titled *Meltdown Summer Sampler*. The single featured "Meltdown" along with four live tracks.

"House of Jazz"

"House of Jazz" is a track that sets the stage with a lively and energetic tone, and which describes imagery to convey a world of excess, spectacle, and rock 'n' roll music. George Young's production expertise shines through in "House of Jazz." The track exudes a warm, vintage sound, evoking the spirit of classic rock 'n' roll. It is another song from *Stiff Upper Lip* that showcases the trademark blend of raw energy and straightforward lyricism against AC/DC's classic rock sound. The lyrics describe provocative descriptions, likely referencing the wild, unrestrained atmosphere associated with the rock and roll lifestyle. The lyrics are filled with phrases that evoke a sense of boldness and rebellion, like "Humdinger" and "Bell ringer," setting the tone for a song that's about indulgence and excess. The use of terms such as "Mud slinger" and "Gold digger" could be commentary on the darker aspects of fame and the music industry, where criticism and exploitation are common. The chorus, "Come into the house of jazz," is an invitation to enter into this world of uninhibited expression and perhaps a metaphor for the experience of rock music itself. The "house of jazz" here doesn't necessarily denote the jazz music genre but rather seems to symbolize a space of musical freedom, energy, and perhaps even chaos, much like the environment portrayed throughout AC/DC's music.

"Hold Me Back"

"Hold Me Back" is another great track from this album, which revisits AC/DC's early rock influences by the general vibe and groove of the song. The lyrics embody the band's classic themes of unbridled freedom, defiance, and a larger-than-life approach to living. This song, like many of AC/DC's tracks, celebrates an unrestrained lifestyle, filled with bold imagery and an assertion of personal power. In this song, the repeated phrase "Can't hold me back" serves as a powerful anthem of self-assertion and resistance against any form of control or limitation. This line is the core of the song's message, emphasizing the idea of being unstoppable and uncontainable. The lyrics are sprinkled with references to symbols of excess and indulgence, like a "big fat Cadillac" and a "honky tonk big ball hit to thrill," which are typical of the band's style, highlighting a life lived at full throttle. The references to a "honk that'll blow the avenue" and a "hot dog kickin' all bend my thing" contribute to this imagery of excess and boastfulness, possibly indicating a life led without concern for norms or conventions. The song also contains playful and slightly nonsensical lines like "Got a sugar looking woman with a bald-headed man," which add a sense of whimsy and irreverence. A special aspect of this track is that Angus provides backing vocals towards the later part of the song. In essence, "Hold Me Back" is a celebration of personal freedom and defiance. It's about living life on one's own terms, loudly and proudly, and resisting any attempt to be constrained. This aligns perfectly with AC/DC's characteristic musical ethos of high-energy, rebellious rock.

"Safe in New York City"

"Safe in New York City" was the second single to be released from the album, which featured the non-album B-side "Cyberspace." The track combines a sense of danger and exhilaration with a paradoxical feeling of safety within the bustling environment of New York City. This is further emphasized by the raw energy of the music, which portrays the fast-paced lifestyle of the city, aligning with the band's characteristic hard rock style. The song portrays the city as a place of wild, unrestrained energy, encapsulated in the vivid nightlife and the frenetic pace of urban life ("Don't mess with this place, it will eat you alive"). The repeated chorus, "I feel safe in New York City," serves as an ironic statement, given the city's reputation for hustle, bustle, and occasional peril. This repetition creates a powerful and somewhat contradictory image of finding comfort in the midst of chaos and unpredictability. The lyrics also touch upon themes of adventure and sexual experiences, as seen in lines like "Need a little rockin' in my big limousine" and "Got a lip-smacking honey to suck off the jam." The descriptions of the city and its various characters, from the "thing in the tight-assed jeans" to the lively depiction of the city's dive bars, paint New York as a vibrant, living entity. This portrayal aligns with the song's underlying theme of vitality and living life to the fullest in the face of potential danger. The verses of the song paint a picture of indulgence and excess, with references to nightlife, luxury, and a sense of invincibility. I've thought perhaps Angus wrote the song about New York allowing him to otherwise "blend in with the noise" of the populated city and crowded fast-paced streets, without being instantly recognized. The closing line, "I feel safe in a cage in New York City, throw away the key," adds an intriguing twist to the song, which might suggest that true safety is found in being removed from the chaos.

"Can't Stand Still"

Another track from the album that revisits AC/DC's early rock music influences is "Can't Stand Still." The song is a lively and exuberant track that captures the essence of restlessness and the pursuit of pleasure. The lyrics convey a sense of living in the moment, seizing opportunities for joy and pleasure whenever they arise. The opening lines about seeing a pretty woman and getting a thrill suggest an immediate and powerful attraction. The phrase "tailor made to order" implies that the woman fits the ideal qualities, sparking an intense reaction ("you know I can't stand still"). The lyrics are straightforward and focus on the theme of being constantly in motion, whether it's in response to attraction, enjoyment, or the simple thrill of living life to the fullest. The repeated line, "You know I can't stand still," serves as a mantra, emphasizing an insatiable appetite for excitement and action. The song speaks to the allure of attractive women, the joy of parties, and the pleasures of indulgence (like "sippin' honey"). These elements are not just sources of enjoyment but catalysts for restless energy. The imagery of "dancin' on the water" further adds a sense of dynamic, almost reckless abandon, portraying a character who is irresistibly drawn to life's temptations and joys. Musically, the energy of the song aligns with its themes. The rhythm and pace mirror the restless, unstoppable groove described in the lyrics. In essence, "Can't Stand Still" is a celebration of unbridled joy and the relentless pursuit of what makes one feel alive, encapsulated in a high-energy, rock-driven soundtrack that is quintessentially AC/DC. One great aspect about this track is that Brian Johnson was able to record the entire vocal track of the song in a single take, which was captured at the very end of the song, with the applause and Brian saying, "Thank you lads, thank you lads." The song's overall tone is one of exuberance and a zest for life and is a song that celebrates an unbridled love for life, expressed through a restless pursuit of pleasure, attraction, and social engagement.

"Can't Stop Rock 'n' Roll"

"Can't Stop Rock 'n' Roll" is a song that celebrates the enduring power and spirit of rock music. It has been a while since AC/DC's last rock anthem, which I believe is what they were shooting for with this track. The straightforward lyrics are an assertive declaration that rock 'n' roll, as a genre and a movement, cannot be silenced or halted, regardless of external factors or opinions. The song opens with a rejection of dishonesty and pretense, as indicated by lines like "Don't you give me no line" and

"Don't you play me no jive." This could be interpreted as a metaphor for the authenticity that rock 'n' roll represents, contrasting with what the band perceives as superficiality or inauthenticity in other aspects of life or music. The chorus, "You can't stop rock 'n' roll," is a straightforward and powerful message. It's both a celebration of the genre's longevity and a battle cry against any forces that seek to diminish its impact or presence. The repetitive nature of this chorus emphasizes the unyielding and unstoppable character of rock music. The song's simplicity in lyrics, with its repetitive chorus and straightforward verses reinforces the song's message, making it both an anthem and a declaration of the timeless power of rock 'n' roll. "Can't Stop Rock 'n' Roll" is a tribute to the enduring spirit of rock music, asserting its continual relevance and impact in the face of changing musical landscapes and trends.

"Satellite Blues"

As the third single from AC/DC's *Stiff Upper Lip*, "Satellite Blues" was released the following year (January 2001) during the Stiff Upper Lip World Tour. The song melds themes of technology and human desire with a classic rock 'n' roll energy. The lyrics metaphorically use the imagery of satellite and television technology to express feelings of attraction and excitement. The song opens with vivid descriptions of a woman's captivating movements, likened to the dynamism of a live performance, and this energy is compared to the excitement generated by new technology, specifically the "new satellite blues." The repeated chorus, "New satellite blues," symbolizes both the fascination and the frustration that come with technological advances. On one hand, the satellite represents a connection to something thrilling and new, much like the woman's allure in the song. On the other hand, the term "blues" traditionally signifies a feeling of melancholy or frustration, which in this context could reflect the overwhelming or unsatisfying nature of constant media and technological bombardment. References to the satellite dish running hot and the box set for pumping suggest an overload of information and stimuli, paralleling the intense attraction being felt. The line "Can't get nothin' on the dial, The frickin' thing gone wild" further indicates a sense of being overwhelmed or lost in the torrent of technology and information. The song uses vivid imagery and clever wordplay to create a song that's not just about physical attraction, but also comments on the overwhelming nature of modern media and technology. It captures the essence of being captivated by something (or someone) that is simultaneously exhilarating and overpowering.

"Damned"

"Damned" is a powerful expression of the conflict between individuality and authoritarian control, likely related to military enlistment by the references found in the lyrics. The song features a classic AC/DC guitar riff and crisp production. The lyrics portray a scenario where the individual is subjected to strict rules and regulations, likely representing a metaphor for any system of control, whether it be military, institutional, or societal. The repeated phrase "I'll be damned" reflects a defiant stance against these constraints. The song starts with a series of prohibitions ("Don't smoke don't fight don't light no cigarettes, or you'll wind up in the can"), setting a tone of strict control and prohibition, suggesting a situation where personal freedom is heavily restricted. The reference to being a "guest of Uncle Sam" hints at a military or governmental context, where obedience and conformity are demanded. The chorus, "I'll be damned if I drink or smoke, Damned if I steal your joke," and similar lines, illustrate the paradox of trying to conform to strict standards. The phrase "damned if I do, damned if I don't" captures the sense of inescapability and the feeling of being judged or penalized regardless of one's actions, essentially a catch-22 situation. The song's tone is one of irony and defiance, acknowledging the absurdity of the situation they are in, where every action seems to lead to condemnation. Despite the oppressive environment described, the song carries an undercurrent of rebellion. Overall, this track is a powerful expression of the conflict between individuality and authoritarian control, much like many AC/DC songs over the years that celebrate individual freedom.

"Come and Get It"

"Come and Get It" is a straightforward track that portrays seeking pleasure without restraint or apology and living life on one's own terms. The song's narrative revolves around indulging in life's "finer things," whether that's fast cars, nightlife, or sexual encounters. The song's opening lines ("Picking up the sleaze in my car, Hell no distance too far") suggest a determined pursuit of pleasure, regardless of the effort or distance involved. The repeated line "If you want it come and get it" serves as a bold invitation, embodying a carefree and assertive attitude towards fulfilling one's desires. The references to driving "Hell no distance too far" and "burning down the road in the night" suggest a relentless pursuit of excitement and pleasure, unbound by limitations or conventions. References to drinking ("Suckin' up the juice in the bar, downin' every shooter so far") and sexual encounters

("I've got my filly wrapped in red, upon my double decker bed") portray a lifestyle of indulgence and sensual pleasures. This song also speaks to the idea of living life on one's own terms, without concern for societal norms or expectations. The lines "These are the finer things in life, don't think you live in paradise" imply a contrast between the uninhibited pursuit of pleasure and a more conventional, restrained approach to life. This also might be ironic, contrasting the conventional idea of the "finer things" with the raw and possibly debaucherous scenes described in the song. Musically, the energetic and driving rhythm of the song complements its themes, embodying the spirit of rock 'n' roll as a symbol of freedom and rebellion. In essence, "Come and Get It" is a celebration of hedonistic pleasure, characterized by a direct and uncompromising approach to satisfying one's desires, which is a hallmark of AC/DC's music style and lyrics.

"All Screwed Up"

"All Screwed Up" is a great, rocking track that deals with themes of confrontation, frustration, and the chaotic nature of certain relationships. The lyrics paint a picture of situations that are tumultuous and problematic, characterized by a lack of clarity, betrayal, and a sense of disillusionment. The song's straightforward and raw style effectively conveys the emotional intensity of these themes. The repeated line "It's all screwed up" suggests a sense of frustration or disappointment, potentially in a relationship or interaction that has gone awry. The song portrays a scenario where toughness and roughness are met with challenges and disappointments. Lines like "You think you're kinda tough, you're walkin' kinda rough" and "Take you out to kick some butt, work you over, screw you nuts" suggest a confrontational or aggressive approach to life. However, this approach does not seem to yield positive results, as indicated by the outcomes described in the song ("Then you're out of luck," "Then she pushed you out the door"). Musically, the song's driving rhythm and hard rock sound reinforce the themes of chaos and frustration. "All Screwed Up" is thus a reflection of life's messier, more tumultuous side, capturing the essence of feeling overwhelmed and outmatched in a world that often seems disordered and unruly.

"Give It Up"

"Give It Up," the closing track from the album, serves as a thunderous finale to this fine album. The song kicks off with a grooving drum beat and has an energetic, rebellious vibe, encapsulating themes of defiance and liberation. The lyrics convey a message of breaking free from constraints and living life on one's own terms—again, much like many of AC/DC's songs throughout their discography. The phrase "Give it up" is repeated throughout the song, but instead of implying surrender, it seems to champion the idea of letting go of inhibitions and embracing a more unrestrained way of living. The song opens with a declaration against conflict and ambiguity ("Well there be no words of fighting around here, 'cause I have no manners, 'cause it ain't clear"). This sets the stage for a narrative that rejects the conventional or the expected. The lines about the storm and the inability to be stopped ("Well there's a big storm a howlin' around here, there be no one to sinning, and no beer") further emphasize this theme of unstoppable force and determination. The lyrics also suggest a celebration of the present moment and indulgence in life's pleasures ("I'm going crazy on a wedding night; take your pick of anything you like"). Musically, the song's driving beat and rhythmic intensity complement its themes, adding to the overall sense of urgency and dynamism. The overall tone of the song combines assertiveness with a sense of playfulness and enjoyment: "I'm ready to rock, yeah I'm gonna whip it, ready to rock, yea I'm gonna stick it." It reflects an attitude of confidently facing challenges while also embracing the joys and pleasures of life. "Give It Up" embodies a spirit of defiance and liberation, emphasizing themes of defiance, determination, and a call to action or change.

Interesting Facts

The *Stiff Upper Lip* album cover featured a bronzed statue of Angus, which would become part of AC/DC's live stage show during the tour, complete with glowing eyes and spewing smoke. During the tour, a video reel was run at the beginning of each show that brought the Angus statue to life in a chaotic, yet humorous scenario as the giant Angus statue stomped around the city, wreaking havoc and destruction.

16

Black Ice

Release date:	October 17, 2008 (U.K.)
	October 20, 2008 (U.S.)
Current edition:	Sony/ Columbia, CD, LP
Personnel:	Brian Johnson, lead vocals
	Angus Young, lead guitar
	Malcolm Young, rhythm guitar
	Cliff Williams, bass guitar
	Phil Rudd, drums
Duration:	55:38
Recorded at:	The Warehouse Studios, Vancouver, BC, Canada
Produced by:	Brendan O'Brien
Chart position:	#1 Australian Albums
	#1 U.K. Albums
	#1 U.S. *Billboard* 200

Notable info: *Black Ice* reached #1 in twenty-nine countries, making it the Columbia Records' biggest charting album to date. This would be the final album featuring Malcolm Young on rhythm guitar. *Black Ice* is certified 2x platinum in the USA, 5x platinum in Australia, 5x platinum in Germany, 4x platinum in Switzerland, 4x platinum in Denmark, 3x platinum in Austria, with multiple multi-platinum, platinum, and gold certifications in several other countries.

After an eight-year-long hiatus, AC/DC delivered *Black Ice*, their fifteenth studio album on October 20, 2008. It was unfortunately an extremely long wait since 2000's *Stiff Upper Lip* and was allegedly due to certain health issues with both Malcolm and Cliff, which contributed to the delays. Although the wait was extremely long, it was well worth the wait. Produced by Brendan O'Brien, *Black Ice* is a pure rock 'n' roll release that combines the band's trademark thunderous riffs with a contemporary energy. The album consisted of fifteen tracks, which was the most songs released on an AC/DC studio album to date. The recording process mostly involved live studio recordings, with minimal overdubs and effects used to maintain the authenticity of the tracks. The album kicks off with the hard-hitting "Rock 'n' Roll Train," the first single from the album and a track that immediately sets the tone for the rest of the record. Tracks like "Big Jack," "War Machine," and "Black Ice" showcase the band's ability to craft songs that resonate with both longtime fans and a new generation of listeners. *Black Ice* not only marked a musical resurgence for AC/DC but also held historical significance as the final studio album to feature rhythm guitarist and founder Malcolm Young. His contributions to the album, especially in crafting the album's solid foundation with his unmistakable rhythm guitar work, underscored the profound impact he had on AC/DC's sound. The album stands as a poignant tribute to Malcolm Young's enduring legacy within the band and to AC/DC's signature guitar tone and sound. The release was supported by an extensive marketing campaign, which included displays of AC/DC memorabilia and in North America was released exclusively through Walmart. Upon its release, *Black Ice* catapulted to #1 in twenty-nine countries around the world and quickly rose to platinum sales status, marking AC/DC's triumphant return to the top of the charts as the world's most dominating force in rock music. The album distributed over 6 million copies by December that year. Naysayers in the music industry who were publicly decrying that rock music was dead were quickly proven wrong by AC/DC's world domination of the charts. The track "War Machine" won the Best Hard Rock Performance category at the Grammys and was also nominated for many other awards, including Brit, Juno, and ARIA music awards. The Black Ice World Tour was AC/DC's most successful, grossing $441.6 million and becoming the second highest-grossing concert tour of all time as of that year. Three concerts from this tour in Buenos Aires were released as the DVD *Live at River Plate* in 2011. The album was also Columbia Records' biggest debut album since Nielsen SoundScan began tracking sales data for *Billboard* in 1991 and was the second best-selling album worldwide in 2008. *Black Ice* not only solidified AC/DC's reputation as timeless legends of rock music but would later become a farewell to their founding member Malcolm Young, who would pass away three years later.

"Rock 'n' Roll Train"

Originally titled "Runaway Train," which was also the original intention for the album title, the song later morphed to "Rock 'n' Roll Train" and would be the first single from *Black Ice*. The track opens with the unmistakable trademark guitar tone of Angus Young, who is then joined by Malcolm and the rest of the band. Overall, "Rock 'n' Roll Train" stays true to AC/DC's style—straightforward, high-energy, guitar-driven rock 'n' roll. The lyrics embody the spirit of rock 'n' roll rebellion and the pursuit of freedom along with sexual innuendos typical of many AC/DC songs: "One hot southern belle, son of a devil, a school boy's spelling bee, a school girl with a fantasy." The recurring phrase "Runaway train (Running right off the track)" serves as a powerful metaphor for uncontrolled, wild freedom, which is a consistent theme with many AC/DC tracks over the years. The chorus is instantly memorable, with catchy lines like "Running right off the track" making it the perfect lead-off single from the album that would ultimately re-crown AC/DC as the biggest band in the world. On the Black Ice World Tour, the song would be the opening track in the set list and would feature a gigantic train that would crash out onto the stage. The single was also issued on both 7-inch vinyl and CD formats, with "War Machine" as the B-side.

"Skies on Fire"

The song kicks off with a thunderous drumbeat, courtesy of Phil Rudd, setting the tone for the high-energy guitars of Angus and Malcolm. The lyrics are relatively simple and direct, a common trait in AC/DC's songs. Brian Johnson's vocals are nothing short of electric. His signature gravelly voice cuts through the mix, delivering the lyrics with raw power and intensity. The chorus, "Skies on fire, Flames burn higher," can be interpreted as a metaphor for intense, possibly destructive emotions or situations, the imagery of a sky ablaze could symbolize turmoil, passion, or even a sense of impending doom, which coincides with the sound of the music of this track. Overall, "Skies on Fire" seems to revolve around themes of upheaval, change, and the dynamics of a relationship or personal interaction. The song, like many of AC/DC's songs, focuses more on creating a mood and invoking imagery rather than telling a detailed narrative. The straightforward and repetitive nature of the lyrics, combined with the band's signature hard rock sounding musical style, makes the song an embodiment of their rock ethos—direct, impactful, and emotionally charged.

"Big Jack"

True to AC/DC's signature style of straightforward rock 'n' roll, "Big Jack," the second single from *Black Ice*, revolves around a character by the name of "Big Jack" who is portrayed as a hard-working, hard-living, and somewhat rogue figure. The fellow is portrayed as a possibly blue-collar or working-class hero who is dedicated and industrious. References to his reputation and behavior, such as "Always into trouble, got to turn the other way" and "Always likes to party and he likes the girls to play," suggest a typical rock 'n' roll lifestyle—one filled with parties, women, and perhaps a penchant for getting into trouble. This portrayal fits the archetype of a rock star or a rebel, which is central to many of AC/DC's songs. The chorus, with lines like "Big Jack, Big Jack, you know it's only natural, he gets you up to scratch" and "Big Jack, look out Jack, He's always at your back," indicates that Big Jack is a formidable, influential presence. The phrase "gets you up to scratch" could imply that he brings out the best in others or stirs things up, adding excitement or intensity to situations. "Big Jack" is a classic-sounding AC/DC song that celebrates a larger-than-life character living on his own terms. The lyrics are filled with machismo and a sense of invincibility, embodying the spirit of rock 'n' roll. The song doesn't delve into deep storytelling but instead focuses on creating a vivid picture of a charismatic and unapologetic individual.

"Anything Goes"

"Anything Goes," the third single from *Black Ice*, is fairly out of the ordinary when it comes to AC/DC's catalog; the track has a very commercial sound to it, although it still keeps the band's straightforward rock style. The lyrics focus on themes of freedom, desire, temptation, and the typical rock 'n' roll lifestyle. The opening lines, "Got a taste of a rocking band, standing there holding out your hand," immediately set the scene in a rock concert environment. This imagery is quintessential AC/DC, celebrating the energy and excitement of live rock music. The song seems to center around a female character, described with phrases like "She is like a spinning dynamo," suggesting that she is full of energy, unstoppable, and perhaps a bit unpredictable. The character could symbolize the wild spirit of rock 'n' roll itself—powerful, unrestrained, and captivating. The repeated chorus, "There she goes she goes, and nobody knows, where she goes, she goes," emphasizes the mysterious and free-spirited nature of this woman. The idea that "nobody knows" where she goes adds an element of mystery and independence, highlighting a lifestyle that defies convention and predictability. "Anything Goes" is about the excitement and unpredictability of the rock 'n' roll world, embodied by a charismatic female figure. The lyrics are less about telling a detailed story and more about creating an atmosphere that captures the essence of the rock music scene—dynamic, loud, and thrilling. The production on "Anything Goes" is polished, allowing each instrument to shine through while maintaining the energy that defines AC/DC's signature sound. The mix is well-balanced, capturing the nuances of the guitars, the pounding rhythm section, and Brian Johnson's vocals.

"War Machine"

Right from the get-go, "War Machine" kicks off with AC/DC's signature, unmistakable guitar tone with a great riff and foot-stomping beat. Much like other AC/DC songs, the track revolves around themes of power, aggression, and defiance. The repeated chorus, "War machine (war machine)," is a powerful metaphor, possibly representing an unstoppable force or an entity that thrives in aggressive situations. This could be a metaphor for the band itself, known for its powerful and relentless style, or it could symbolize a person who embodies similar qualities of strength and aggression. Brian Johnson's commanding presence and delivery make you feel like you're on the front lines of a musical battlefield. The lines "Push your foot to the floor, don't need no more, you've been kickin' all around, while you're messin' about" suggest a sense of urgency and unbridled energy. This could be interpreted as living life with intensity, a common theme in rock music that celebrates the idea of living fully and fiercely. "War Machine" would be part of the set list during the Black Ice World Tour and was accompanied by an animated AC/DC-themed video during the performance of the song.

"Smash 'n' Grab"

"Smash 'n' Grab" is another track from *Black Ice* that is a straightforward, hard rocker with a no-nonsense lyrical approach. Lyrically, "Smash 'n' Grab" embodies the wild and carefree nature of rock 'n' roll. The song captures the spirit of seizing the moment and embracing the thrill of the rock 'n' roll lifestyle. The song, like many in AC/DC's catalog, is steeped in the themes of rebelliousness, raw energy, and where the pursuit of immediate gratification and living life on one's own terms is often glorified. The references to "steal the money" and "shoot 'em right down" are more metaphorical than literal, embodying the band's trademark rebellious spirit. It's about challenging the status quo and taking what one believes they deserve, albeit not through actual violence or theft, but through a metaphorical smashing of barriers and grabbing of opportunities. Overall, "Smash 'n' Grab" sticks to the band's formula of hard-hitting, high-energy rock with themes of challenging the status quo.

"Spoilin' for a Fight"

Another otherwise straightforward rocker, "Spoilin' for a Fight" is a song that epitomizes the band's hard-edged, rock 'n' roll style. The song is infused with themes of confrontation, determination, and a raw, unyielding energy that has been a hallmark of AC/DC's music. "Spoilin' for a Fight" encapsulates the exhilarating thrill of embracing conflict and standing up for what you believe in. The lyrics paint a picture of defiance and determination, with lines like "Spoilin' for a fight, trying to make it right." The opening line, "I see trouble coming man," sets the tone for the entire song. It suggests a premonition of conflict or challenges ahead, but instead of avoiding it, Brian seems to embrace this impending trouble with a kind of rugged enthusiasm. The song reflects the mindset of being unafraid to face challenges head-on and living a life on the edge. The line "You better stand your ground, and keep out of my town" adds a territorial aspect to the song, perhaps reflecting the band's own journey and struggles in the music industry.

"Wheels"

"Wheels" is likely a nod to Brian Johnson's passion for car racing, but with lyrics that focus around an attractive and perhaps dangerous woman through the use of metaphors. The song is a high-adrenaline rock track that creates visuals of a high-speed pursuit. The lyrics "Flyin' down the road, ready to explode" and "Burnin' down the road, hitting overload" depict a high-energy, intense scenario, almost akin to a high-speed chase. The recurring use of "Wheels" as a metaphor is central to the song. Wheels are described as "Spinnin' around my brain, driving you insane," and "Rolling 'round my head, going through the red," creating a sense of uncontrollable motion and perhaps the chaotic, overwhelming nature of the rock 'n' roll lifestyle or a tumultuous relationship. The song uses references of spinning wheels to convey themes of risk, intensity, and the overwhelming nature of certain experiences or relationships.

"Decibel"

"Decibel" is essentially a lyrical tribute to the raw power and energy of rock 'n' roll music. The song employs a straightforward structure to emphasize its central theme—the sheer force of rock music, embodied in the concept of decibels, a measure of sound intensity. The lyrics portray a carefree, energetic atmosphere: "Take up all your time, kick up your heels, lookin' fine." This introduction sets the stage for a narrative that is both exuberant and rebellious, consistent with AC/DC's signature style. The lines "You come riding blind, you come rollin' back a while" could signify an immersion in the moment, typical of rock 'n' roll culture's emphasis on living in the present. Central to the song is the chorus "Decibel, decibel," which is not just a repeated word but a symbol. Decibels here represent the loudness and the raw, unadulterated nature of rock music. "Decibel" is a homage to the spirit of rock 'n' roll. It's about the sound, the intensity, and the communal experience of music. AC/DC uses straightforward, yet powerful lyrics to convey a message that is at the heart of their music—a celebration of the unyielding and passionate nature of rock 'n' roll, which essentially is what AC/DC is all about.

"Stormy May Day"

"Stormy May Day" stands out as a unique and captivating track on *Black Ice*. What sets this song apart is the introduction of slide guitar, a rare and unexpected addition courtesy of Angus Young. The song uses vivid meteorological imagery to convey a sense of impending danger and chaos. The lyrics paint a picture of a severe storm, using this as a metaphor to explore themes of turmoil and distress. The opening lines, "The storm is raging, winds are howling," immediately set a tone of unrest and turbulence. The phrase "The water's calling, rescue you" suggests a search for salvation or escape in times of trouble. One could almost wonder if lyrically this song was referencing some of the health-related issues faced by Malcolm Young at the time. Lightning and thunder are recurring motifs in the song, symbolizing moments of intense, possibly frightening change. Phrases like "A flash of lightning, a times a frightening" and "A clap of thunder, a split us under" evoke the sudden and disruptive nature of life's challenges. "Mayday" is an international distress signal, which, coupled with "stormy rain day," emphasizes the sense of crisis. It's not just a description of bad weather but a call for help in a dire situation. The lyrics also touch on the communal aspect of facing hardships: "A call for help you hope they get you through." Towards the end, "The sky is darkening, the dogs are barking" further adds to the ominous atmosphere, signifying a climax or a peak in the tumultuous events described. The song encapsulates a mood of desperation, coupled with a faint glimmer of hope for rescue or relief. Although the track is fairly short (3:10), "Stormy May Day" is an emotionally powerful sounding song from the album.

"She Likes Rock 'n' Roll"

"She Likes Rock 'n' Roll" is another track that celebrates rock music, focusing on the joy and energy of the genre. The song starts with "A little game of falling down, you rock 'n' roll when the call come 'round," setting the scene for a carefree and spontaneous attitude towards life, a recurring theme in AC/DC songs and in rock music in general. The phrase "Made in the shade and you wished it'd turn around" suggests a desire for change or excitement, which rock 'n' roll provides. Central to the song is the chorus, "She digs rock 'n' roll, she likes rock 'n' roll," indicating not just a preference for a music genre but an embrace of the rock and roll lifestyle. It's about the connection and shared enthusiasm for this style of music and what it represents—freedom, rebellion, and enjoyment. The repetition of "You want rock 'n' roll, I need rock 'n' roll" emphasizes the importance of rock music, which is not just an interest but is a vital part of life. Additionally, the lyrics "We are a gang coming down, we're gonna rock all night, rockin' rollin' all the time" reflect the communal aspect of rock music. It's about being part of a group, sharing experiences, and enjoying music together. The lines "She gives rock 'n' roll, she lives rock 'n' roll" further personify rock 'n' roll, suggesting it's not just music but a way of life, a sentiment shared by many AC/DC fans worldwide, myself included. It's something that gives and takes, influencing and shaping the lives of those who engage with it.

"Money Made"

"Money Made" was released as the fourth and final single from *Black Ice*. The song kicks off with a really great groove and catchy and memorable guitar riff of interplay between Angus and Malcolm. The song's repetitive structure and lyrics emphasize the relentless, almost monotonous drive for financial success. The repeated phrase "Work work money made" serves as the song's backbone, symbolizing the endless cycle of labor for financial gain. This repetition underscores the song's critique of a work-obsessed culture where the pursuit of money becomes the primary focus of life. The narrative, set in Los Angeles, "Then went down to LA, they roped 'em in, she couldn't get away," emphasizes the seductive, yet trapping nature of a lifestyle centered around money. The imagery of being "roped in" and unable to escape reflects the constraints that a life focused solely on financial gain can impose. Luxury and excess are highlighted in "Spending cash all about, the die was cast," indicating a lifestyle where spending and extravagance are paramount. However, the phrase "There's no burning out amount of money made" implies that no amount of wealth can ultimately satisfy the endless desire for more. Later verses, "Can't bring me into Hollywood, see you livin' it up, it feels mighty good," indicate a critical view of Hollywood's culture of wealth and superficiality. The lyrics caution against being lured by this flashy lifestyle, hinting at the hollowness beneath the surface. "Money Made" provides a critique of the endless pursuit of wealth, depicting it as a cycle that is both alluring and entrapping. AC/DC uses this song to comment on the superficiality and ultimate dissatisfaction that can come from a life focused solely on financial gain, contrasting it with the more grounded and authentic values often celebrated in rock music. Having met the members of AC/DC several times, I can say from my own experience, this sentiment is true to their own nature as they are the most humble, nicest, and down-to-earth people one could imagine—despite their massive success, fame, and fortune, they have always stayed true to themselves and to their fans.

"Rock 'n' Roll Dream"

"Rock 'n' Roll Dream" presents a contemplative and somewhat somber reflection that can be interpreted in various ways, including possibly alluding to the challenges faced by Malcolm Young, although his dementia diagnosis was not publicly known at the time. When reading the lyrics of this song, this is what I've always personally felt the song was reflecting on. The opening lines, "Deep water all around me, and circle sharks all about," set a tone of being surrounded by challenges or threats. This imagery of being in deep water and encircled by sharks could symbolize a sense of being overwhelmed or facing significant difficulties, which could be related to personal struggles, possibly including health issues like Malcolm Young's condition. The lyrics "Deep in trouble, and I may turn around, man up and one man down" suggest a situation of distress and adversity, possibly hinting at the band's internal challenges or personal battles of its members. The line "Man up and one man down" could be interpreted as a reference to Malcolm, who was dealing with health issues at the time of the album's recording. It can be seen as a recognition of the challenges faced by Malcolm and the band's determination to carry on despite the difficulties. The chorus repeats the phrase "I could be in a rock 'n' roll dream," which can be seen as a manifestation of the band's aspirations and dreams coming true. It reflects the essence of the rock and roll lifestyle and the euphoria that comes with being on stage and performing. Further, the verse "You come up and you don't know why, where goes a woman with a warm embrace, does a man walk in the hard rain?" paints a picture of confusion and seeking comfort in tough times. This could be a metaphor for seeking solace in the familiar (rock 'n' roll) amid personal turmoil. Lastly, the repeated phrase "Deep water all around, 'round, 'round" towards the end of the song reinforces the theme of being engulfed by challenges but also suggests a cyclical, ongoing struggle, possibly again hinting at Malcolm's health struggles. This track, based on my assessment of the lyrics, serves as a tribute to Malcolm Young's resilience in the face of his health issues and the band's determination to continue their musical journey.

"Rocking All the Way"

"Rocking All the Way" is a really great track from *Black Ice*; actually, it is one of my favorites from the album. The song grooves and has a great guitar riff and beat that is high-energy and is characterized by classic rock themes of excitement, seduction, and danger. The overall tone of the song captures AC/DC's signature sound and straightforward approach. The opening lines, "Well, one mad shuffle, he says two women is trouble," set the stage for a narrative about complex relationships and the troubles they can bring, as observed throughout AC/DC's song repertoire. The song revolves around a female character, who is described as bold and assertive: "She's rockin' all the way, she's comin' out my way." This portrayal of a woman who is confident, assertive, and in control, aligns with the band's often edgy and provocative style. The lyrics "She's sexy in her boots, tear up all the news, shoot you in the back, driving you mad" depict a femme fatale-like figure. She is captivating and perhaps dangerous, hinting at the allure and peril of the rock 'n' roll lifestyle. The advice "Come on hear me out, and take my advice, she won't stop until you're in her sights" suggests a warning or a sense of being overpowered by this woman's presence, further adding to the song's theme of irresistible attraction and potential danger. "Rocking All the Way" is a quintessential AC/DC song that combines themes of allure, danger, and the uninhibited spirit of rock 'n' roll. The lyrics celebrate a powerful, enigmatic female figure, embodying the energy and rebellion with the overall vibe of the music.

"Black Ice"

"Black Ice," the title track and last of the album (also my favorite from the album), is a song that showcases AC/DC's enduring power and musical prowess. The song has a fantastic guitar riff and a really great groove to it, and it was another track from the album performed live during the Black Ice World Tour. The song's cryptic lyrics paint a vivid picture of a dangerous and seductive force, delving into themes of danger, temptation, and the inevitable encounter with one's darker side. The song employs stark, vivid imagery and metaphors to convey a sense of foreboding and confrontation with peril. Angus once spoke about the song and the album title in general and indicated that he was inspired by the idea from the warnings of black ice they used to hear about growing up in Scotland. The opening line, "Well, the devil may care, you toss him back and be a man," immediately introduces the theme of dealing with temptation or evil (personified by the devil). This sets the tone for a song about facing and overcoming daunting challenges or dangerous situations. The repeated phrase "Black ice" serves as a central metaphor. Black ice, known for being deceptively dangerous because it's transparent and hard to see, symbolizes unforeseen or hidden dangers in life. The lines "End of it all, end of the line, end of the road" associated with black ice suggest a finality or a point of no return, enhancing the song's ominous tone. In "Don't you know I live it down, when the devil come a callin' I ain't gonna be around," there is a declaration of resistance or avoidance of these dangers. The song then takes a more aggressive and sinister turn with "I'll kick, I creep crawl down your street, I'll gouge your eyes out," which is quite a surprising line, which could otherwise symbolize a readiness to tackle or confront challenges head on rather than a figurative reference. Overall, "Black Ice" is the perfect conclusion to a brilliant album—an album that to me is one of the band's best in twenty-five years.

Interesting Facts

AC/DC went above and beyond for the Black Ice World Tour, having a giant train constructed for the tour that would emerge from the stage at the start of every night for the opening track in the set, "Rock 'n' Roll Train." A massive promotional campaign was launched for the tour that included multiple fan-centered events including Sony Music sponsored contests, a Rock 'n' Roll Caravan event for the tour kick off, a dress rehearsal concert at Wachovia Arena in Wilkes-Barre, Pennsylvania, on October 26, 2008 where the band performed a partial setlist, and numerous other cool fan-interactive events.

17

Rock or Bust

Release date:	November 28, 2014 (U.K.)
	November 28, 2014 (U.S.)
Current edition:	Sony/ Columbia, CD, LP
Personnel:	Brian Johnson, lead vocals
	Angus Young, lead guitar
	Stevie Young, rhythm guitar
	Cliff Williams, bass guitar
	Phil Rudd, drums
Duration:	34:55
Recorded at:	The Warehouse Studios, Vancouver, BC, Canada
Produced by:	Brendan O'Brien
Chart position:	#1 Australian Albums
	#1 U.K. Albums
	#3 U.S. *Billboard* 200

Notable info: This would be the first album featuring Stevie Young on rhythm guitar. *Rock or Bust* is certified gold in the USA, platinum in Australia, 3x platinum in France, 3x platinum in Germany, with multiple multi-platinum, platinum, and gold certifications in other countries.

AC/DC's sixteenth studio album, *Rock or Bust*, released on November 28, 2014 arrived amid tumultuous times for the band, with the departure of founding member and rhythm guitarist Malcolm Young due to health issues. With this album, AC/DC took the straightforward approach of a writing a solid, hard rock album, which included an appropriate, simple, yet really cool album cover depicting a 3D AC/DC logo made of rock that explodes when you rotate the cover. Produced by Brendan O'Brien, *Rock or Bust* also marked the debut of rhythm guitarist Stevie Young, Malcolm Young's nephew, who had previously filled in for Malcolm during the North American leg of the Blow Up Your Video Tour in 1988. Stevie was also formerly the rhythm guitarist of the band The Starfighters who had toured as the opening act for AC/DC in the early 1980s. Stevie's seamless integration into the band ensured that the album retained the classic AC/DC sound, demonstrating the familial bonds that run deep within the band's history. The album features eleven tracks that encapsulate the band's trademark style of high-energy rock 'n' roll. Songs like the title track "Rock or Bust," "Play Ball," and "Emission Control" are imbued with the band's classic themes of rebellion, partying, and unapologetic fun. The album's lyrical themes touch on familiar AC/DC territory—the thrill of rock 'n' roll, the pursuit of pleasure, and the resilience in the face of adversity. Tracks like "Miss Adventure," "Baptism by Fire," and the title track showcase the band's ability to craft songs that are both timeless and contemporary, proving that AC/DC's musical formula is as potent as ever. *Rock or Bust* debuted at #1 in twelve countries, showcasing the enduring global appeal and unstoppable force of AC/DC. The album, while not diverging significantly from their established formula, showcases the band's commitment to their roots and their ability to deliver solid rock music consistently.

"Rock or Bust"

Appropriate as the album's opener, the title track "Rock or Bust" is a vibrant rock anthem that celebrates AC/DC's enduring spirit and unyielding commitment to rock music. The lyrics are straightforward and exude a strong sense of loyalty and dedication to the genre of rock 'n' roll. The opening riff is unmistakably AC/DC, with their characteristic guitar tone and sound. From the onset, "Hey yeah, are you ready, we be a guitar band, we play across the land," the song establishes AC/DC's identity as the quintessential rock band. The reference to being a "guitar band" highlights the significance of guitar-driven music in rock, a hallmark of AC/DC's style and perhaps even a nod to the song by Australian legend Stevie Wright, formerly of The Easybeats. The chorus, "In rock we trust, it's rock or bust," is a bold declaration of the band's unwavering commitment to rock music. Quite frankly, "In Rock We Trust" could have also made a perfect title for this song and album. The song expresses a profound love for rock music, suggesting that it is not just a genre but a way of life. "Rock or Bust" is an emphatic statement about AC/DC's dedication to rock music. The lyrics are a celebration of the genre's power, the communal experience of rock concerts, and the band's identity as unwavering ambassadors of rock 'n' roll. It served as testament to AC/DC's longevity and commanding presence in rock music after a long, six-year gap from their previous album *Black Ice*.

"Play Ball"

"Play Ball," the first single released from the album, kicks off with a catchy guitar riff and combines straightforward rock rhythms and lyrics that are characteristic of AC/DC's style. This is a high-energy track that uses the metaphor of a ball game to convey a sense of wild, unrestrained fun and revelry. The opening lines "Listen, pick me up, fill my cup, pour me another round" immediately set a tone of indulgence and celebration. The chorus, "Let's play ball, shootin' down the walls, yeah, let's play ball, baby, battin' down the stalls," uses the language of a baseball game as a metaphor for engaging in lively and possibly raucous activities. The references to "shooting down the walls" and "battin' down the stalls" imply a breaking free from constraints or norms, embracing a more wild and free-spirited approach. Lines like "I'm on the loose, make it feel alright" and "I'm in the mood, because the night is mine" emphasize a sense of liberation and seizing the moment. This aligns with the band's frequent themes of living in the present and enjoying life to the fullest. The overall sound is polished, yet retains the raw edge and organic feel that has become synonymous with AC/DC's music

"Rock the Blues Away"

"Rock the Blues Away" was actually the first song that was recorded for the album, and producer Brendan O'Brien recalled: "It was just fun; it sounds like these guys. It sounds like AC/DC." The track is likely somewhat of a tribute to Malcolm Young, who was forced to retire from the band due to his critical health issues. "Rock the Blues Away" encapsulates a classic rock ethos of leisure, camaraderie, and using music as an escape from troubles. The lyrics are upbeat and celebratory, focusing on the simple joys of life and the therapeutic power of rock music. Angus Young told *The Sun*: "'Rock the Blues Away' is an up track that reminds me of growing up in Australia, I loved being on the beach and that song was inspired by taking me back to the beach hearing rock 'n' roll on the radio." The song begins with a casual, everyday scene: "Drivin' in my car, headed for the local bar, pickin' up my girl tonight." This sets a relaxed and happy tone, suggesting a night out filled with simple pleasures and good company. The chorus, "We won't get the blues because we, Rock the blues away, up all night and day, drink the night away, until the light of day," is central to the song's theme. It conveys the idea that rock music serves as a remedy for the blues—a way to chase away sadness or troubles. The repeated phrase "Rock the blues away" emphasizes the healing or uplifting power of music. The lines "And when I'm on the way back home, I listen to the radio, I hear some great rock sounds, that make you wanna sing out loud" further reinforce the idea that rock music is a constant companion and a source of joy. It underscores the band's appreciation for the genre not just as musicians but as fans who find solace and happiness in their music.

"Miss Adventure"

"Miss Adventure" presents a playful, flirtatious narrative centered around a charismatic and alluring female. The song is infused with the band's typical rock 'n' roll energy and incorporates themes of attraction, desire, and a bit of mystery. The introduction sets the stage for a song about pursuit and engagement, with an emphasis on directness and intensity. The character "Miss Adventure" is introduced as "Miss adventure, hot surprise, bare essential, yeah that's nice." This description paints her as a figure of excitement and allure, with an element of unpredictability. The lines "She eye you up, she eye you down, Oh, she make you, make you stand up proud" depict the power of "Miss Adventure's" presence and the sexual effect she has on those around her. In "Want some pie, but cat got your tongue, feelin' like some hot cross buns," there's a playful use of language and imagery, suggesting teasing and flirtation. These lines add a light-hearted, somewhat cheeky tone to the song. The song concludes with repeated references to "Miss Adventure," reinforcing her as the central figure of intrigue and fascination The song combines AC/DC's signature high-energy music with witty, engaging lyrics to create a portrait of a seductive and captivating woman.

"Dogs of War"

"Dogs of War" explores the theme of mercenary soldiers and the harsh realities of their lives. The song has a really great riff and groove to it, that features AC/DC's trademark sound, but also with ominous overtones. The song uses the metaphor of "dogs of war" to describe soldiers of fortune, conveying a sense of aggression, survival, and the complexities of warfare. The repetitive chorus "Dogs of war (Soldier of fortune)" immediately establishes the central theme. The chorus is powerful and resonates with the guitar riff of the song. The phrase "dogs of war" traditionally refers to soldiers who fight not out of loyalty to a country or cause, but for personal gain. This label carries connotations of ruthlessness and a readiness to engage in conflict. The lyrics "You be a fightin' man, make all the cash you can, don't mix and feel your tide, they wanna risk their lives" alludes to this sentiment. In "Takin' all you can, riskin' ain't in the plan, feel the boots upon the ground, trouble brewin' all around," the song highlights the precarious nature of being a soldier of fortune. While they aim to gain as much as possible, these soldiers are constantly surrounded by danger and uncertainty. Towards the end, "Marchin' through the nightness, those mercenary men" encapsulates the relentless, often unseen struggles faced by these individuals. The imagery of marching through darkness could symbolize the moral ambiguities and the isolated journey of mercenaries.

"Got Some Rock & Roll Thunder"

"Got Some Rock & Roll Thunder" is a celebration of the spirit and energy of rock 'n' roll. The song encapsulates the essence of AC/DC's music—a source of empowerment, joy, and rejuvenation, highlighting rock 'n' roll's ability to transform and invigorate. It blends the themes of rock music and the power of thunder together to create a vibrant and energetic track that celebrates the invigorating power of rock music. The lyrics convey a sense of freedom, rejuvenation, and the transformative effect of rock music. The song opens with "Well, I'm headin' on out, down to a major town, I'm gettin' hungry, I'm gettin' mean, I'm gettin' down on easy street." This introduction sets a tone of anticipation and excitement, suggesting a journey or escape to a place where the narrator can fully immerse themselves in the rock and roll experience. The recurring phrase "I got some rock and roll thunder" serves as the song's core theme. "Got Some Rock & Roll Thunder" symbolizes the powerful, electrifying impact of rock music. Lyrics like "I been workin', deep and rolled, I get high on rock and roll" express the transformative effect of rock music, providing an escape from the mundane or challenging aspects of everyday life. The idea of getting "high" on rock 'n' roll suggests a euphoric, uplifting experience. The song positions rock music as a remedy or a source of strength.

"Hard Times"

Likely another track that serves as a testament to the challenges and difficulties faced by the band in the wake of Malcolm's forced retirement, "Hard Times" explores the theme of resilience and perseverance in the face of challenges. The song captures the sadness and resilience likely felt by AC/DC due to Malcolm Young's medical condition and subsequent absence. The lyrics convey a gritty determination to overcome difficulties and maintain a sense of freedom and autonomy. The refrain "They try to hold you down, but they can't push you 'round, tryin' to hold you back, gettin' on the right track" reflects the theme of defiance and persistence. It suggests that despite external pressures or obstacles, one remains determined to stay on course and not be deterred. "Hard times, blue and sad, don't you cross the line, Run, run, make it fun, freein' up the time" captures the essence of coping with difficult periods. The song advises not to cross into despair and to find ways to make the best of the situation. Towards the end, "Hard times, these hard times sure ain't been good to me, hard times, hard times, sure been misery" acknowledges the toll that these struggles can take. However, the overall tone of the song remains defiant and hopeful rather than resigned. The song serves as a tribute to the band's unwavering resilience, showcasing their ability to find strength in the face of adversity. It acknowledges sadness and pain while ultimately embracing a sense of determination and hope.

"Baptism by Fire"

"Baptism by Fire" is a high-octane track that embodies the spirit of rock 'n' roll revelry and transformation. This track was part of the Rock or Bust World Tour setlist along with the title track, "Play Ball," and "Got Some Rock & Roll Thunder." The song uses vivid imagery and energetic language to convey themes of excitement, change, and the exhilarating power of music. The song is fast paced, with an energetic drive and upbeat tempo. The lyrics start with an invitation to celebrate: "Let's get the party started, and lady do your tricks." This sets a tone of uninhibited fun and enjoyment, characteristic of many AC/DC songs. The phrase "Baptism by the fire" implies undergoing a significant change or initiation, likely through the power of rock music. Lines like "We're gonna shock the nation, make 'em flip their lids" and "You hear a clap of thunder, or feel her lightning strike" portray the impact of their music as both shocking and electrifying, but also with a metaphor of a night of passion with "You get you pistons firing, it's lady fortune's night." "Baptism by Fire" is a metaphorical exploration of transformation through the exhilarating power of rock 'n' roll. The song captures the essence of AC/DC's music as a force for excitement, change, and empowerment, encouraging listeners to embrace the intensity and thrill of the rock 'n' roll experience.

"Rock the House"

"Rock the House" kicks off with an almost Led Zeppelin-style volley between the music and vocals. Brian Johnson's commanding vocals undeniable presence and range on this track. It is a high-energy song that embodies the raw and vibrant essence of rock 'n' roll. The lyrics are infused with themes of passion, excitement, and the powerful impact of music and attraction. The song opens with an intense and suggestive tone: "Mistress, mistress, all night long, hey, ooh keep on coming, hard and strong." These lines set the stage for a narrative about an intense, sexual experience, typical of the band's direct and unapologetic style. The chorus "Rock the house, Rock this house, Rock, rock, rock and then roll" is a straightforward celebration of rock music's ability to energize and invigorate. Lines like "Hot to the touch, hot to the taste, oozin' out on my plate" and "She's gonna push it all the way down, gonna kick up her heels, make you scream" convey a sense of intensity and abandon. The song also includes vivid imagery of a dynamic and commanding female presence: "She gonna kick her legs high in the air, she gonna shake it down the hot, wet, wild fare." This portrayal of a powerful, uninhibited woman aligns with many of AC/DC's songs throughout their career. "Rock the House" celebrates rock 'n' roll music through themes of passion, energy, and excitement.

"Sweet Candy"

"Sweet Candy" is a song that vividly portrays a scene of seduction and allure, centered around a charismatic and enticing woman named Candy. The lyrics paint a vivid picture of Candy, a captivating performer who entrances her audience with her alluring moves. The song describes a dancer who expertly slides down a pole, performs backflips, and crawls across the floor, leaving the crowd in awe of her skill and sensuality. The imagery captures the essence of an artist who knows how to captivate and command attention through her dynamic stage presence. The lyrics focus on her captivating performance and the reaction it elicits from her audience. Throughout the song, the chorus "Sweet Candy, clap and kneel" repeats, creating a rhythmic and hypnotic effect. Towards the end, "She really rolls the dice, panting in wait, yeah, she knows just what she done, and she gives it all and shakes" conveys a sense of risk and excitement associated with Candy's performance. The idea of "rolling the dice" implies a gamble or taking chances, adding to the song's theme of seduction and allure. The song combines AC/DC's characteristic rock energy with evocative lyrics that celebrate the allure and power of feminine charisma and sensuality.

"Emission Control"

"Emission Control," the closing track from *Rock or Bust*, is a high-energy rock song with sexually suggestive lyrics that use the metaphor of a car's emission control system to explore themes of desire and control. The song kicks off with a unique sounding guitar riff that distinguishes it from the rest of the album. The opening lines, "Here's my mission, to seek you out, you're up for grabs, honey, breathe in, don't make a sound," set a tone of pursuit and anticipation. The language is direct and assertive, suggesting a chase or hunt in the context of a romantic or sexual encounter. The chorus, "Come in emission control, Emission control, it's good for the soul, yeah," plays on the double-entendre of "emission control." In one sense, it refers to a vehicle's emission control system, but it's also used here to imply sexual control or release. The phrase "It's good for the soul" adds a lighthearted, enjoyable aspect to this metaphor. Lines such as "Turn on emission, the engine comes alive, she takes to pairing mama, like a lion ready to strike" further develop this metaphor. The engine coming alive symbolizes arousal, and the comparison to a lion ready to strike adds a sense of primal energy and instinct. Towards the end, the repetition of "Giving it up, raising it up" serves to build intensity, mirroring the escalating excitement suggested by the song's content. "Emission Control" is a classic AC/DC song that uses innuendo and metaphor to explore themes of desire, control, and release. The song's playful and suggestive lyrics are set to the backdrop of AC/DC's signature rock sound, creating a track that is both provocative and energetically engaging.

Interesting Facts

Shortly after the release of the album, Phil Rudd found himself involved in some legal trouble, which resulted in a sudden replacement drummer (Bob Richards), who filled in and appeared in the promotional video for the title track of the album. Shortly after, the band re-hired drummer Chris Slade as the drummer for the Rock or Bust World Tour, which ran from April 2015 through September 2016. Brian Johnson was facing hearing loss issues toward the last leg of the tour, which resulted in him stepping down and the rescheduling of those shows. The band hired Axl Rose (Guns N' Roses) to fill in for the remaining rescheduled tour dates to finish out the tour. Cliff Williams announced that he would retire from the band at the conclusion of the tour due to disinterest.

18

Power Up

Release date:	November 13, 2020 (U.K.)
	November 13, 2020 (U.S.)
Current edition:	Sony/ Columbia, CD, LP
Personnel:	Brian Johnson, lead vocals
	Angus Young, lead guitar
	Malcolm Young, rhythm guitar
	Cliff Williams, bass guitar
	Phil Rudd, drums
Duration:	41:03
Recorded at:	The Warehouse Studios, Vancouver, BC, Canada
Produced by:	Brendan O'Brien
Chart position:	#1 Australian Albums
	#1 U.K. Albums
	#1 U.S. *Billboard* 200

Notable info: *Power Up* reached #1 in twenty-one countries worldwide. *Power Up* is certified 2x platinum in France, with multiple platinum and gold certification in other countries.

Power Up, AC/DC's seventeenth studio album, was released on November 13, 2020. It featured a return of the classic lineup, including the much-celebrated reunion with Brian Johnson on vocals, Phil Rudd on drums, and Cliff Williams on bass. The title *Power Up* (PWRUP) serves as a testament to AC/DC's overall theme as a band since the very beginning—hard-hitting, high-voltage rock 'n' roll. The album marks a significant comeback for the band, following a period of uncertainty and lineup changes, including the tragic loss of founding member Malcolm Young in 2017. The album serves as a tribute to Malcolm, with his brother Angus Young incorporating many of Malcolm's unused guitar riffs and ideas into the album's composition. Chris Slade had been recruited during the previous

Rock or Bust World Tour to replace Phil Rudd, who was facing legal issues at the time. Brian had to step down during the last portion of the Rock or Bust World Tour due to hearing issues and Cliff Williams chose to retire at the conclusion of the tour. But with *Power Up*, AC/DC were back in full swing with the classic *Back in Black* lineup of Brian, Cliff, and Phil. Produced by Brendan O'Brien, the album delivers a powerful resurgence of the band's signature sound, characterized by driving rhythms, high-energy guitar riffs, and anthemic choruses. The album kicks off with the electrifying "Realize," immediately signaling that the band hasn't lost an ounce of their trademark power. The album's title is a fitting descriptor of the music within—a powerful surge of classic AC/DC energy that refuses to wane. Tracks like "Shot in the Dark," "No Man's Land," and "Demon Fire" showcase the band's ability to craft sold rock tracks that seamlessly blend their signature guitar tones with relentless, foot-stomping rhythms. Brian Johnson's vocals, as gritty and distinctive as ever, add an extra layer of dynamism to the album. Despite the absence of Malcolm and the challenges faced by the music industry, the album soared to the top of the charts globally, underscoring AC/DC's unwavering commitment and relevance as the world's #1 rock 'n' roll band of all time. The album was very successful, hitting #1 in twenty-one countries and was later Grammy nominated for best rock album, with "Shot in the Dark" nominated for best rock performance and best music video.

"Realize"

"Realize," the opening track and second single released from *Power Up*, announces the band's triumphant return to the rock scene following the tragic loss of rhythm guitarist Malcolm Young. This electrifying song serves as a powerful statement of resilience, capturing the essence of AC/DC's signature sound while offering a fresh perspective. The lyrics are infused with a sense of energy and dynamism, characteristic of the band's hard rock style. The opening guitar riff that features interplay between Angus Young and Stevie Young sets the stage for the song, which is unmistakably AC/DC. The opening lines, "The moment you realize, those moments just pass you by, gonna take you to paradise," set the tone for a song about realization and seizing the moment. Throughout the song, phrases like "And your eyes playin' tricks on you, and your mind will seek the truth, you know you're gonna make it through" delve into the theme of self-realization and discovery. The lines "I got the power to electrify, make or break or satisfy" further reinforce the idea of possessing a transformative power. The use of "electrify" adds to the sense of excitement and vitality inherent in the song and at the same time pays homage to AC/DC's electric sound. "Realize" stands tall as the opening track of AC/DC's *Power Up*, marking a triumphant return for the band after the loss of Malcolm Young and resonating with the band's enduring appeal as icons of rock music. The track showcases AC/DC's ability to create music that resonates with fans old and new, reaffirming their status as one of rock's most enduring and influential acts.

"Rejection"

"Rejection" continues the flow of Power Up nicely; it is a track that is about the aggressive pursuit of one's desires. The lyrics revolve around a central theme of demand and retribution; ""If you reject me, I'll take what I want" and "Disrespect me, and you get burned." A menacing and relentless attitude is depicted throughout the song, like "You better give me what I want, or I'll come for you." Interestingly, the song shifts away from materialistic desires, as indicated by the line "Now, I don't want your money or greed, you better give me just what I need," which is likely referring to romantic attraction as with many AC/DC tracks in their catalog. Musically, this song mirrors its lyrical intensity with AC/DC's signature hard rock sound, marked by driving rhythms and powerful guitar riffs and is a really great segway after the great introduction of "Realize" before it. The aggressive tone of the lyrics is complemented by an equally forceful musical arrangement, enhancing the song's raw and confrontational mood, especially with Brian Johnson's raspy delivery. "Rejection" encapsulates the theme of dominance and the threat of retribution in the face of opposition, embodying a more menacing and forceful aspect of AC/DC's musical persona.

"Shot in the Dark"

"Shot in the Dark," the first single from *Power Up*, is a track that rekindles the classic AC/DC sound and also injects a fresh dose of energy, proving that the band still knows how to rock 'n' roll. It kicks off with Brian Johnson's unmistakable gravelly voice, marking a triumphant and highly anticipated return to the band since the last portion of the Rock or Bust World Tour in 2015. The song is about celebrating life's thrilling moments and serves as an anthem for seizing pleasure and excitement in the midst of the ordinary. The lyrics capture the essence of AC/DC's signature rebellious spirit, with lines like "A shot in the dark, beats a walk in the park" serving as an anthem for taking risks and living life to the fullest. The song cleverly uses the imagery of "electric sparks" and a "shot in the dark" to convey the idea of sudden, intense pleasure and the thrill of the unexpected. Phrases like "You got a long night coming" and "Your mission is to party 'til the broad daylight" evoke a sense of anticipation for a night full of potential and unbridled energy. Musically, the track features great guitar riffs from Angus and Stevie Young, complemented nicely by the rhythm section of Phil Rudd and Cliff Williams. Brendan O'Brien, the producer, succeeds in capturing the essence of AC/DC's iconic sound while giving it a slightly modern touch, which resonates throughout the whole album. The song would be performed live for the first time at the Power Trip festival in Indio, California, in October 2023.

"Through the Mists of Time"

"Through the Mists of Time," a heartfelt tribute to the late guitarist and AC/DC founder Malcolm Young, is a poignant reflection on memory, legacy, and the passage of time. The song was released as the fifth and final single from *Power Up*, which was available as a "Record Store Day" limited edition 12-inch vinyl picture disc (with "Witch's Spell" as the B-side). The band also released a fantastic promo video for the song. The lyrics are steeped in imagery that evokes a sense of nostalgia and introspection while paying homage to their influential co-founder. The opening lines, "See dark shadows on the walls, see the pictures, some hang, some fall," immediately set a contemplative mood, suggesting the persistence and yet the fragility of memories. The repeated references to "painted faces" and "painted ladies" allude to images from the past, possibly representing people and moments that have left a lasting impact. These images, frozen in time, serve as a connection to bygone days, highlighting the theme of reminiscing. The phrase "through the mists of time" symbolizes the journey back through memories, with "mists" representing the unclear, ethereal nature of the past. The lyric "From a mansion high" could symbolize a place of prominence or a metaphorical pedestal on which memories or significant figures from the past are placed. This can be seen as a nod to Malcolm Young's stature and importance in the band's history and in the hearts of those who remember him. The song is a heartfelt homage to Malcolm Young, reflecting on the enduring nature of his influence and the bittersweet reality of looking back through the "mists of time." The lyrics balance a sense of loss with a celebration of his legacy, capturing the emotional depth of remembrance and the enduring impact they have left behind. The track serves as a sentimental tribute to

Malcolm Young, reminiscing about the band's journey and the indelible mark he left on their music and their lives. This heartfelt tribute not only honors the memory of Malcolm Young but also offers solace and reflection to fans worldwide. AC/DC's dedication and passion shine brightly in this track, ensuring that Malcolm Young's spirit will forever live on through their music.

"Kick You When You're Down"

"Kick You When You're Down," one of my favorites from *Power Up*, features a less than traditional sounding AC/DC riff, which works really great in this song. The lyrics delve into themes of adversity, betrayal, and resilience, much like some of the other songs on the album. The song begins with a vivid metaphor of someone "slipping down the wall," symbolizing a person in a declining or precarious situation. The rhetorical question of "Why do they kick you when you're down" repeated through the song serves as the central theme of the song, reflecting the human tendency to harm or exploit others who are most vulnerable. The lyrics also explore relationships and their complexities. Lines like "Hey, mama, why are you beating on my head?" and "Hey, hey, woman, why do you kick me outta bed?" suggest intimate betrayals. The reference to a "shady lady" who thinks "money grows on trees" further suggests deceit and materialism, adding to the sense of disillusionment and mistrust. The song captures the frustration and defiance of facing adversity, especially when that adversity is compounded by the actions of others.

"Witch's Spell"

"Witch's Spell," the fourth single from *Power Up*, was released on June 9, 2021 and was available as the B-side to "Through the Mists of Time," which was released as a limited edition 12-inch vinyl picture disc. The song is rich in mystical and enigmatic imagery, with lyrics that create an atmosphere of mystery and intrigue of witchcraft, revolving around the theme of being entrapped in a witch's spell. As typical with many AC/DC tracks, the subject is metaphorical, and in this instance refers to being mesmerized and enchanted by a woman's beauty and sexual attractiveness. The opening lines, "Let me tell you your fortune, it could be sinister, or maybe not," immediately set the tone for a narrative that is unpredictable and potentially ominous. The line "Like a leopard, can't change its own spots" implies that the nature of the witch's spell is unalterable, hinting at the inescapable consequences of getting caught in her enchantment. The lyrics use supernatural themes to enhance the mystical aura of the song; "My blaze in the night sky, see the witch's flight" conjures the classic image of a witch flying through the night sky. The chorus, "Caught in a witch's spell, got a tale to tell," signifies being irresistibly drawn into a situation that is both compelling and potentially dangerous. This theme of enchantment is reinforced by references to traditional elements of witchcraft, such as crystal balls, almanacs, potions, and snake oil, all of which add to the song's mystical allure. The reference to a "good time maker who likes it hot" implies that the witch revels in indulgence and excitement. "Witch's Spell" is a captivating exploration of enchantment and the mystical, while weaving a tale of being under the irresistible influence of a powerful and enchanting woman.

"Demon Fire"

"Demon Fire" was the third single released from *Power Up*. Although it was not available as a physical media single (vinyl or CD), the song did feature a great animated promo video that accompanied its release. The song presents a narrative steeped in themes of danger, rebellion, and seductive thrill of temptation. From the outset, the song sets a tone of menacing allure with lines like "He loves to drive 'em crazy with his evil lips" and "Great guns are blazing, what a deadly trip." These phrases paint a picture of a character who is both enticing and dangerous, someone who thrives on chaos and intensity. The character's background, "born of no family, born of no creed, yeah, raised by a jackal, raised a bad seed," further emphasizes their outsider status and inherent malevolence. After the intro, the song features a really great boogie-rock guitar riff and has a fast-paced groove that drives it forward. The promo video for the song depicts a black car racing through roads, which really works well and illustrates the scenes derived from the sound of the music, which features a boogie-infused rock riff courtesy of Angus and Stevie Young. The chorus, "Demon fire, is all you desire," encapsulates the song's central theme: the irresistible draw of something both fearsome and captivating. The repeated invocation of "demon fire" serves as a metaphor for an uncontrollable and consuming passion or drive, something that both entices and overwhelms. Throughout the song, there are references to power and control, as seen in lines like "Seeking all power, gonna hunt you down." This suggests a relentless pursuit of dominance and the thrill of the hunt, further adding to the character's formidable and intimidating persona. The repeated warnings to "better look around, hear that evil sound" add a sense of urgency and caution, advising the listener of the imminent danger posed by this "demon fire." The use of the phrase "all drenched in grime" and references to "bad intentions" reinforce the sense of something dark and malevolent at work. The themes of liberation, indulgence, and the pursuit of unadulterated pleasure resonate throughout the track.

"Wild Reputation"

"Wild Reputation" is another favorite track of mine from *Power Up*, which features another fantastic guitar riff, where Angus and Stevie Young play complementary riffs that flow together really nicely. The song captures the essence of rebelliousness and defiance against societal judgment and misconceptions, much like many songs from AC/DC's repertoire. The song's lyrics portray a character who is misunderstood and judged unfairly by those in a small, close-minded community, represented by the "one-horse town." The song opens with the setting of this small town where there is the feeling of being alienated and judged: "They try to pull you down, and make you feel out of place." This imagery suggests a place where conformity is expected and anything different is met with disdain or suspicion. Central to the song is the chorus, "Got a wild reputation," which is repeated multiple times, emphasizing the character's infamous status in the eyes of the townspeople. It suggests a history or a persona that is larger than life, and possibly misunderstood. The lines "On a hot, summer day, dollar bills come your way, somebody robbed the bank, ooh, they picked you out of the ranks" indicate a scenario of being wrongly accused due to their reputation. This situation highlights the prejudice and quick judgment often faced by those who are perceived as outsiders or non-conformists. The defiant tone of the lyrics, particularly in "You better keep away, don't get in my face, oh, yeah" and "When I'm comin' down main street, get outta my way, I ain't stoppin' for nobody," showcases the resistance to being downtrodden or defined by others. This defiance is a key aspect of the song, representing a refusal to be victimized by others' perceptions. The song embraces the allure of danger, living life to the fullest, and defying expectations.

"No Man's Land"

And yet another favorite track of mine from *Power Up*, "No Man's Land" has that great, classic AC/DC sound courtesy of the guitar riff and tight rhythm section. "No Man's Land" delves into themes of struggle, escape, and the relentless pursuit of freedom. The song's lyrics portray a sense of urgency and desperation, with the desire to break free from a stifling situation. The song begins with a call to action, "Come on need, you gotta get on board, come on, noon train," suggesting a narrow window of opportunity for escape. The repeated references to the "noon train" symbolize a chance for liberation, a means to leave behind a confining circumstance. The lines "I've tried and I found no way to get out, I said I tried and I found, there's no comin' back for me" express a sense of entrapment and the difficulty of breaking free. The repeated attempts and failures to escape emphasize the gravity of the situation and the seemingly inescapable nature of the predicament. Central to the song is the chorus, "Know you gotta get away, (No man's land), fight and live another day," which encapsulates the song's central themes of resilience and survival. No man's land serves as a metaphor for a place of uncertainty and danger, a zone between safety and peril where one's fate hangs in the balance. The imagery of being "Caught in a hard rain" and "In the middle of the fray" further illustrates the challenges and adversities that are being faced. These lines convey a sense of being overwhelmed and caught in a tumultuous situation, yet there remains a determination to persevere and escape. The repeated exhortation to "Fly, fly, fly away" underscores the longing for freedom and the need to escape the confines of "no man's land." "No Man's Land" is a song about the intense desire for escape and the relentless pursuit of liberation from confining circumstances. It explores themes of struggle, resilience, and the indomitable human spirit in the face of adversity.

"Systems Down"

"Systems Down" is a powerful song that uses vivid, fiery imagery to convey themes of destruction, chaos, and the inevitable collapse of systems. The lyrics paint a picture of a world or system in the throes of a catastrophic breakdown, with a focus on the intensity and inevitability of this process. The song opens with the word "Unchained," immediately setting a tone of something being released or set free, but in a potentially uncontrollable and destructive manner. The lines "Feel it burning up the heat, see the flames scorching everything it seeks" use the imagery of fire to symbolize the destructive power at play. The chorus, "Systems (systems), Are going down, systems, are burning out, and they all fall down," reinforces the theme of systemic failure and collapse. The repetition of the word "systems" emphasizes the scale of the breakdown, suggesting that it's not just isolated incidents but a widespread, fundamental failure.

Maybe computers? Maybe entire nation infrastructure? Difficult to comprehend, but we can assume. The second verse continues with the imagery of an untamed force, "Untamed like a tiger searching feed." This metaphor conveys the idea of a primal, unstoppable force of nature that is both powerful and indifferent to the destruction it causes. Throughout the song, there's a sense of impending doom and an acknowledgment of the powerlessness to stop the unfolding disaster. Phrases like "This furnace is about to blast" and "Who knows if this place implodes" suggest an awareness of the imminent catastrophe. Overall, the song reflects themes of destruction, chaos, and the inescapable nature of systemic failures. Whether AC/DC penned this song literally in reference to actual computer systems and technology or are referring to something else altogether (society perhaps?) is unknown and can only be assumed.

"Money Shot"

"Money Shot" is a song about the healing and invigorating power of rock 'n' roll, using playful metaphors to convey a message about finding joy and release in music. The song embodies AC/DC's characteristic blend of humor, energy, and a slightly rebellious spirit. The lyrics employ a dialogue format between a "doctor" and a "lady," using the concept of a "money shot" as a metaphorical remedy. The song opens with an evocation of the rock 'n' roll spirit: "Feel in the rock 'n' roll mood, gonna make it feel good." This sets the tone for a song about indulgence and the liberating power of music. The phrase "Might be a little dangerous, I believe, I believe, you will see, it could be, contagious" suggests that the allure and thrill of rock 'n' roll are both enticing and infectious. Central to the song is the recurring phrase "Doctor, what's the antidote?, lady, try the money shot." This back-and-forth represents a conversation about finding a cure or solution, albeit in a tongue-in-cheek manner. The "money shot" metaphor, while suggestive, is used here to symbolize a potent, perhaps unconventional, remedy or solution to the lady's ailment, which in the context of the song, seems to be a need for excitement or release. The lyrics "I got a good prescription, for the state of your condition, you gotta take it three times a day, or as much, as much as you need" further play on the theme of healing or relief through music and enjoyment. The "prescription" and "diagnosis" metaphorically suggest that indulging in the joy and energy of rock 'n' roll can be a therapeutic experience. Towards the end, the lines "Now take this down, gonna send you on your way, 'cause I believe I solved your case, I'll give you your relief" imply a resolution to the lady's search for relief. The doctor, symbolizing the voice of rock 'n' roll, assures a solution through the "money shot," reinforcing the theme of music as a source of liberation and joy.

"Code Red"

The final track on *Power Up*, "Code Red" is a high-energy song that delves into themes of urgency, conflict, and the thrill of danger. The song kicks off with a great boogie blues rock riff and groove. The lyrics are filled with vivid, combative imagery, conveying a sense of being on the edge and ready for action. The song opens with "Loading up the battery, raising up insanity, beating out the old-time blues," setting a tone of preparation for an intense experience or confrontation. The imagery of charging up and gearing up for battle pervades the song, suggesting a state of heightened alertness and readiness. The chorus, "Station to station, yeah, code red, battle stations, ooh, code red," uses the military term "code red" to signify a critical situation requiring immediate response. This sense of urgency is echoed throughout the song, with references to being in a high-stakes scenario where quick, decisive action is necessary. Lines like "Speeding up the road, tearing up the Highway Code, ain't gonna slow me down" and "No need to hesitate, ain't coming up late, hit the brakes, don't mess with fate" further emphasize a reckless abandon and a disregard for rules in the face of urgency. This defiance and determination to push forward, regardless of obstacles, is a key element of the song. The lyrics also contain elements of warfare and combat, as seen in "Hard fight, rough night, dead in your sight, fire light, fire bright, fire in the night." These lines paint a picture of a battleground, where every moment is filled with tension and the potential for conflict. "Code Red" captures the essence of adrenaline-fueled readiness, the exhilaration of being on the brink of action, and embracing the thrill and danger of a confrontational situation. The song concludes *Power Up* nicely, delivering what AC/DC fans have always come to love and expect: hard rock 'n' roll in its truest and purest form.

Interesting Facts

On October 7, AC/DC performed their first live show in eight years in Indio, California, at the Power Trip, a three-day festival featuring Iron Maiden, Guns N' Roses, Judas Priest, AC/DC, Tool, and Metallica. It featured the album line up, minus Phil Rudd, and was the first time that any of the tracks from *Power Up* were performed live. The set list featured "Shot in the Dark" and "Demon Fire." In February 2024, AC/DC announced the Power Up Tour, with European dates, and the first show took place on May 17, 2024 (Gelsenkirchen, Germany), though with substitute drummer Matt Laug (Alanis Morissette, Alice Cooper, Slash's Snakepit) and bass player Chris Chaney (Jane's Addiction, Alanis Morissette). The tour concluded in Dublin, Ireland, on August 17, 2024. AC/DC continued the Power Up world tour in North America from April 10 through May 28, 2025, and at the time of writing they are returning to Europe for a second leg starting on June 26 in Prague, and set to conclude on August 21 in Edinburgh. Rumors suggest another possible North American leg, plus dates in South America and Australia to follow.

19

Non-Album Tracks (*Bonfire*, *Backtracks*, & B-Sides)

Non-Album Releases

The original debut AC/DC single, "Can I Sit Next to You, Girl," was released in July 1974 in Australia (and later in New Zealand) featuring an early AC/DC lineup of Angus and Malcolm Young, Dave Evans on vocals, Colin Burgess on drums, and George Young on bass guitar. The B-side to the single was "Rockin' in the Parlour." The single was produced by George Young and Harry Vanda and released on Albert/EMI in Australia and later on Polydor in New Zealand. "Can I Sit Next to You, Girl" peaked in the Australian Top 50 and would later be re-recorded with Bon Scott on vocals and released as part of *T.N.T.* in Australia in 1975. These two tracks were never commercially re-issued by AC/DC but are otherwise available as part of various compilation albums over the years. The original vinyl singles are extremely rare and highly collectible.

"Can I Sit Next to You, Girl"

In the annals of AC/DC's illustrious career, their original version of "Can I Sit Next to You, Girl" stands as a testament to the band's early potential and the raw energy that would come to define their signature sound. Released as a single in 1974 exclusively in Australia and New Zealand, this track features the original AC/DC lineup, with Dave Evans on vocals, showcasing a different style compared to the band's later work with Bon Scott and Brian Johnson. Colin Burgess, AC/DC's first drummer, recorded the song, however, George Young recorded the bass parts instead of the original AC/DC bassist, Larry Van Kriedt. This song, with its light-hearted and straightforward lyrics, reflects the early rock 'n' roll influence in AC/DC's music. The original version's uniqueness lies in its exploration of blues-infused rock, paving the way for the band's future evolution. The song's narrative is simple: the singer meets a girl at the Odeon (a reference to a popular movie theater chain) and tries to woo her with his charm and lines. The chorus, "Can I sit next to you, girl, can I sit next to you," is a direct and uncomplicated expression of his interest in her. This straightforward approach is characteristic of early rock 'n' roll, where lyrics often revolved around romantic pursuits and social interactions in dance halls and movie theaters. The lines, "At intermission we were doing alright, 'Till this guy came up and stood by her side," introduce a slight twist, where the singer faces a bit of competition for the girl's attention. However, he remains confident, as indicated by his response to the situation and his continued attempts to charm her. The repetition of the phrase "Can I sit next to you, girl" throughout the song serves as both a chorus and a hook. It emphasizes the singer's persistence and focus on his simple objective—to sit next to the girl he's interested in. This kind of repetitive, catchy chorus is a hallmark of early rock songs, designed to be memorable and singable. The song's structure, with its repeated chorus and simple, catchy melody, is indicative of the early rock 'n' roll style that AC/DC started with before developing their harder rock sound. It's less about the complexity of the music or depth of the lyrics and more about creating a fun, energetic, and engaging song. Overall, the song showcases the early roots of AC/DC in the simple, straightforward style of rock 'n' roll, likely heavily influenced and mentored by producers Harry Vanda and George Young.

"Rockin' in the Parlour"

"Rockin' in the Parlour" was released in July 1974 as the B-side of AC/DC's first single, "Can I Sit Next to You, Girl," and remains a rarity to this day. This song holds a special place in the band's history as it was part of their initial foray into the recording industry and still remains an elusive track in AC/DC's discography, as it has never been commercially reissued or available aside from the original version, which is now highly rare and collectible (and its appearance on an early Australian various artists LP). Similar musically to the original version of "Can I Sit Next to You, Girl," the song exudes a sense of youthful exuberance and rebellious spirit, which is a common theme in many rock 'n' roll songs. The lyrics speak of meeting a girl and quickly engaging in a lively, spontaneous party, which reflects the carefree and spontaneous nature of youth. The lyrics are straightforward and lack complex metaphors, which is typical of many early rock songs. The song is primarily about having fun and enjoying the moment. This aligns with the general ethos of rock music, which often prioritizes enjoyment and living in the moment. "Rockin' in the Parlour" is a vibrant and energetic song that reflects the early style of AC/DC, who were still finding their sound, which was likely heavily influenced by The Easybeats and producers Harry Vanda and George Young. It showcases the band's raw and straightforward approach to rock music, emphasizing themes of youth, rebellion, and the pursuit of enjoyment.

Bonfire

Released in 1997, the *Bonfire* box set was a tribute to Bon Scott and featured previously unreleased tracks as part of the CD titled *Volts* included in the set. The *Volts* CD primarily consisted of demo versions of songs that would ultimately be revised and recorded for *Highway to Hell*, including the track "Dirty Eyes," which was an early version of "Whole Lotta Rosie." "Dirty Eyes" was recorded in London at Vineyard Studios in 1976 along with the songs "Carry Me Home" and "Love at First Feel," all of which were originally intended for a possible EP. The *Bonfire* box set also included a 2CD set of AC/DC's live performance from Paris, France, from December 9, 1979, which is the soundtrack to the *Let There be Rock* AC/DC movie. *Bonfire* also featured the AC/DC live performance from *Live from the Atlantic Studios* from December 7, 1977, which was previously only available as a limited promotional-only vinyl LP. A copy of *Back in Black* (CD) was also included in the box set. *Bonfire* was produced by Vanda and Young. The title *Bonfire* was Bon Scott's own creation as he once said: "when I'm a fucking big shot I'm calling my solo album *Bonfire*."

"Dirty Eyes"

Within the expansive *Bonfire* box set released in 1997 lies a hidden gem for AC/DC fans and enthusiasts—the original demo version of the song "Dirty Eyes." This early incarnation later evolved into the iconic hit "Whole Lotta Rosie," which appears on both versions of their album *Let There Be Rock*, albeit with different lyrics. The song was recorded in London, England, in 1976 along with "Carry Me Home" and "Love at First Feel." The lyrics are filled with direct and sensual imagery, focusing on physical attraction and desire. The repeated references to the subject's "dirty eyes" suggest a raw, unfiltered attraction. The song heavily relies on the repetition of key phrases, such as "dirty eyes" and descriptions of heavy breathing. This repetition not only emphasizes the song's central themes but also contributes to its rhythmic and hypnotic quality. The use of words like "hypnotize" and "mesmerize" adds a layer of intensity to the song, suggesting a deep and irresistible attraction. The song has an overall simple structure, which would eventually evolve into the classic AC/DC track "Whole Lotta Rosie" as heard on *Let There Be Rock*. The track offers a glimpse into AC/DC's songwriting prowess and their ability to shape a raw idea into an enduring rock anthem.

"Touch Too Much"

Much like "Dirty Eyes," the original demo version of "Touch Too Much," first recorded in July 1977, features a radically different arrangement and lyrics compared to its later incarnation on *Highway to Hell.* Both lyrically and musically, the song is completely different than what ultimately ended up on the album two years later, and this rare gem was included as part of the *Bonfire* box set in 1997 (as part of the *Volts* CD). From the first chords, "Touch Too Much (Demo Version)" immediately distinguishes itself from its well-known counterpart. The demo version retains the classic AC/DC sound and Angus and Malcolm's unmistakable guitar tone. The lyrics in the demo convey a more subtle approach to the theme of desire and temptation, showcasing a less polished but equally captivating exploration of longing and forbidden allure. Bon Scott's expressive vocals bring these lyrics to life, evoking a mix of vulnerability and raw emotion. The song speaks of a night of excess, with imagery like "bottles on the floor" and "the room is spinning 'round." This reflects a common rock and roll theme of indulgence and the consequences that come with it. The lyrics describe a struggle to "find the light" and "searching for the switch," suggesting a sense of disorientation and loss of control. The repetition of "She had a touch, a touch too much" implies an overwhelming attraction that is almost too intense to handle. The themes in the song align with the stereotypical rock and roll lifestyle, which often includes elements of partying, sexual encounters, and a sense of living on the edge. These types of themes are found throughout the majority of the songs in AC/DC's catalog.

"If You Want Blood (You've Got It)"

"If You Want Blood (You've Got It)" is notable for its title, which was borrowed from AC/DC's live album of the previous year. Another rare gem, included as part of the *Bonfire* box set release from 1997 (*Volts*), the original demo version of the song provides fans with another glimpse into AC/DC's creative writing process. The demo version of the song is quite similar to the final version that was recorded for *Highway to Hell*, though with a slightly slower tempo and slightly different lyrics. The overall context of the track is the same, using metaphorical imagery to symbolize the band's challenges in everyday life. It features themes of confrontation, aggression, and the struggles of the working man, conveyed through direct language and violent imagery. The song exemplifies the band's straightforward and energetic style, which resonates strongly with its hard rock ethos. The lyrics are straightforward and direct, making the song accessible and relatable. AC/DC is known for its unpretentious and direct approach to songwriting, which is evident in this song as well.

"Back Seat Confidential"

Another hidden gem nestled in the *Bonfire* box set from 1997 is the demo of "Back Seat Confidential," an early recording that eventually transformed into "Beating Around the Bush" which is featured on *Highway to Hell* (albeit with different lyrics). Overall, the song embodies the classic rock themes of youthful rebellion, the rock 'n' roll lifestyle, and romantic adventure, presented in AC/DC's signature straightforward and energetic style. The song's playful and sensual imagery, combined with its direct language, captures the essence of the band's approach to storytelling in their music. The song starts with a scene of a young man with a woman, feeling good on a Saturday night, which sets the tone for a story of youthful adventure and rebellion. This theme is common in many rock songs, particularly those by AC/DC, and reflects a sense of freedom and nonconformity. The setting in the song—a drive-in show and the back seat of a car—reflects the classic rock 'n' roll lifestyle of the 1970s. This lifestyle often includes elements of spontaneity, romance, and a carefree attitude. The lyrics depict a playful and sensual scenario, emphasizing a light-hearted approach to romance and physical attraction. This approach is consistent with many of AC/DC's songs, which often have a strong sexual undercurrent.

"Get It Hot"

The demo version of "Get It Hot" is different from the track of the same title on *Highway to Hell*, with the primary similarity being the title itself. Another song contained within the *Bonfire* box set from 1997 (*Volts*), the demo version of the song features distinctly different lyrics and musical arrangement. The differences in tempo, lyrics, and overall execution highlight the band's commitment to honing their material until it reaches its full potential. The lyrics begin with a depiction of a carefree and easygoing lifestyle, characterized by lines like "No money, Easy going, nothin' gonna get me down." This reflects a common theme in rock music that emphasizes living in the moment and enjoying life without worries. The song captures the spirit of youth with references to young women and nights out, highlighting the energy and vibrancy of young adulthood. The language used in the song is straightforward and devoid of complex metaphors, making it accessible and relatable. The song conveys a sense of adventure and risk, particularly in the lines "Someday baby, I'm gonna get shot" and "Here I come, ready or not," as well as desire and romantic interests during the chorus. The overall tone of the song is playful and flirtatious, with a focus on romantic encounters and the joys of attraction and connection. The straightforward and direct lyrics, combined with themes of desire, adventure, and inclusivity, reflect the band's signature approach to rock music.

Backtracks

Released in 2009, *Backtracks* is a box set release that includes various rarities of both studio and live recordings. *Backtracks* is an almost complete rarities box set, as it features most of AC/DC's B-side and otherwise non-album tracks that were previously unavailable aside from Australian-only albums, vinyl 7-inch or 12-inch singles, EPs, and CD singles over the years. These tracks include rare AC/DC songs such as "Carry Me Home," "Love Song," "Who Made Who (Collector's edition mix)," "Snake Eye," and many others. *Backtracks* was available in different formats, including a deluxe edition that came with a hardcover coffee table book, three CDs, two DVDs, and an LP all housed within a working 1-watt guitar amplifier. The standard edition includes two CDs and one DVD.

"Fling Thing"

"Fling Thing," an instrumental B-side to AC/DC's Australian "Jailbreak" single in 1976, offers a unique and captivating experience for fans of the band. It takes the foundation of the traditional Scottish song "Loch Lomond" and showcases AC/DC's ability to infuse their signature rock sound with elements of traditional folk music. By embracing their roots (Angus, Malcolm, and Bon were all born in Scotland, but immigrated to Australia at an early age), while injecting their signature sound, AC/DC pays homage to the past while making it their own. The band performed it live during the 1978 If You Want Blood Tour at the Glasgow Apollo Theater, but it has not performed it again since. Angus did perform a short intro of the melody during The Razors Edge World Tour in Glasgow, which was released as the track titled "Bonny" on *AC/DC Live* in 1992. The original studio version of the song would also be included as the B-side of the "Jailbreak" 7-inch single released in the UK.

"Carry Me Home"

"Carry Me Home" remained one of AC/DC's most elusive tracks for decades, as it was only available as part of the Australian-only "Dog Eat Dog" 7-inch single (Albert AP-1140) until it ultimately became available commercially as part of the *Backtracks* box set release from 2009. The song was recorded in the UK in 1976 along with "Dirty Eyes" and "Love at First Feel," and possibly another track (possibly "Cold Hearted Man," but not confirmed), originally intended for an EP at the time. One of my favorite non-album tracks, "Carry Me Home" opens with a driving guitar riff that sets a relentless pace, showcasing AC/DC's trademark sound with bluesey undertones. Bon Scott's vocal performance on "Carry Me Home" is a testament to his commanding stage presence and unique vocal style.

The lyrics of the song paint a vivid picture of a night out, characterized by drinking and revelry: "I don't know what it is you're trying to prove, well it should be you but it's me who can hardly move." The song describes the physical and emotional toll of a night out drinking ("My arms and legs are aching and my head's about to blow"). This reflects the consequences of indulgence, a common cautionary tale in rock lyrics. The chorus, "Oh won't you carry me home," conveys a sense of desperation and dependence, highlighting the vulnerability that can come with excessive drinking. The lyrics contrast the current condition with that of his female companion who seems more in control ("You drank all your booze and half of mine"). This contrast adds depth to the narrative, showing different responses to the same environment. The song is structured as a narrative, telling the story of a night out gone too far, which is almost like an omen for Bon's tragic fate in 1980.

"Snake Eye"

Originally released as a B-side on the "Heatseeker" single in 1988, this non-album gem would become available globally as part of the *Backtracks* box set in 2009. Personally, it surprises me that the song was held back as a B-side as I prefer it over many of the tracks that were included on *Blow Up Your Video*. The song features a great riff and hard-hitting rhythm section. "Snake Eye" uses the metaphor of a snake to convey themes of vigilance, danger, and perhaps betrayal. The lyrics suggest a scenario where someone is being closely watched, as seen in lines like "I'll be watching, every move you make, when you hear the rattle, better be awake." This creates a sense of paranoia and tension. The song has a predatory and menacing tone, reflected in the way the lyrics describe the snake's behavior and intentions. This could be a metaphor for a person or situation that is perceived as threatening. The repeated warnings, "better be awake" and "look out," imply that danger is imminent. The song's menacing tone, combined with its direct language and repetitive structure, creates a powerful and engaging narrative that aligns with AC/DC's signature rock style.

"Borrowed Time"

As with "Snake Eye," I personally find it surprising that "Borrowed Time" was not included on *Blow Up Your Video* as it is also one of my favorites from those recordings. The song is another gem originally released exclusively on the 12-inch vinyl and CD single for "That's the Way I Wanna Rock 'n' Roll" in 1988 and would also make its way as part of the *Backtracks* box set in 2009. "Borrowed Time" seems to reflect a common theme found throughout AC/DC's music: a celebration of freedom, rebelliousness, and living life on one's own terms. The lyrics "Got the word, getting ready, gonna get my pay from, I'm in light, when the action is hot" suggest a readiness to seize opportunities and indulge in the exhilaration of the moment. This aligns with AC/DC's ethos of high-energy rock 'n' roll, often characterized by a pursuit of excitement and pleasure. The chorus, "Cause I'm living on a borrowed time do it your way, I'll do it mine," emphasizes individualism and the notion of living life fully, aware that it might not last forever. The idea of "borrowed time" implies an awareness of life's fleeting nature, encouraging a seize-the-day attitude. Moreover, the line "Don't need a shove, don't need a sign" reiterates a disdain for external guidance or societal norms, a recurring motif in AC/DC's music. Despite its status as a B-side, "Borrowed Time" captures the essence of AC/DC's sonic identity, making it a standout addition to their discography.

"Down on the Borderline"

"Down on the Borderline" was originally recorded during the sessions for AC/DC's 1988 album *Blow Up Your Video*. This non-album B-side remained buried until its release in 1990 as part of the Australian-only "Moneytalks" vinyl single and CD, which are now rare and collectible. Later, it found its place among the tracks of the *Backtracks* box set in 2009. Another gem and yet another of my favorite tracks from the *Blow Up Your Video* sessions, the song resonates with AC/DC's classic themes of desire, the seductive danger of the high life, and the allure of what is just out of reach. The song opens with a depiction of a woman from high society, described as an "idle child" who never had to work physically. This portrayal sets a tone of luxury and perhaps a sense of detachment from everyday struggles. The chorus, "On the borderline, she's a danger sign, on the borderline, getting out of line, on the borderline, but it feels so good," suggests a sense of risk and excitement associated with this woman. The phrase "on the borderline" could imply being on the edge of socially acceptable behavior or teetering on the brink of something dangerous yet enticing. Lyrics like "She can spread them round and she shows them off, with a neon sign saying don't you touch" further paint a picture of a woman who is both alluring and untouchable, increasing the sense of forbidden desire. The line "You know I shoot the dice to claim my dream, you pull them in without a thought to me" might reflect a sense of recklessness and the risks taken in the pursuit of desire, indicative of the band's frequent exploration of themes like gambling and taking chances.

"Big Gun"

"Big Gun" was written and released as a single in 1993 and was part of the soundtrack for the film *Last Action Hero*, starring Arnold Schwarzenegger. The song would be the last studio recording to feature Chris Slade on drums and was produced by Rick Rubin, who had been asking to produce AC/DC for years; they figured it would be a good opportunity to try him out as a producer. Its lyrics reflect themes of power, aggression, and the glamorization of violence, particularly in the context of Hollywood and the media. The opening lines, "Riot on the radio, pictures on the TV, invader man take what he can, shootout on the silver screen," set the stage for *Last Action Hero*. The chorus, with its repetition of "Big gun, Big gun number one, Big gun, Big gun kick the hell out of you," emphasizes the idea of dominance through firepower. The term "big gun" serves as a metaphor for power and the ability to control or intimidate others. It aligns with the band's often hard-edged, defiant stance in their music. The lines "Terminators, Uzi makers, shootin' up Hollywood" further this theme by alluding to action movies and their glorification of gun violence. The mention of "Terminators" is likely a direct reference to Schwarzenegger's famous role, tying the song more closely to its usage in *Last Action Hero*. The lyrics employ metaphors of guns and violence to comment on the nature of power and control, which are appropriate for the theme of the movie. The song fits within AC/DC's larger body of work, which often features themes of power, rebellion, and a hard-edged approach to societal issues. "Big Gun" seamlessly integrates into the world of *Last Action Hero*, amplifying the film's adrenaline-pumping action sequences. The track was originally released as a single on both vinyl and CD with different packaging in certain countries and would eventually become available as part of the *Backtracks* box set in 2009.

"Cyberspace"

Originally released exclusively on the "Safe in New York City" CD single in 2001, this song would also be included as part of the *Backtracks* box set in 2009. "Cyberspace" is a high-energy track that metaphorically explores the concept of escapism and freedom, themes often present in rock music. The song uses the metaphor of "cyberspace"—a term popularized in the late twentieth century to describe the virtual world of computers and the internet—as a realm of unbounded possibility and liberation. The lyrics start with "High tail in your face, black hole rockin' the place, Hong Kong videos, big bang mad to blow," suggesting a chaotic and fast-paced environment. The reference to "Hong Kong videos" and "big bang" could be seen as a nod to the overwhelming and explosive nature of information and entertainment in the digital age. The song uses phrases that convey a sense of breaking loose, with the imagery of a "hot star burning it up" and a "full moon running amok" evoking a feeling of exhilarating chaos. The song is infused with imagery of speed, energy, and liberation, consistent with AC/DC's trademark style of hard-hitting, rebellious rock music.

Interesting Facts

Although it was never officially released, AC/DC recorded a song, "I'm a Rebel," written by Angus and Malcolm's elder brother Alex Young (Grapefruit). The song was recorded in Hamburg, Germany, with Alex on vocals, Bon on backing vocals, and Angus and Malcolm on guitars. The German heavy metal band Accept recorded a cover of this song, which is the title track of their 1980 album.

Bibliography

AC/DC Live at Donington (DVD), Angus and Malcolm Young interviews, 2003

"AC/DC Tour History—19 Mar. 1977 Southend (Kursaal Ballroom)," (n.d.), www.ac-dc.net/archive/acdc_tour_history.php?date_id=776

Barton, G., and Rasmussen, J., "Hell's Bells," *Classic Rock* (Special Edition), July 2019

"Behind the early hits," *Music Spotlight: The Ultimate Guide to AC/DC* (2023), p. 43

Benitez-Eves, T., "The Meaning Behind AC/DC's Bon Scott Tribute 'Hells Bells'," *American Songwriter*, 2023, retrieved November 11, 2023, americansongwriter.com/the-meaning-behind-ac-dcs-bon-scott-tribute-hells-bells/

Benitez-Eves, T., "Behind the meaning of 'You shook me all night long' by AC/DC," *American Songwriter*, January 15, 2023, americansongwriter.com/behind-the-meaning-of-you-shook-me-all-night-long-by-ac-dc/

blabbermouth.net, "AC/DC's 'Black Ice Tour' is Second-Highest-Grossing concert tour in history," (n.d.), web.archive.org/web/20100729131739/http://www.roadrunnerrecords.com/blabbermouth.net/news.aspx?mode=Article&newsitemID=143523

Canyon, L., "For Those About to Rock track by track," *Sounds*, 1981

Colby, J., "AC/DC's Angus Young & Brian Johnson," *Guitar*, December 1985

Di Perna, A., "Angus & Malcolm Young talk dirty," *Guitar World*, November 1994

Engleheart, M., and Durieux, A., *AC/DC: Maximum Rock N Roll* (2006), pp. 92–93

Family Jewels (2-disc DVD set), video footage and liner notes, 2005

Greene, A., "Exclusive: Angus Young, Brian Johnson, and Cliff Williams on the Resurrection of AC/DC," *Rolling Stone*, October 6, 2020, www.rollingstone.com/music/music-features/acdc-interview-brian-johnson-angus-young-power-up-1070834/

HellTonicGooseII, "acdcbehindthemusic 7 [Video]," YouTube, July 11, 2007, www.youtube.com/watch?v=UrOPijv4b_A

"Inside Albert Productions with Fifa Riccobono," Ep. 338, www.thevinylguide.com/episodes/ep338-inside-albert-productions-with-fifa-riccobono

Landrum, J., "AC/DC—'Hells Bells' Lyrics Meaning," *Melodyinsight*, September 24, 2023, retrieved December 21, 2023, melodyinsight.com/ac-dc-hells-bells-lyrics-meaning/

McDonald, A., "AC/DC—Highway To Hell (Lyrics Review and Song Meaning)," October 20, 2019, justrandomthings.com/2019/10/20/ac-dc-highway-to-hell-lyrics-review-and-song-meaning/

"Meaning of Little Lover by AC/DC," (n.d.), www.songtell.com/ac-dc/little-lover

Minsker, E., Hussey, A., Bloom, M., and Monroe, J., "Grammy nominations 2022: See the full list here," *Pitchfork*, April 3, 2022, pitchfork.com/news/grammy-nominations-2022-see-the-full-list/

"News from the Lab Archive: January 2004 to September 2015," (n.d.), archive.f-secure.com/weblog/archives/00002403.html

noise11.com/news/ac-dc-to-release-limited-edition-record-store-day-through-the-mists-of-time-single-20210604

Ozden, E., "Angus Young's Regret On AC/DC's 'Love Song' Rock Celebrities," (March 1, 2022), rockcelebrities.net/angus-youngs-regret-on-ac-dcs-love-song/

Putterford, M. "The shorts remain the same," *RIP Magazine*, 1990

Rock, C., "Angus Young reveals that a British poet inspired one of AC/DC's biggest anthems," *Louder*, February 24, 2021, www.loudersound.com/news/angus-young-reveals-that-a-british-poet-inspired-one-of-acdcs-biggest-anthems

Sheppard, D., "Famous last words: Angus Young," *Q*, issue #137, February 1998

Sidney, "Unmasking the Legacy of AC/DC's 'What Do You Do For Money Honey'," *The Velvet Underground*, August 4, 2023, retrieved December 21, 2023, www.velvetunderground.com/unmasking-the-legacy-of-ac-dcs-what-do-you-do-for-money-honey/

Sloan, B., "Ice memories for AC/DC's Angus Young," *Daily Record*, July 1, 2012, www.dailyrecord.co.uk/entertainment/music/music-news/ice-memories-for-acdcs-angus-young-995285

Ultimate Classic Rock, "AC/DC Producer Brendan O'Brien Talks 'Rock or Bust' [Video]", YouTube, January 5, 2015, retrieved February 1, 2024, www.youtube.com/watch?v=2pBjjJWXzRE

Wall, M., "AC/DC: The Making Of Highway To Hell", loudersound.com, November 6, 2013

Wall, M., "Let there be light! Let there be sound! Let there be rock!" *Classic Rock*, issue #170, May 2012

Wall, M., "For Whom the Bell Tolls," *Classic Rock* (Special Edition), July 2023

Walthall, C., "A deeper look behind the story and meaning of 'Back in Black' by AC/DC," *American Songwriter*, May 3, 2022, americansongwriter.com/a-deeper-look-behind-the-story-and-meaning-of-back-in-black-by-ac-dc/

Yates, H., "Rock 'n Roll Train," *Classic Rock* (Special Edition), July 2023